The Bible Handbook of Difficult Verses

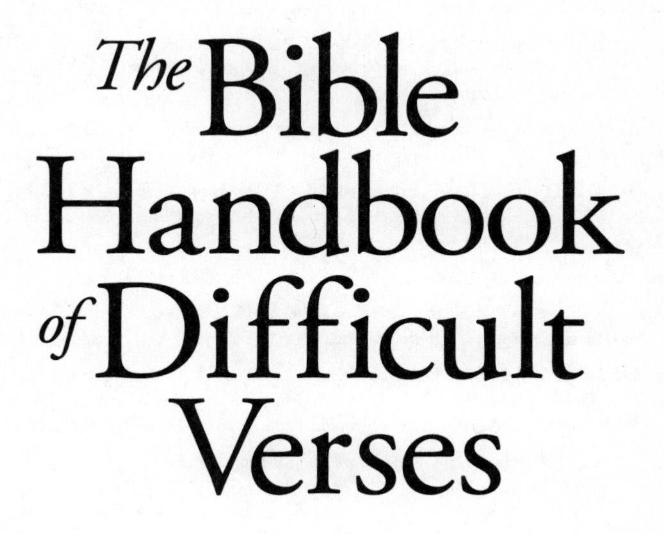

JOSH McDOWELL
SEAN McDOWELL

Cover by Koechel Peterson & Associates, Inc., Minneapolis, Minnesota

THE BIBLE HANDBOOK OF DIFFICULT VERSES

Published by Harvest House Publishers
Eugene, Oregon 97402
www.harvesthousepublishers.com

ISBN 978-0-7369-4944-6

Library of Congress Cataloging-in-Publication Data
McDowell, Josh.
The Bible handbook of difficult verses / Josh McDowell and Sean McDowell.
p. cm.
ISBN 978-0-7369-4944-6 (pbk.)
ISBN 978-0-7369-4945-3 (eBook)
1. Bible—Criticism, interpretation, etc.—Miscellanea. 2. Apologetics—Miscellanea. I. McDowell, Sean. II. Title.
BS511.3.M3365 2013
220.6—dc23

2012033401

Printed in the United States of America

13 14 15 16 17 18 19 20 21 / LB-JH / 10 9 8 7 6 5 4 3 2 1

Contents

The Prophets: Isaiah–Malachi

Difficult Passages from...

The Gospels/Narratives: Matthew–Acts

Difficult Passages from...

Paul's Letters: Romans–Philemon

Difficult Passages from...

Acknowledgments

We wish to recognize the following individuals for their valuable contribution to this handbook.

Dave Bellis, my (Josh's) friend and colleague for 36 years, for collaboration with us on all the passages covered in this handbook, researching the answers, writing the rough draft, and folding in all our edits and revisions to create the final draft. We recognize Dave's insights and knowledge of Scripture and are deeply grateful for his contribution.

Ken Turner for reviewing the manuscript and providing helpful insight in his areas of expertise.

Becky Bellis for laboring at the computer to ready the manuscript.

Terry Glaspey of Harvest House for his vision and guidance in shaping the direction and tone of this work.

Paul Gossard of Harvest House for the expert editing and insight he brought to the manuscript completion.

Josh McDowell
Sean McDowell

How to Use This Handbook

Have you ever read a passage in the Bible and thought, *Now, what does that mean?* Or perhaps the passage made sense but you wondered, *Is that really relevant to us today?* And then there are critics today that scoff at the idea of taking the Bible seriously. Some contend that it is riddled with inaccuracies, errors, and out-of-date laws and teachings that border on the ridiculous for a modern society.

The apostle Paul said to "live wisely among those who are not believers, and make the most of every opportunity. Let your conversation be gracious and attractive so that you will have the right response for everyone" (Colossians 4:5-6). Having the right answer for everyone isn't easy. Sometimes when we're stuck about what this passage means or how that scripture is to be applied, we may be tempted to say, "We take these things by faith."

But again Paul reminds us that "if someone asks about your Christian hope, always be ready to explain it. But do this in a gentle and respectful way" (1 Peter 3:15-16). What we hope to have done in this *Bible Handbook of Difficult Verses* is provide "the right answer" to help you "be ready to explain it." We won't be answering every possible question there is about what the Bible teaches. What we will do is offer answers by trusted scholars who have given much study and thought to many of the tough issues of the Bible. Not all scholars agree on how to explain certain passages. So we will, at times, provide differing opinions and interpretations by various scholars on both sides of the issue.

We will not shy away from some of the tough issues of Scripture either. We will tackle passages that are difficult to understand, some that have commonly been misinterpreted, and portions of the Bible that some believe contain mistakes, errors, or contradictions. Our hope is that the explanation of over 240 passages in this handbook will, first and foremost, give you a deeper love for God and his Word. And then we hope it provides you with answers to your questions to equip you to confidently explain your faith to others.

Use this handbook as you would a Bible commentary or study Bible. When you are studying your Bible and come across a passage you have questions about, check to see if it is covered in this handbook. You can also check out the various issues, subjects, or Scripture passages covered by consulting the indexes.

Not all passages we cover require the same amount of explanation. Some only require concise answers. Others take more space to explain a more complex issue. We have tried in each case to provide satisfying answers to the questions surrounding each Scripture passage listed.

Before we begin, we want to establish six "ground rules" in approaching any difficult or hard-to-understand passage of Scripture. This will provide a context or grid within which we examine and understand the Bible. We cover these six "ground rules" by answering six questions about the Bible.

1. Is the Bible Inspired by God?

When the apostle Paul said that "all Scripture is inspired by God" (2 Timothy 3:16) he did not mean that the Bible was merely an inspirational book. He used a specific word in the Greek language—*theopneustos,* which literally means "God-breathed" (*theos,* God; *pneō,* to breathe). All of Scripture is "God-breathed," which means the written words in the Bible are from God. That is why we refer to Scripture as the Word of God.

Jesus referred to Scripture this way when he told the Pharisees that they were misusing scriptural teaching. He said, "So you cancel the word of God [Scripture] for the sake of your own tradition" (Matthew 15:6). The apostle Paul explained how the Jewish people "have been entrusted with the very words of God" (Romans 1:3 NIV). So when you read the Bible you are not simply reading an inspirational book; you are reading words from God.

While Scripture is God's Word, it doesn't mean that God penned the words himself or put people into a trance and used their hands and pens to write out his thoughts and ideas. Rather, he chose people who had a spiritual relationship with him to be his spokesmen. And he spoke through them to write down his words and message through their unique personalities.

So when it is said that Scripture is inspired by God it means he superintended what he wanted to be said through men as his instruments. The apostle Paul said, "When we tell you these things, we do not use words that come from human wisdom. Instead, we speak words given to us by the Spirit, using the Spirit's words to explain spiritual truths" (1 Corinthians 2:13). The apostle Peter made the same point when he wrote that "no prophecy in Scripture ever came from the prophet's own understanding, or from human initiative. No, those prophets were moved by the Holy Spirit and they spoke from God" (2 Peter 1:20-21).

God's Word spoken and written by his prophets and apostles is what is referred to as a special revelation. Scripture was inspired by him so he could reveal his thoughts, words, and promises in order that we could have them preserved from generation to generation. So the Bible is a special revelation of God, written by human authors who were inspired directly by him. And because of that the Bible carries power and weight, or what we might call authority. Behind the Scripture stands the Sovereign God of the universe. And when he speaks, his Word defines the essence of authority. *So when we try to explain the meaning of Scripture passages we are mindful that we are explaining God's authoritative, inspired words.*

2. Is the Bible Without Error?

Conservative Christian theologians do say that the Bible is without error (*inerrant*). But what they mean is, when all the facts are known, the Scriptures as they were penned by the authors in the original writings and as properly interpreted will be shown to be true and not false in all they affirm. This would naturally be the case if God is actually the author of Scripture. It stands to reason that if he inspired certain men to reveal his words, he would be sure not to contradict himself, so that his Word would be error-free.

There were 40-some authors of the 66 books of the Bible. It was a complex process for God to communicate his message through such a diverse group of men over the span of about 1500 years. Yet he miraculously brought his Word together. It was as if he were composing a perfect musical masterpiece using a 40-piece orchestra. Think of a master maestro who has created a marvelous musical composition. He uses different instruments for different purposes: the percussion instruments set the rhythm, the trumpets call us to action, the violins and cellos soothe us, the flutes lift our spirits, and so on. In the hands of the maestro the varied instruments produce a symphony of sounds that move the mind, heart, and emotions of the hearer with the message of the music. In a similar way, God used the different authors to impart his message clearly to us, no matter who we are or how varied our human experiences might be.

Not only did God speak through spokesmen with varied human experiences, he also expressed his Word in a number of literary styles and forms. At times, the Bible reads like a novel, and at other times like a book of laws. The Scripture moves from the mournful laments of Jeremiah to the exalted poetry of Isaiah and the Psalms. The Bible uses this wide range of literary forms to communicate clearly to its human audience. God's Word is full of historical narratives, parables, letters, allegories, metaphors, similes, satire, and hyperbole. One of the keys to accurately understanding the Bible is knowing the proper rules for interpreting various genres.

Because God spoke his words through humans, the Scripture is textured not only with varying literary forms and styles, but also the different human perspectives, emotions, and cultures of his spokesmen. In so communicating, God captures the full character of those he spoke through, from the tight-knit logic of a scholar (Paul, in his epistles) to the priestly perspective of a theologian (the writer of Hebrews) to the poetic talents of a musician (David, in the Psalms) to the despair and agony of a people (Jeremiah, in Lamentations). *So as we unpackage a passage we will be mindful that God's truth is being presented through the lens of its human spokesman yet still conveys the exact, error-free message God wants us to receive.*

3. Does the Bible Contain Any Mistakes?

Although the original writings of Scripture are without error, none of the original autographs are in existence today. What we have today are copies of what was originally penned. In fact, we have thousands of copies. (Hundreds of millions, if you count modern printed versions of the Bible.)

Because there were no printing presses at the time Scripture was being written (nor were there any for more than another thousand years), men had to handwrite copies to preserve the documents from one generation to another. And while those who made the copies (scribes) did their best to copy accurately, some errors were made. But just because there were copying mistakes does not mean the Bible is full of contradictions and errors. Because when you examine the "errors" it is often clear how they were made and that they do not alter the intended meaning of the text.

For example, some manuscripts of the New Testament spell the name John with one "n"; other times it is spelled with two. This technically constitutes a variation. And whenever a particular "variant" like this occurs, critics consider it an error or contradiction. But of course that type of "error" in no way changes the meaning of God's Word.

Because we are dealing only with copies of the original manuscripts and not the originals themselves, we are bound to have some copying errors. *So as we examine passages we will at times point out these "errors" and try to determine just how they may have occurred.*

As we consider these errors or apparent contradictions, it stands to reason that those copies that are closer to the originals are more likely to have fewer copying errors. Because if one error is made in copying down a manuscript, future manuscript copies are going to reproduce that error. The earlier manuscripts tend to be more accurate because they are closer to the original. So it becomes evident when and how these errors came about. But we didn't know just how amazingly accurate the Old Testament copies were until the discovery of the Dead Sea Scrolls in 1947.

Before 1947, the oldest complete Hebrew manuscript in our possession dated to AD 900. But with the discovery of more than 800 manuscripts in caves on the west side of the Dead Sea, we came into possession of Old Testament manuscripts dated by paleographers to around 125 BC. These scrolls were therefore a thousand years older than any previously known manuscripts.

But here's the exciting part: Once the Dead Sea Scrolls were compared with later manuscript copies, the then-current Hebrew Bible proved to be identical, word for word, in more than 95 percent of the text. The other 5 percent consisted mainly of spelling variations. For example, of the 166 words in Isaiah 53, only 17 letters were in question. Of those, 10 letters were a matter of spelling, and 4 were stylistic changes; the remaining 3 letters comprised the word *light*, which was added in verse 11.

In other words, the greatest manuscript discovery of all time revealed that a thousand years of copying the Old Testament had produced only very minor variations, none of which altered the clear meaning of the text or brought the manuscript's fundamental integrity into question.[1]

4. Is What We Have Today Truly God's Word?

Today our complete Bible is comprised of 39 books of the Old Testament and 27 books of the New Testament. But how do we know those are the God-inspired books God prepared for us? Maybe some God-inspired books were overlooked. How do we know we have all the writings that were inspired by God?

Determining what writings were inspired by God (God-breathed) was not a specific event, but rather a process over time. People required some time to recognize which writings were God-inspired and to establish a process to know for sure which books were his Word. The 66 books accepted as God's inspired word are referred to as the *canon* of Scripture. *Canon* comes from the Greek word *kanōn,* meaning "rule" or "principle." In other words there was a very high standard or measuring tool needed to deem a writing "inspired by God."

Contrary to what some modern critics say, early Jewish and church leaders did not create the canon. In other words, a group of religious leaders did not determine which books would be called Scripture, the inspired Word of God. Rather, those leaders merely recognized or discovered which books were "God-breathed" from their very inception. A writing was not given the authority of being Scripture just because the early Jewish or Christian leaders accepted it as such. Instead, it was accepted by the leaders and the people because it was clear to them that God himself had given the writing its divine authority.

From what we find in biblical and church history we can see at least four guiding principles or rules that qualified a letter or book to be recognized as a divinely inspired writing:

1. The writing was authored by a prophet or apostle of God or someone connected with them.
2. The message of the book was consistent with what had already been revealed about God.
3. The writing clearly evidenced the confirming presence of God.
4. The book was widely accepted by the church from an early date.[2]

By as early as the 300s BC, and certainly no later than 150 BC, all the 39 books of the Old Testament had been written, collected, and officially recognized as canonical books.[3] The Hebrew text of these 39 books was originally divided into 24 books: five books of the Law (of Moses), eight Prophets, and eleven Writings.

By the 200s and 300s AD, church elders began to set criteria for recognizing writings of the apostles as inspired by God. In AD 367, Athanasius of Alexandria provided the first official list of the 27 books of the New Testament we have today. And by the late 300s there was consensus. All 27 books were canonized by the councils of Hippo (AD 393) and Carthage (AD 397). Remember, this was not a group of church elders authorizing a collection of religious writings—rather, they were recognizing that this collection of books was authorized by God as his Word. *So as we deal with the many passages in this handbook, we accept that the 66 books of the Bible are God's final word.*

5. Is the Bible Historically Accurate and Reliable?

Some people think the Bible can be trusted on moral issues but is not to be fully trusted on matters of history. This propagates the idea that the Bible is a spiritual book that has little to do with historical events.

However, many of the truths of the Bible are rooted in history. For example, it is crucial that Jesus was a historical person and that the bodily resurrection was a historical reality. Because as the apostle Paul puts it, "If Christ has not been raised, then your faith is useless and you are still guilty of your sins" (1 Corinthians 15:17).

The Bible is largely a historical book that reveals who God is, who humans are, how humans became separated from God, and how his redemptive plan was put in place to restore his lost children to a relationship with him. And it is vitally important that his words have been accurately passed down from generation to generation. So the question is: Can we be confident that what was inspired by God and written down has been in fact preserved as an accurate record of history?

Of course what we have today as the Bible are printed copies translated from ancient handwritten copies of yet other copies of the original. This is because, as we stated earlier, the Bible was composed and transmitted in an era before printing presses. All manuscripts had to be written by hand. Over time, the ink would fade, and the material the manuscript was written on would deteriorate. So if a document was to be preserved and passed down to the next generation, new copies had to be made, else the document would be lost forever. Of course, these copies were made just like the originals—by hand with fading ink on deteriorating materials.

As mentioned, this opens up the probability of human error in the hand-copied reproductions. A weary copier, blurry-eyed from lack of sleep, could have skipped a few words or left out a sentence or miscopied some numbers. Critics say that the Bible is a collection of outdated writings that are riddled with inaccuracies and distortions. So, how can we be sure that the Bibles available to us today reflect an accurate transmission of the originals?

God has not left us to wonder. He has miraculously supervised the transmission of the Scriptures to ensure they were relayed accurately from one generation to another.

Transmission of the Old Testament

One of the ways God ensured that the Old Testament would be relayed accurately was by choosing, calling, and cultivating a nation of men and women who took the Book of the Law very seriously. God commanded and instilled in the Jewish people a great reverence for the Scriptures. That attitude became such a part of their identity that a class of Jewish scholars called the *Sopherim*, from a Hebrew word meaning "scribes," arose between the fifth and third centuries BC. These custodians of the Hebrew Scriptures dedicated themselves to carefully preserving the ancient manuscripts and producing new copies when necessary.

The Sopherim were eclipsed by the *Talmudic* scribes, who guarded, interpreted, and commented on the sacred texts from about AD 100 to 500. The Talmudic scribes were followed by the better-known *Masoretic* scribes (about AD 500 to 900).

The Talmudic scribes, for example, established detailed and stringent disciplines for copying a manuscript. Their rules were so rigorous that when a new copy was complete, they would give the reproduction equal authority to that of its parent because they were thoroughly convinced they had an exact duplicate.

The Transmission of the New Testament

But while there were expert Hebrew scribes who made copies of the Old Testament manuscripts, that is not the case with the New Testament. There are several reasons for this: 1) The official Jewish leadership did not endorse Christianity; 2) the letters and histories circulated by the New Testament writers were not at the time thought of as official Scripture; and 3) the documents were not written in the Hebrew language, but rather in forms of Greek and Aramaic. Thus, the same formal disciplines were not followed in the transmission of these writings from one generation to another. In the case of the New Testament, God did a new thing to ensure that his Word would be accurately preserved for us and our children.

Historians evaluate the textual reliability of ancient literature according to two standards: 1) the time interval between the original and the earliest copy, and 2) how many manuscript copies are available.

For example, virtually everything we know today about Julius Caesar's exploits in the Gallic Wars (58 to 51 BC) is derived from ten manuscript copies of Caesar's work *The Gallic Wars*. The earliest of these copies dates to a little less than a thousand years from the time the original was written. Our modern text of Livy's *History of Rome* relies on 1 partial manuscript and 19 much later copies that are dated from 400 to 1000 years *after* the original writing.

By comparison, the text of Homer's *Iliad* is much more reliable. It has an estimated 1757 manuscript copies in existence today, with a mere 400-year time gap between the date of composition and the earliest of these copies.

The textual evidence for Livy and Homer is considered more than adequate for historians to use in validating the originals, but this evidence pales in comparison to what God performed in the case of the New Testament text.

Using this accepted standard for evaluating the textual reliability of ancient writings, the New Testament stands alone. It has no equal. No other book of the ancient world can even approach its textual reliability.

Nearly *25,000* manuscripts or fragments of manuscripts of the New Testament repose in the libraries and universities of the world in languages such as Coptic, Latin, and Armenian. Among these are nearly 5800 Greek manuscripts of the New Testament, which is over three times as many as for the *Iliad*. The earliest of these discovered so far is a fragment of John's Gospel, located in the John Rylands Library of the University of Manchester, England; it has been dated to within *50 years* of when the apostle John penned the original.[4] As this book goes to publication there is compelling evidence that a recently found portion of Mark's Gospel dates from the first century.

We can be confident that the text of the New Testament and Old Testament has been handed down over the centuries with precision and accuracy. *So when we discuss the writings of Scripture in this handbook, we are working from the premise that we are dealing with what was accurately written down initially.*

6. How Do We Interpret the Bible to Know What It Means for Us Today?

Let's face it, the Bible was written in a time and place vastly different from twenty-first-century North America. The customs, traditions, and overall culture were nowhere near ours today. What they were facing and how they dealt with issues of life often don't relate to us. So how can the teachings of the Bible be relevant to our lives today?

It is true that the Old Testament was written over a period from 3400 to 1900 years ago. The cultures were different; there is no question about that. What people did and how they expressed themselves don't much resemble the speech and activities of our modern world.

It is also true that the New Testament, for example, commanded that men greet their Christian brothers with a "holy kiss." It instructed slave owners on how to treat their slaves and how slaves should respond to their masters. During biblical times daughters were given away to men in arranged marriages, and wives had no legal rights.

But with all these cultural differences, the Bible is still extremely relevant to us today. And to interpret and understand the relevancy of Scripture to our lives involves a two-step process. The first step is *to determine what the specific passages meant for those who first spoke them or wrote them down, and what the passages meant to those who heard them or read them*. This is when the historical or cultural setting of Scripture becomes important. Because the Bible was written in various time periods, we must understand its historical context. How a given truth applies to us must be understood through the attitudes, settings, lifestyle, and political structure of the times in which it was given. We properly understand the Bible when we learn *what* was said, *who* said it, *how* it was said, *where* it was said, *when* it was said, and *why* it was said.

In this first step we need to remember that nothing spoken or written in Scripture was spoken or written directly to us living in the twenty-first century. Moses and the prophets were speaking to the children of Israel. Jesus was speaking to his disciples, the crowds, and various individuals. When the apostles wrote the Gospels and when Paul, Peter, James, and others wrote the other books of the New Testament, they were writing them for certain hearers or readers of their time.

The point is, they wrote what they wrote within a historical context, to an audience considerably different from us today. But even though the words of Scripture may not have been written specifically *to* us in the twenty-first century, that doesn't mean they weren't written *for* us as well as for the original recipients. So because God was revealing himself and his truth to a specific audience within a specific time in history, our first task is to interpret what he intended to communicate to them at the time.

But then comes the second very important step: *understanding what universal, relevant truth God is revealing to us right now*. This is when we attempt to draw out God's meaning from the text. We are not to create the meaning ourselves or read into a text what *we* think it is teaching. When people impose their particular slant on a passage or inject their own ideas, it is not hard to see how we can end up having different and contradictory views on a particular truth. But much of this can be avoided if we follow a process to discover God's meaning of a truth. This process is called *exegesis*.

Exegesis is from the Greek word *exegeomai,* which means to make known, to unfold in teaching, to declare by making known. The word is used by John when he says that Jesus "has *revealed* God to us" (John 1:18). The New American Standard Bible translates this phrase as "he has *explained* him."

To properly interpret, or explain, the meaning of a passage of Scripture we must engage in this process of exegesis. We do this by asking various questions about the passage to determine answers to *what, where, why, how,* and so on. And in the process we

1. examine the text to understand its grammatical construction;
2. understand the meaning of individual words—literally, figuratively, culturally, and so on;
3. discover the historical context, such as the author, cultural setting, time frame, and so on;
4. examine the message within the context of paragraphs, chapters, individual books, and the entire scope of scriptural truth; and
5. understand that the timeless truth applied to those it was first written to and then understand how that timeless truth applies to us today.

Thus, to exegete a passage means we must understand the meaning of words and put those words within context—a literary, historical, and theological context. And if we read a passage out of its literary, historical, or theological context we are in danger of reading another meaning into the text that simply isn't there. Scholars call this *eisegesis,* or "reading into." Most errors of interpretation come from reading into Scripture a meaning that just isn't there. And much of that can be avoided by reading the text within context.

As we stated before, the Scripture may not have been specifically written *to* us in the twenty-first century, but that doesn't mean it wasn't written *for* us—it was. But to understand what God is saying to us today we must understand it within its context and then properly apply his truth to our own culture and personal lives.

When we read the Bible we are entering into the past. The Scriptures were written over a 1500-year span. Within that time frame significant cultural, political, and sociological changes took place. *So throughout this handbook we will attempt to understand the meaning of the words and discover the literary, historical, and theological context, so we will be in a position to better understand even what the difficult verses of the Bible are saying to us. And as we do, we trust that the meaning of God's Word will be revealed and applied to your life.*

The Pentateuch
Genesis–Deuteronomy

Difficult Verses *from* *the* Book *of* Genesis

Passage:
In the beginning...(Genesis 1:1).

Difficulty: Doesn't science claim the universe is eternal? If so, how can it have a beginning?

Explanation: The First Law of Thermodynamics states that matter and energy can be changed from one form to another, but it cannot be created or destroyed. For centuries scientists believed the universe was uncaused and eternal.

In the early part of the twentieth century the scientific community was confronted with the ramifications of Albert Einstein's general theory of relativity. Like most scientists of the day, Einstein assumed the universe was static and eternal. Yet his mathematical equation of relativity pointed strongly toward a universe that was either expanding or contracting. While this seemed to unsettle him, Einstein later accepted that the universe had a finite past. Why did he change his mind?

In 1929 cosmologist Edwin Hubble used his hundred-inch telescope to demonstrate that light from distant galaxies were shifting toward the red end of the light spectrum. This meant that the universe was expanding in all directions. This was a powerful confirmation of Einstein's findings that the universe is not static but at some point in time had a beginning.[1] This first moment of existence is now referred to as the *singularity*, which is an edge or boundary to space-time itself. According to Professor Paul Davies at Oregon State University, "For this reason most cosmologists think of the initial singularity as the beginning of the universe."[2]

This doesn't mean that all scientists necessarily accept God as the best explanation for the beginning of the universe, but most now believe that the universe began to exist at a finite point in the past. It appears that many in the scientific community have caught up with the biblical declaration that "in the beginning..." (Genesis 1:1).

Passage:

In the beginning God created the heavens and the earth (Genesis 1:1).

Difficulty: Is there any evidence that God did in fact create the universe?

Explanation: There is solid evidence that the universe had a beginning (see previous *Explanation*), but that doesn't prove that God gave the universe its beginning, right? And while many scientists now concede that the universe had a beginning, this doesn't address who or what caused it. But there *is* evidence to confirm what Christians believe: that God is the Creator of the universe as Scripture states.

One of the evidences that God created the universe is what is often referred to as the first-cause argument for God's existence, or the cosmological argument.

The idea is that everything that begins to exist must have a cause. So if you go back in time far enough you will find the first cause—and that cause will be an Intelligent Creator. Actually this argument has three premises:

1. Whatever begins to exist has a cause.
2. The universe began to exist.
3. Therefore the universe has a cause.

The first premise seems self-evidently true. Can *you* think of something that comes from nothing? Some try to evade this problem by defining "nothing" as a quantum vacuum. But even vacuums aren't technically nothing. They have energy and quantum particles, which is *something*. We have no empirical evidence of something emerging without a cause from absolute nothing. The ancient Greeks were right when they said, "Out of nothing, nothing comes." It certainly seems more reasonable than to not believe that things that begin to exist have a cause.

The second premise finds support from the second law of thermodynamics (see question on Genesis 1:1 for additional scientific evidence). That law states that usable energy within a closed system will eventually run down. Since the universe is a closed system, its usable energy will eventually run down and the universe will reach a state of equilibrium known as "heat death." But the energy has not run down yet. Why not? The answer is simple: The past is finite. If the past were eternal, then the universe would have already run down at some point in the past.

The last premise builds off the previous two: The universe has a cause. This can lead us then to a conclusion based on the question, "Who caused the cause?" We can derive our answer from the origins of time, space, and matter. It is logical to conclude that since time, space, and matter did not exist prior to the beginning of the universe, then the "cause" of the universe had to be timeless, spaceless, and immaterial. Further, this "cause" could not be physical or subject to natural law since that would presuppose its existence involved time, space, and matter. This then leads us to conclude that the timeless, spaceless, immaterial "cause" was in fact God. (For more details and other evidences for the existence of God see the book *Is God Just a Human Invention?* by Sean McDowell and Jonathan Morrow, described in the back pages of this book.)

Passage:

God said, "Let there be light," and there was light (Genesis 1:3).

Difficulty: Isn't it contradictory to say light was created on the first day, yet the sun wasn't created until the fourth day?

Explanation: Some have suggested that on the first day God created light, as well as all other types of what is called electromagnetic radiation (EMR). Some who hold this view believe God created the light of the sun and moon on the first day, but it only became visible on the fourth day as the atmosphere of the Earth became transparent.

Visible light is just a small part of the entire spectrum of EMR. The visible light range or wavelength of what we can see with the naked eye is from about 380 nanometers (NM) to about 740 NM. But the electromagnetic spectrum is much broader. It extends from low frequencies used for radio broadcasts, which we cannot see to very high frequencies of gamma radiation, which again are beyond our vision. This means electromagnetic radiation covers wavelengths from thousands of kilometers down to a fraction of the size of an atom. What we see with the human eye is only a very small part of the electromagnetic spectrum.

Scientists say that the electromagnetic spectrum in principle is infinite and continuous. Indeed, while Einstein's theory of relativity predicts that time, space, and mass can all change due to relativistic effects, the speed of EMR is always constant in all frames of reference. Perhaps that is why Jesus so aptly referred to himself as the "light of the world" (John 8:12)—God as the constant, infinite, and continuous one brings his light to every dimension of the universe, from the distant stars to a fraction of the diameter of a proton.

On the very first day of creation God may have very well brought into existence the miraculous phenomenon of light along with the entire spectrum of electromagnetic radiation, ranging from the lowest of the low in frequency to the highest of the high. Then on the fourth day (Genesis 1:14-18), God formed the sun, moon, and stars to warm Planet Earth and radiate light throughout the visible universe.

The other possible response to this question involves asking a question about the nature of Genesis—"Was Moses trying to offer a scientific chronology of the creation event?" In other words, is the Genesis 1 creation account meant as a scientific account of the sequence and manner of creation? If yes, then some explanation such as the above is necessary. If no, then this difficulty disappears. See answer to Genesis 2:1-4 for alternative ways of understanding the creation account.

Passage:

God said, "Let us make human beings in our image, to be like ourselves" (Genesis 1:26).

Difficulty: Why does God refer to himself as "us"?

Explanation: Some people suggest that God, being a Trinity (Father, Son, and Holy Spirit), is actually speaking among the three persons of the Godhead and therefore refers to himself as us. We know, for example, that the Holy Spirit, the third person of the Trinity, was at creation for it says in Genesis 1 that "the Spirit of God was hovering over the surface of the water" (verse 2). Scripture also states that Jesus was at creation. "Through him God created everything in the heavenly realms and on earth...He existed before anything else, and he holds all creation together" (Colossians 1:15-17).

We can then clearly conclude from other passages of Scripture that the three persons of the Godhead were present and actively engaged in creation of all things. So since God is Trinity, is that why God said, "Let *us* make human beings in *our* image?" The short answer is "Maybe."

There are three possible explanations for the plural pronoun in this passage. The first option is, as we have seen, that the "us" and "our" passages refer to the Trinity. However, one difficulty with this interpretation is that the word "us" is actually part of a Hebrew verb, not a pronoun. The "our" is the first plural pronoun. As a result, some scholars believe the "us" is literarily meant to signal that the creation of humanity is special, rather than indicate the numerical plurality of the Creator.

The second option is that the Hebrew word *elohim* gives a more encompassing, grand, and majestic context of the person of God. The plural name *elohim* is in the *majestic plural* (the *royal "we"*) and should lead us to remember that God cannot be placed in a narrow singular box. As the prophet Isaiah wrote,

> "My thoughts are nothing like your thoughts," says the LORD. "And my ways are far beyond anything you could imagine. For just as the heavens are higher than the earth, so my ways are higher than your ways and my thoughts are higher than your thoughts" (Isaiah 55:8-9).

The third option is that the "us" refers to God and his heavenly court (that is, angels). While this interpretation does have some difficulties, it is a possible view held by a number of respectable evangelical scholars.

Regardless of the proper interpretation of this passage, this in no way lessens the truth that God is triune. God has revealed his character progressively throughout history, and most fully in the person of Jesus Christ (John 14:7-9).

Passage:

God said, "Let us make human beings in our image, to be like ourselves. They will reign over the fish in the sea, the birds in the sky, the livestock, all the wild animals on the earth, and the small animals that scurry along the ground." So God created human beings in his own image. In the image of God he created them; male and female he created them (Genesis 1:26-27).

Difficulty: How are we humans like God? We don't have the infinite characteristics of God of knowing everything and having all power, so what does it really mean to be created in God's image?

Explanation: Scripture teaches us that 1) God has life without beginning or end (eternal, see Isaiah 40:28); 2) God is almighty and powerful (omnipotent, see Job 42:2); 3) God is ever-present (omnipresent, see Jeremiah 23:23-24); 4) God knows all (omniscient, see Isaiah 46:9-10); and 5) God is constant and will not change (immutable, see Psalm 102:26-27). And none of these Godlike characteristics has been passed on to his human creation. And being created in God's image doesn't mean we look like him either, because "God is Spirit, so those who worship him must worship in spirit and in truth" (John 4:24). We are physical beings—God is not. So what part of his image did we inherit from our Creator?

Before there were humans, before the material universe or time and space existed as we know it, God existed eternally as a loving relational being. He is relational by his very nature, three personalities blended in perfect harmony—Father, Son, and Holy Spirit. While he is the infinite one and we as humans are finite, we bear his relational image.

We have inherited his relational ability to love in a way that other creatures cannot. Scripture says, "Love comes from God...for God is love" (1 John 4:7-8).

As part of God's relational image we have inherited the ability to communicate our thoughts, intents, and feelings to others through complex language. Scripture repeatedly uses the phrase "God said," showing us that relationships mean communication to others. The ability to express and enhance relationships by communicating is another way we reflect the image of God.

We have inherited his sense of value for human relationships and for life itself. God said, "Honor your father and mother...you must not murder...you must not commit adultery...you must not steal... you must not testify falsely...you must not covet your neighbor's wife" (Deuteronomy 5:16-21). From God's giving of the law at Mount Sinai up through the early church and beyond, it was understood and taught that life is sacred at every stage. Promoting social justice, taking care of the poor, and defending human rights find their basis in each of us because we are purposely created in God's relational image—with value, dignity, and worth.

We have inherited God's sense of satisfaction and joy in accomplishing things through relationships. After each creative act in Genesis, this relational God "saw that it was good" (Genesis 1:10). The Father, Son, and Holy Spirit found joy in their collective creative acts as the Master of the universe.

We inherited from the Master of the universe the charge to "reign" over all the creatures of the earth (Genesis 1:26). God told the first humans that in relationship with one another they were also to live in proper relationship with their home—Earth. God said to be stewards of the earth and "to tend and watch over it" (Genesis 2:15). So God instilled within his human creation an environmental responsibility to relate lovingly to the planet they inherited.

God placed humans on a plateau above the rest of creation when he fashioned them in his relational image and likeness. To summarize, this Godlikeness bestowed upon the human race certain gifts and obligations:

- to love God and one another as persons

- to effectively communicate through complex language
- to be creative
- to think logically
- to make moral decisions
- to defend the dignity, value, and worth of all human life, to be the protector of peace and harmony among all people, and to preserve the unity and sanctity of marriage between a man and a woman and the family
- to rule over and be the steward of creation

It is this relational dimension with all its ramifications that distinguishes us as created in God's image and gives us special meaning.

Passage:

God created human beings in his own image. In the image of God he created them; male and female he created them. Then God blessed them and said, "Be fruitful and multiply. Fill the earth and govern it" (Genesis 1:27-28).

Difficulty: Doesn't the science of genetics refute the concept that the entire population of the world came from just one couple?

Explanation: Over the past couple of decades researchers have used "population genetics" to estimate initial population size of the human species. By studying human genetic diversity in the present day, they have tried to extrapolate back to determine the minimum size of the original population of humans necessary to produce the diversity we observe today. Some have argued that it is impossible for civilization to have come from one human couple.

Dr. Francis S. Collins is a physician and geneticist who in 2007 formed the San Diego–based BioLogos Foundation. It is an organization that promotes theistic evolution among evangelicals. Dennis R. Venema, PhD, a BioLogos senior fellow for science and biology chairman at Trinity Western University, is a writer for BioLogos. He too is a theistic evolutionist who is trying to promote harmony of Darwinian science and faith within the evangelical community.

Dr. Venema claims that human population "was definitely never as small as two." He contends that "our species diverged as a population. The data are absolutely clear on that."[3] He asserts that to reach the level of genetic diversity we see today, the inital population of humans would have had to be several thousand individuals at minimum—not one couple.

Not all biologists, however, agree with Dr. Venema. Dr. Ann Gauger is senior research scientist at the Biologic Institute, a pro–intelligent design research lab based near Seattle, Washington. She earned a PhD in biology from the University of Washington, and later did postdoctoral work at Harvard. In the chapter "The Science of Adam and Eve" in the 2012 book *Science and Human Origins*, Gauger finds that Venema's arguments were based upon a now outdated study of genes involved in the human immune system that was published by the geneticist Francisco Ayala in 1995.

According to Gauger, these population genetics studies make many assumptions—including a constant background mutation rate, lack of natural selection, lack of migration, and a constant population size. If any of those assumptions are wrong then the conclusions could be meaningless. Gauger reanalyzed Ayala's data and found that he failed to control two of the assumptions, and analyzed a portion of the gene known to experience an unusually high mutation rate, causing him to dramatically overestimate the required initial population sizes.

When the analysis is done properly, Gauger found that "a first couple could have carried sufficient genetic diversity to account for" the genetic diversity we observe today in humans for this gene.[4] Gauger further found that more recent research reveals this gene shows conflicting phylogenetic patterns, which "cannot be explained by common ancestry" of humans and apes.[5]

Likewise, Dr. C. John Collins, professor of Old Testament at Covenant Theological Seminary, questions these population genomics figures. He cites 2006 research from Canada, France, and Japan that "indicates ambiguity about the rate of changes in genetic diversity that have been used thus far to calculate primordial population sizes."[6]

Theorizing about how many people it would initially take in the deep past to generate observed human genetic diversity today, according to Collins and Gauger, is far from an exact science.

Another factor that geneticists usually fail to consider is the original genome of the first man and woman, Adam and Eve. From a creationist's point of view, the optimal DNA and genetic diversity of the first couple formed by the hand of God is impossible to quantify because it has been lost to time, and potentially radically changed since the Fall. But it does seem plausible that Adam and Eve had a physiology and genotype different from our own today. After all, Adam lived to be 930 years old—so clearly his biology was different from ours. So their biological makeup may have been such that their genetic diversity was not comparable to humans today. If that is the case there might be no genetic reason why an initial pair of two humans couldn't have led to present-day human genetic diversity in a short period of time.

Passage:

God said, "Be fruitful and multiply. Fill the earth and govern it" (Genesis 1:28).

Difficulty: Didn't God ordain sexual relations between a husband and wife for the sole purpose of procreation?

Explanation: There are those who believe that the only time a husband and wife should engage in sexual intercourse is for the purpose of procreation. However, Scripture identifies at least two other reasons God gave humans the gift of sex.

"God said, 'It is not good for the man to be alone. I will make a helper who is just right for him'...Now the man and his wife were both naked, but they felt no shame" (Genesis 2:18,25). God also designed sex within marriage to bring two people together emotionally, to remove their aloneness, and to create a bonding and oneness.

Certainly sex was given to us to reproduce and have a family, but one of its additional purposes is to bring a married couple fully together spiritually, relationally, and biologically for a lifetime. When expressed properly sex can meet the desire and need for intimacy for a husband and wife. That is why Jesus said, "Since they [a married couple] are no longer two but one, let no one split apart what God has joined together" (Matthew 19:6). Sexual relationship is designed to express the oneness of marriage and intimacy of the husband and wife relationship.

Another purpose of sex within marriage is the recreational factor. Procreation and intimacy are very important factors of sex, but marital sex was made for our pleasure as well. King Solomon put it this way:

> Let your wife be a fountain of blessing for you. Rejoice in the wife of your youth. She is a loving deer, a graceful doe. Let her breasts satisfy you always. May you always be captivated by her love (Proverbs 5:18-19).

Sex between a committed husband and wife is designed for pleasure—to playfully enjoy each other as well as to express and deepen their intimacy and to "be fruitful and multiply."

> **Passage:**
>
> The creation of the heavens and the earth and everything in them was completed. On the seventh day God had finished his work of creation, so he rested from all his work. And God blessed the seventh day and declared it holy, because it was the day when he rested from all his work of creation. This is the account of the creation of the heavens and the earth (Genesis 2:1-4).
>
> **Difficulty:** Did God create the world in six 24-hour days, or is the world billions of years old as the standard scientific dating suggests?

Explanation: There is a wide variety of theories Christians have presented and understood for the duration of creation in Genesis. Here are a few of the more common explanations:

The *gap theory* postulates that eons passed between Genesis 1:1 and Genesis 1:2—possibly leaving plant and animal remains in the fossils we now find. Part of this theory postulates that Satan was cast down to earth and destroyed it, rendering the earth "formless and empty" as described in Genesis 1:2. This is partially based on the assumption that God would never create something as chaotic as is described in the second verse of the chapter. The time then between verses 1 and 2 could have been millions of years. This view has grown out of favor in scholarly circles.

The *day-age theory* holds that each day of creation embraced extended periods of time. This theory turns on the scientific data for an older earth as well as the definition of the Hebrew word *yom* or "day" for the six days of creation in Genesis 1. Does *day* mean 24 hours or a period of time in general, as in "the day of trouble" (Psalm 20:1 NASB)? Those that support this theory say that a day is not limited to 24 hours. They also point to Peter who said, "A day is like a thousand years to the Lord" (2 Peter 3:8).

The *progressive creation theory* suggests that God may have guided a general evolutionary process and intervened at strategic points—such as imparting life into the first cell or breathing a soul into hominids. This theory usually utilizes some form of the day-age theory to explain the six days of creation. It is important to recognize the difference between this view and Darwin's theory. Progressive creation implies that God was involved in *guiding* the process to a desired end. Thus, progressive creationists embrace intelligent design. In contrast, Darwinian evolution lacks any intelligent design and is entirely materialistic.

The *24-hour solar day theory* is that God created everything at full maturity in six 24-hour solar days (this view is usually associated with *young-earth creationism*). This means that the universe and all within it has the appearance of having gone through a development stage. Examples of this would be Adam and Eve, created fully developed, and the wine Jesus created in Cana, fully fermented in an instant of time. This would explain the earth's appearance of millions of years of age, while in reality it was recently created within only thousands of years. Young-earth creationists believe the fossil evidence and geological data can also be explained by appealing to Noah's universal Flood.

The Earth is typically viewed as somewhere between 6000 and 10,000 years old.

The *framework view theory* regards the seven days of creation as a figurative framework. While Genesis 1 records real historical events, such as God creating light or animals, they are recorded in a nonsequential literary structure of a seven-day week. Framework view proponents note how creation days form a framework of two parallel triads. The first triad (days 1-3) includes the creation of the "creation kingdoms" of light (day 1), sky and seas (day 2), and dry land and vegetation (day 3). The second triad (days 4-6) includes the creation of "creature kings" who exercise dominion over those kingdoms. Thus, God creates luminaries (day 4), sea creatures and winged creatures (day 5), and land animals and man (day 6). Framework view supporters observe that the temptation accounts of Jesus in the Gospels are recorded in different chronological order (Matthew 4:1-11; Luke 4:1-13), yet this does not diminish the historicity of the temptation itself.[7]

There are others, such as Dr. John H. Walton, Professor of Old Testament at Wheaton College, who believe we mistakenly read modern concerns about the material origins of life into the Genesis account. Walton contends Genesis 1 was not written to give us a scientific explanation of the origin of the universe. Rather it focuses on metaphysical questions of how God ordered the universe. He asserts that the biblical record describes how the cosmos was created as God's temple—a place he wished to reside with his creation. According to Dr. Walton, days 1-3 establish functions of the universe, while days 4-6 establish functionaries—the vehicle through which the created world was to operate. Day 7 was the day God took up residence within his created world. Walton contends that in the Hebrew mind Genesis 1 is presenting the cosmos in its original state as God's residency in his temple with his creation.

There are yet others, like Dr. John Sailhamer, a Hebrew and Old Testament scholar at Southeastern Baptist Theological Seminary, who propose a kind of "modified gap theory." He contends that the word *beginning* can refer to an indefinite and possibly long period of time. Sailhamer believes, while the functioning universe was created sometime "in the beginning," God's declaration of life (Genesis 1:3) is the advent of sunrise and cities. He sees Genesis 1:2 and the following material as describing God preparing the Promised Land for his chosen people.

We recognize there are well-meaning, thoughtful, and Bible-believing Christians who disagree about the age of the earth and how Genesis 1 is to be interpreted. While these are important matters, they are *not* essential questions that should divide Christians. The most important truth Genesis 1–2 offers is that the personal God is the Creator of all and that humans are his special creation with whom he wants a relationship.

Passage:

The LORD God took the man and put him into the Garden of Eden to cultivate it and keep it. The LORD God commanded the man, saying, "From any tree of the garden you may eat freely; but from the tree of the knowledge of good and evil you shall not eat, for in the day you eat from it you will surely die" (Genesis 2:15-17 NASB).

Difficulty: It is clear that Adam didn't die on the day that he sinned—in fact he lived to be 930 years old. So how can this Scripture passage be accurate?

Explanation: Both Adam and Eve did suffer "death" on the day they disobeyed God. But to understand what that death was, we must understand a little of the nature of God and his relationship with the first human couple.

Scripture tells us that God is all-powerful (see Job 42:2) and has life without end—he is eternal (see Isaiah 40:28). Jesus said, "The Father has life in himself, and he has granted that same life-giving power to his Son" (John 5:26). And it is God the Son, known also as the Word, through whom God created everything, "and nothing was created except through him. The Word gave life to everything that was created"

(John 1:3-4). Adam and Eve got their life from God and were continually dependent on him to sustain their life.

Within God there is not only life, but love, joy, peace, goodness, and everything that brings happiness, meaning, and purpose to our existence. "Whatever is good and perfect," James said, "comes down to us from God" (James 1:17). So if Adam and Eve were dependent upon God, as was everything else, for the sustaining of life, love, joy, goodness, and so on, what would happen if they somehow become disconnected from that very source of life and love? They would die—be separated from life and love.

God is not only the eternal creator and sustainer of life; his core nature is also holy and pure. "The LORD is good and does what is right" (Psalm 25:8). "The LORD is just! He is my rock! There is no evil in him" (Psalm 92:15). He is "the one who is holy and true..." (Revelation 3:7).

God is perfectly holy and without sin. And to be in relationship with sin would be in violation of his nature. The Bible says of him, "Your eyes are too pure to look on evil; you cannot tolerate wrong" (Habakkuk 1:13 NIV). He is so holy that he "cannot allow sin in any form" (Habakkuk 1:13 NLT). So to preserve his holiness there is only one thing he can do when confronted with sin, and that is to separate himself from it.

The reason Scripture says that the "wages of sin is death" (Romans 6:23) is because God, the sustenance of life, has separated himself from those who are sinful. "When Adam sinned," the Bible says, "sin entered the world. Adam's sin brought death [separation from God], so death spread to everyone, for everyone sinned" (Romans 5:12).

It's true that Adam and Eve did not physically die on the day they disobeyed God. But they died spiritually that day because they became relationally separated from God. And the physical death process began immediately. Their relational separation from God separated them from him as the eternal life source, and it was only a matter of time until they would physically die. So on the very day Adam and Eve sinned they did die spiritually, and their separation from God eventually resulted in physical death.

Passage:

The Lord God said, "It is not good for the man to be alone. I will make a helper who is just right for him"... While the man slept, the Lord God took out one of the man's ribs and closed up the opening. Then the Lord God made the woman from the rib and he brought her to the man. "At last!" the man exclaimed. "This one is bone of my bone, and flesh from my flesh! She will be called 'woman,' because she was taken from man" (Genesis 2:18,21-23).

Difficulty: Since God created a woman out of a man to be his "helper," does this indicate that women are not on equal par with men?

Explanation: God said, "'Let us make human beings in our image, to be like ourselves'...male and female he created them" (Genesis 1:26-27). The woman was made in the same image and likeness of God as the man. Men were not given a more superior image of God, with God somehow creating women in a lesser image. Men and women equally share his image.

The Bible also says God made woman as man's "helper." Some have thought this helper role means that God created women as servants or assistants to men. However, the Hebrew word translated as "helper" is *ezer*. It denotes one who surrounds, protects, or aids. It is this same word that Jacob used of God when he said, "May the God of your father *help* you" (Genesis 49:25). Moses used it when he said, "The God of my ancestors was my *helper*" (Exodus 18:4).

The psalmist David used it repeatedly in passages like "We put our hope in the Lord. He is our *help* and our shield" (Psalm 33:20). God is primarily portrayed by the Old Testament writers as the *ezer*—the one who surrounds us and helps us. This by no means is a lowly servant role. Rather, it is a lofty role to bring help to one who needs it. And many men today will admit they need the aid and help of not only God, but the expert aid and help of a woman in the person of a wife. When God created a female as a Godlike equal to help the male, it was a highly esteemed role, not one of a inferiority or servitude. God considered the man to be in need of a woman and that didn't mean he was inferior either. Women are not inferior for being a counterpart or companion to men, and men are not weak for needing women.

Genesis actually has a uniquely *high* value of women. There are hundreds of other creation accounts in the ancient Near East besides Genesis. And yet Genesis uniquely climaxes with the creation of women. The Babylonians, Sumerians, and Mesopotamians did not even think women worthy of mention in their creation accounts, and yet the biblical account has the woman being the final act of a progressive creation. The Bible values women.

Passage:

Adam said, This is now bone of my bones, and flesh of my flesh: she shall be called Woman...And Adam called his wife's name Eve; because she was the mother of all living (Genesis 2:23; 3:20 KJV).

Difficulty: Were Adam and Eve real people or simply a biblical allegory to teach us about good and evil?

Explanation: As we saw in response to Genesis 1:27-28, there are no good genetic reasons why we ought to reject belief in Adam and Eve. Despite what the Bible clearly teaches on this matter, there is a growing number of Christians who question whether Adam and Eve were real historical figures. They see Adam, Eve, and the creation story as metaphorical, a story in which the first couple is a figurative representation of how primitive humanity interacted with divine revelation. Many who take this view, like those associated with the BioLogos Foundation, which promotes theistic evolution, twist Scripture to align with evolutionary theory.

For example, Peter Enns, formerly a senior fellow with the BioLogos Foundation, contends that a literal Adam as a special creation without evolutionary forebears is "at odds with everything else we know about the past from the natural sciences and cultural remains." As he reads the early chapters of Genesis, he says, "The Bible itself invites a symbolic reading by using cosmic battle imagery and by drawing parallels between Adam and Israel." After scanning various interpretations of Genesis, Enns joins those who see the Genesis passages on Adam as "a story of Israelite origins," not the origin of all humanity, in which case there is no essential conflict with evolutionary theory.[8]

A *Christianity Today* magazine cover story stated that commentary on Genesis by British evangelist Derek Kidner proposed a "tentative" concept that could fit with geneticists' theory of human origination with a larger population. He thought it conceivable that "pre-Adamites" and "Adamites" from the same genetic stock existed simultaneously but with "no natural bridge from animal to man." After God conferred his image upon Adam, he did the same with the others who then existed, "to bring them into the same realm of being." In Kidner's view, Adam's "headship of humanity extended, if that was the case, outwards to his contemporaries as well as onwards to his offspring, and his disobedience disinherited both alike."[9]

There are other explanations to address the "population genomics" issue without denying there was a literal Adam and Eve that lived in the Garden of Eden (see *Explanation* of Genesis 1:27-28). To try to reinterpret the Genesis story to bring it in line with Darwinian evolution invites many problems of biblical interpretation.

In Genesis 2 it states, "This is the account of the creation of the heavens and the earth" (Genesis 2:4). The phrase "this is the account" (literally "these are the generations") is repeated throughout Genesis. In chapter 5 it says, "This is the written account of the descendants of Adam. When God created human beings, he made them to be like himself…" (Genesis 5:1). This "written account" is providing us with a historical record of Adam's genealogy through Seth that traces ten generations to Noah. Then in chapter 6 it says, "This is the account of Noah and his family…" (Genesis 6:9). And we read another ten generations from Noah to Abram.

If Adam and Eve didn't actually exist, that means the historical "written accounts" are not historical records at all. In fact, if Adam wasn't a real person then the apostle Paul was seriously mistaken.

Because Paul states that "when Adam sinned, sin entered the world. Adam's sin brought death, so death spread to everyone, for everyone sinned" (Romans 5:12). It is clear that Paul believed Adam was a real person of history.

Tim Keller, pastor of Redeemer Presbyterian Church in Manhattan, weighs in on this issue by saying,

> Paul most definitely wanted to teach us that Adam and Eve were real historical figures. When you refuse to take a biblical author literally when he clearly wants you to do so, you have moved away from the traditional understanding of the biblical authority...If Adam doesn't exist, Paul's whole argument—that both sin and grace work "covenantally"—falls apart. You can't say that "Paul was a man of his time" but we can accept his basic teaching about Adam. If you don't believe what he believes about Adam, you are denying the core of Paul's teaching.[10]

Then in Matthew 19:4-6 we have Jesus quoting Genesis 1:27 about Adam and Eve's creation. Was Jesus also seriously mistaken about a literal first couple? And was Luke seriously mistaken too? He provided the account of Jesus' genealogy all the way back to the historical record that "Seth was the son of Adam. Adam was the son of God" (Luke 3:38).

South Carolina pastor Richard Phillips, a blogger with the Alliance of Confessing Evangelicals and chair of the Philadelphia Conference on Reformed Theology, sees serious doctrinal danger if the historical Adam disappears. "Can the Bible's theology be true if the historical events on which the theology is based are false?" he asks.[11] The Bible is not only a theological book. It is also a book about the history of how we as humans were created by God, how sin entered the human race, and how God's miraculous plan is to redeem his lost children and restore everything to his original design.

Passage:

The serpent was the shrewdest of all the wild animals the LORD God had made. One day he asked the woman, "Did God really say you must not eat the fruit from any of the trees in the garden?" (Genesis 3:1).

Difficulty: Where do people get the idea that the serpent in the Garden of Eden was the devil?

Explanation: There are a number of reasons the serpent in the Garden of Eden is considered to be the embodiment of Satan. Revelation describes a time when Michael and his angels went to war with Satan and his angels. This is when the devil was forced out of heaven. Scripture describes him as "this great dragon—the ancient serpent called the devil, or Satan, the one deceiving the whole world" (Revelation 12:9). Later in Revelation it describes a time when Satan was locked in a bottomless pit. "He seized the dragon—the old serpent, who is the devil, Satan—and bound him in chains for a thousand years" (Revelation 20:2).

In both cases Satan is identified as the "old" and "ancient" serpent. Scholars believe this is a clear reference to the serpent in the Garden of Eden.

Another indication that the serpent was Satan is found in verse 15 of Genesis 3. God said, "I will put enmity between you and the woman, and between your seed and her seed; he shall bruise you on the head, and you shall bruise him on the heel" (Genesis 3:15 NASB). This verse is prophetic, for the offspring of the woman is, of course, Christ. The words "you and the *woman*" stand out as both unique and prophetic, for a critical reason.

Genesis 3:15 refers specifically to the offspring of the woman and not the man because Jesus was supernaturally born of a virgin (see Isaiah 7:14). It was Jesus, the perfect Son of God that defeated the old serpent. "For only as a human being could he die, and only by dying could he break the power of the devil, who had the power of death"

(Hebrews 2:14). The old serpent may have been instrumental in Jesus' death, but in the end it was Jesus' victory over death that broke the power of the serpent.

Passage:

He [God] said to the woman, "I will sharpen the pain of your pregnancy, and in pain you will give birth. And you will desire to control your husband, but he will rule over you" (Genesis 3:16).

Difficulty: Was God's curse on women to be forever ruled by men?

Explanation: There were negative consequences of Adam and Eve's disobedience to God. Yet these consequences were extended to all humanity and to Planet Earth. They included spiritual and physical death on all humans, increased physical pain in childbearing for women, husbands ruling over wives, and the cursed ground affecting plant life, making it hard for humans to grow crops. (See Genesis 3:14-19). But these negative consequences were not meant to be accepted as norms. God himself put a plan in motion even before he created humans to reverse these very consequences. He planned to send his Son to not only offer eternal life to humans who were dead in their sin, but to eventually reverse the effects of sin on the entire planet and animal life (see Isaiah 25:7-8 and Isaiah 65:17).

So are we as God's children to sit still and not assist him in his redemptive and restoration plan? Of course not. We have discovered new and improved ways to farm the land and increase crop productivity in order to grow better and healthier crops. We take advantage of modern medical discoveries to ease the pain of the birthing process. We don't accept these negative consequences of sin and simply live with them—we take the initiative to counteract them. And neither should we accept the negative consequences of husbands that rule over their wives. This was not God's intention from the beginning, and it is clear he doesn't want that kind of distorted relationship in marriage now. No one should be lording it over another.

While the New Testament does teach that wives are to submit to their husbands, this is by no means an oppressive act. In fact, Scripture commands that we all submit to one another (see Ephesians 5:21). Jesus made the truth clear that both men and women are to serve one another in Mark 10:42-44, and he included himself: "Even the Son of Man came not to be served but to serve others and give his life as a ransom for many" (Mark 10:45).

Because husbands and wives share different roles doesn't mean women are to be ruled over. Sin brought negative consequences to our relationships, but God doesn't want that to continue. He wants both husbands and wives to respect and love one another as he demonstrated to us through Christ. (For more on the husband and wife relationship see *Explanation* of Ephesians 5:22-23 and Ephesians 5:28.)

Jesus affirmed the rights of women when he spoke to the Samaritan woman (John 4:1-42). He affirmed Mary as she sat at his feet as his disciples did. Jesus gave great praise to the women who anointed him prior to his death (Mark 14:3-9). To Jesus, women were equals in God's eyes. Relationally God sees no significant difference between male and female. As we stated, husbands and wives may have different roles, but this does not make one more superior to rule or one inferior to be ruled over. The apostle Paul made it clear that God did not engage in favoritism when he said,

> You are all children of God through faith in Christ Jesus. And all who have been united with Christ in baptism have put on Christ, like putting on new clothes. There is no longer Jew or Gentile, slave or free, male or female. For you are all one in Christ Jesus (Galatians 3:26-28).

Passage:

The Lord God said, "Look, the human beings have become like us, knowing both good and evil. What if

> they reach out, take fruit from the tree of life, and eat it? Then they will live forever!" So the LORD God banished them from the Garden of Eden...the LORD God stationed mighty cherubim to the east of the Garden of Eden. And he placed a flaming sword that flashed back and forth to guard the way to the tree of life (Genesis 3:22-24).
>
> **Difficulty:** Why would God deny Adam and Eve access to the tree of life that could allow them to live forever?

Explanation: God's original plan was for humans to enjoy an unbroken relationship with him. He wanted Adam and Eve and all their offspring to live a life of joy and happiness that came from him. The perpetual source of all goodness in life was from the holy and perfect nature of God. He wanted humans to experience that kind of existence for all eternity. But he gave them a choice.

God gave the first couple the power to choose between unselfishly loving him and believing that *he* knew what was best, or selfishly loving themselves and believing *they* knew what was best. What he wanted was for humans to trust that he (the infinite God) knew what was best for them (finite humans). He wanted them to unselfishly put him first and learn that his way of living was a way of joy, peace, goodness. If the first couple had followed that way they would have no doubt been given perpetual access to the tree of life.

But since Adam and Eve chose not to trust God, sin entered the world and immeasurable pain and suffering followed. This broke God's heart (see Genesis 6:6). Certainly he wanted humans to live forever, but not in a fallen state of perpetual pain, heartache, selfish warring, jealousy, greed, and separation from him. So he kept them from eating from the tree of life. However, he wasn't satisfied with leaving humans in this state of sin. That is why he implemented a plan of salvation in which his Son would sacrifice himself and become the means of raising his lost children from death to eternal life.

The next time we read of the tree of life is in Revelation, in the description of the new heaven and new earth and the New Jerusalem. The water of life is flowing from God's throne and "on each side of the river grew a tree of life...The leaves were used for medicine to heal the nations" (Revelation 22:2). Once Jesus finally destroys sin and death (see 1 Corinthians 15:24-28) those that have trusted in Christ will have access to the tree of life forever.

Passage:

The Lord God banished them from the Garden of Eden, and he sent Adam out to cultivate the ground from which he had been made (Genesis 3:23).

Difficulty: This is perhaps the saddest passage in all the Bible. What does God do in an attempt to restore "paradise lost"?

Explanation: The 66 books of the Bible tell the story of who God is and who we as human beings are (the creation), what he did in response to human sin and how he forms our purpose in life (the incarnation), and what his mission of restoration is and where we are going (re-creation).

The historical record of the creation, the incarnation (God taking on human form), and God's planned re-creation provide the sweeping story from Genesis to Revelation. The Bible gives us God's response to a fallen human race in three profound declarations.

We identified those three declarations in our book entitled *The Unshakable Truth* (see the back of this book for more information). We offer them here to explain what God did and is doing to restore paradise lost, written in the first person as if God were speaking:

God's Creation Declaration

I am God. I have spoken the world into existence and have delivered my words to you accurately so you can know me and my truth. I have created you in my likeness for the purpose of having a love relationship with you. Out of that relationship you will find joy in knowing who you are, why you are here, and where you are going. However, you have not trusted what I have told you. You have sinned by disobeying my truth, and sin has brought you death—a separation from me. This separation has resulted in the deforming of my image and likeness in you, and as a result you have suffered immensely. Because I am a God of relationships this has broken my heart.

God's Incarnation Declaration

Because I am also a God of redemption and want to regain my relationship with you, I have provided the only solution to your problem of sin and death. I have entered the world in human form on a mission to redeem you and transform you back into my image. This requires that I atone for your sin by laying down my own human life. If you accept my provision for your salvation, which I offer in love and grace, you and I can again enter into a relationship with each other.

God's Re-Creation Declaration

I cannot accomplish my mission to redeem you eternally unless I conquer death through Christ's resurrection and establish my eternal kingdom in a new heaven and a new earth. You are to join us—the Father, the Son, and the Holy Spirit who empowers you—in our mission to first establish our kingdom in the hearts and minds of men and women. We will accomplish this mission through Christ's body, the church; and upon his return all things will be eternally restored to my original design. I will do this because I am also a God of restoration.

When God established a covenant relationship with Abraham—and through him, the children of Israel—he was putting into place his promise of redemption and restoration for the entire human race. Upon Christ's future return his promise to restore paradise lost will be fulfilled.

Passage:

Cain had sexual relations with his wife, and she became pregnant and gave birth to Enoch. Then Cain founded a city, which he named Enoch, after his son (Genesis 4:17).

Difficulty: Where did Cain get his wife, and where did the people come from to build a city?

Explanation: The Bible records only three people on the earth when Cain married (Adam, Eve, and Cain—Abel had been killed). So we don't know for sure when Cain married or who he married. We don't know exactly how many children Adam and Eve had during their lifetime. But we do know that Adam had "other sons and daughters" (Genesis 5:4) and that he lived for 930 years. And we know that the people of that time lived on average over 800 years. So a very sizable population could have developed very rapidly.

Cain no doubt married a sister or niece or grandniece. It appears that at first, sons and daughters of the first couple had to marry each other to populate the earth.

The Scripture simply doesn't tell us at what point in the life of Cain he murdered his brother, married his wife, or built his city. Even a few hundred years might have passed before all of these events took place, allowing for a large population with which to build a city.

All this raises the question of incest. If incest is scripturally forbidden, according to the Mosaic law, how do we explain all this marrying of siblings? Since Adam and Eve were created directly by God, and perfect, it can be presumed that their gene pool was perfect. So marrying relatives and having children would probably not have produced defective offspring.

When sin entered the world, however, death, disease, and destruction followed and this gene pool would have gradually become corrupted. Had sin not entered the world, it's possible that there would have never been a genetic problem with the intermarrying of relatives.

But after hundreds of years, no doubt diseases took their toll on human genetics, which resulted in mutant and defective births of relatives intermarrying. That is probably the reason incest was prohibited in Moses' time. From a biological standpoint it was presumably dangerous and resulted in deformed, moronic, or otherwise defective offspring.

In addition to the biological problem which arises from incest, there is also an ethical one. When God gave the law to Moses incest was declared wrong on moral grounds, and this is more crucial than the biological aspect (see Leviticus 18:16-18).

Passage:

Lamech married two women. The first was named Adah, and the second was named Zillah (Genesis 4:19).

Difficulty: Does the Bible condone polygamy?

Explanation: Scripture does teach us what is right and wrong (2 Timothy 3:16). But the Bible is also the history of people and a nation. It records wars, murder, rape, incest, and a host of other tragic events but does not in every case specifically point out the error and sin. It does, however, in most cases, explain the negative consequences of these actions.

Lamech, the seventh from Adam in the line of Cain, is the first recorded polygamist. His life, however, was marked by murder, rebellion, and defiance. It is clear Lamech was not honoring God's design for marriage as stated in Genesis 2:24. Later God would record his views on the importance of men being married to one woman (the wife of their youth) in Proverbs 5:18-19, Malachi 2:14-15, Mark 10:2-8, and 1 Corinthians 7:2-10.

In the moral law God did forbid polygamy. "While your wife is living, do not marry her sister [literally, "a woman to her sister"] and have sexual relations with her, for they would be rivals" (Leviticus 18:18). The Hebrew text uses the phrase "a woman to her sister" and "a man to his brother" numerous times. This is not referring to a literal sister or brother. Rather in this passage it is like saying "do not take a wife in addition to the one you already have."

The key word in this verse is *rival* (Hebrew *tsarah*). The result of marrying another woman is that it creates a rival wife. Throughout Scripture, whenever polygamy occurred, disastrous consequences followed. Abraham took Hagar in addition to his wife Sarah and Ishmael was born (Genesis 16:3-11). And the rivalry was prophesied by the angel of the Lord: "He [Ishmael] will live in open hostility against all his relatives" (Genesis 16:12). Jacob experienced the negative consequences of having Rachel and Leah as wives (Genesis 30). Hannah, the wife of Elkanah, felt the ridicule of Peninnah as a rival wife (1 Samuel 1:6). While the Scripture is full of examples of polygamy, they were not with God's blessing.

King Solomon perhaps was the "greatest" of polygamists. He had 700 wives and 300 concubines (1 Kings 11:3). Solomon did this in disobedience to God's instructions to the kings of Israel. "'You must not marry them, because they will turn your hearts to their gods.' Yet Solomon insisted on loving them anyway...And in fact, they did turn his heart away from God" (1 Kings 11:2-3). Solomon, like so many in the Old Testament, violated God's original design for one man and one woman to "be one" in marriage and paid the tragic consequences.

In contrast, Seth obeyed God's commands, and his life and his offspring paint a picture of God's blessing. Like Lamech, Enoch was also the seventh from Adam, only in the line of Seth. And it is in the line of Seth that "people first began to worship the LORD by name" (Genesis 4:26). At the age of 65 Enoch became the father of Methuselah, the longest living person recorded in Scripture. And "Enoch lived in close fellowship with God for another 300 years...Then one day he disappeared, because God took him" (Genesis 5:22,24). Lamech reflects disobedience, violence, and destruction while Enoch reflects obedience, closeness to God, and the real hope that death is not our final doom.

Passage:

When Adam was 130 years old, he became the father of a son who was just like him—in his very image. He named his son Seth. After the birth of Seth, Adam lived another 800 years, and he had other sons and daughters. Adam lived 930 years, and then he died (Genesis 5:3-5).

Difficulty: From Adam to Noah people lived an average of over 800 years. How could people live that long?

Explanation: The life expectancy in the U.S. is under 80 years. Some progress has been made within the last two centuries to increase the life span of humans, but adding 20 to 30 years to our lives has not gotten us anywhere near the life span of the first people. To live up to 800 to 900 years seems impossible. So how is it that people prior to Noah lived so long?

The aging process is complex, involving biochemical, endocrinological, nutritional, biological, and atmospheric effects on human life. Research in each of these areas has shown that even subtle changes can increase life expectancy. In the perfect paradise where God created a perfect couple, one would expect the physiological, nutritional, and atmospheric conditions to be perfect. And even after being separated from God due to sin, the natural negative effects on Adam and Eve and their offspring could have been gradual, allowing them to still reap the benefits of the original paradise.

It is significant to notice that there is a clear life span difference between those who lived before the Flood and after the Flood. Prior to the Flood a life span of 900 years was common. After the Flood the life span dropped sharply to 100 to 200 years.

Biochemist Dr. Fazale R. Rana and astrophysicist Dr. Hugh Ross provide some insight on how atmospheric changes could have an effect on life expectancy immediately after the Flood.

> A major astronomical event provides a partial explanation for how God may have acted to reduce the long pre-flood human life spans. Cosmic radiation is one of the main factors that limit human life expectancy. The cosmic radiation coming down to Earth has not been uniform through time, and in fact, most of the deadliest cosmic radiation Earth experiences comes from a fairly recent and nearby (1300 light-years away) event, the Vela supernova. A supernova is a rare celestial phenomenon that is the explosion of most of the material in a star. It is estimated that roughly at the time of the Genesis flood, the Vela supernova erupted.
>
> Prior to the Vela supernova, only a fraction of the current level of deadly cosmic radiation bathed the Earth. Under these lower radiation conditions (coupled with

> complementary biochemical adjustments) life spans of up to 900 years might have been possible. Scientists do acknowledge that this higher-level radiation silently bombarding the Earth since Vela plays a significant role in limiting life expectancy. Moreover, a significant radiation event such as Vela would explain the mathematical curve, the gradual, exponential reduction in life spans, from about 900 to 120 years reported in Genesis.[12]

These two Christian scientists conclude their remarks on the long lifespans recorded in Genesis by saying,

> Scientists' success in altering the life span of selected organisms (such as worms, yeast, and fruit flies) and their emerging ability to increase human life expectancy through biochemical manipulation lend scientific plausibility to the long life spans recorded in Genesis 5. If humans with their limited knowledge and power can alter life spans, how much more so can God? He could have used any of four (or more) subtle alterations in human biochemistry to allow for long life spans. He could have used the Vela supernova or other astronomical events, in combination with complementary biochemical changes, to shorten human longevity.[13]

Passage:

The people began to multiply on the earth, and daughters were born to them. The sons of God saw the beautiful women and took any they wanted as their wives...Then the LORD said, "My Spirit will not put up with humans for such a long time, for they are only mortal flesh. In the future, their normal years will be no more than 120 years." In those days, and for some time after, giant Nephilites lived on the earth, for whenever the sons of God had intercourse with women, they gave birth to children who became the heroes and famous warriors of ancient times (Genesis 6:1-4).

Difficulty: So did angels—fallen angels—have sexual relations with mortal women to create half angel–half human creatures called Nephilites?

Explanation: Prior to AD 500 writers of ancient Jewish and Christian literature commonly interpreted the "sons of God" as fallen angels. First Enoch 7:1-7, a part of Jewish literature that is not accepted as Hebrew Scripture, explains that 200 fallen angels came to earth and bore children with the "daughters of men." Their offspring were called Nephilites and were believed to be a hybrid race between these fallen angels and humans which became powerful warriors.

By the fourth century the book of Enoch had long been rejected and the common view was that the "sons of God" referred to the God-fearing descendants of Seth. And it was those men who married the daughters of the wicked and rebellious line of Cain.

Some believe that since angels are spiritual beings they are not reproductively compatible with human beings. Others contend that we really don't know what angels, fallen or not, can do. And if the fallen angels did produce an evil offspring, perhaps that was another reason God sent the Flood. He wanted to rid the world of such profound evil.

Truth is, there is a case for both views. However, it does seem that whoever the giant Nephilite warriors were, they were destroyed in the Flood.

Passage:

God saw that the earth had become corrupt and was filled with violence. God observed all this corruption in the world, for everyone on earth was corrupt. So God said to Noah, "I have decided to destroy all living creatures, for they have filled the earth with violence. Yes, I will wipe them all out along with the earth!" (Genesis 6:11-13).

Difficulty: God obviously brought judgment upon a wicked world through a flood. Does this mean God brings judgment on people today by sending earthquakes, volcanoes, tornadoes, floods, and every kind of natural disaster?

Explanation: God did bring judgment on the people of Noah's time and destroyed them in the Flood. There are other incidents in Scripture when God withheld rain from Israel (1 Kings 17:1), sent plagues upon Egypt (Exodus 3:19-20), and opened up the ground to swallow the household of Korah, who was rebelling against Moses (Numbers 16:29-33). We see that Jesus had control of the weather, when he calmed the storm for his disciples (Luke 8:24). God is fully in control of every atom of the universe, and he can use the natural elements to accomplish his will, including judgment upon nations, cities, and small towns.

Scripture does say that "each person is destined to die once and after that comes judgment" (Hebrews 9:27). But God is merciful and for the most part reserves his judgment until we face him after death. He definitely has the power to send judgment now, but we shouldn't consider natural disasters as his punishing us.

Remember that the earth was cursed because of sin. The planet seemed to undergo a transition to violence. Now cold air and warm air collide, tumultuous weather patterns form, tornadoes twist, hurricanes swirl, rains fall, floods come, the earth shifts, the ground shakes, and volcanoes erupt. Today the earth experiences 2000 thunderstorms at any one time. Our planet receives a shocking 100 lightning strikes per second—3.6 trillion strikes per year![14] We live on a violent earth.

But God is no more pleased with natural disasters than we are. And he will one day bring peace to a violent earth. Scripture says that "all creation is waiting eagerly for that future day when God will reveal who his children really are" and "when it will join God's children in glorious freedom from death and decay. For we know that all creation has been groaning as in the pains of childbirth up to this present time" (Romans 8:19,20-21).

Meteorologists tell us that floods are the number-one natural-disaster killer. Perhaps the message isn't that God is punishing those who are swept away by floods, but rather we need to be more careful where we build our businesses and homes. Modern construction has enabled levees to be constructed in recent years that have opened up millions of acres for communities to grow around the world. And when these levees overflow or break, low-lying communities are devastated. This isn't to suggest that God can't speak through natural disasters nor judge people by them. But this planet follows the laws of physics and nature. So it is wise when natural tragedy strikes not to cast blame on either the victims or on God.

When natural disasters strike, rather than wondering if God is punishing us personally, it is better to follow Peter's advice to "humble yourselves under the mighty power of God, and at the right time he will lift you up in honor. Give all your worries and cares to God, for he cares about you" (1 Peter 5:6-7).

Passage:

Look! I am about to cover the earth with a flood that will destroy every living thing that breathes. Everything on earth will die (Genesis 6:17).

Difficulty: Was the Flood a localized disaster or a worldwide destruction of all human and animal life?

Explanation: Many geologists and Christian scholars do not believe there was a single universal flood of history, yet acknowledge that there were many devastating local floods in earth's history. On the other hand, there are geologists and Christian scholars who contend that only a worldwide flood could account for the earth's sedimentary layers and the fossils that have been formed.

The Scripture states that "all the underground waters erupted from the earth, and the rain fell in mighty torrents from the sky...Finally, the water covered even the highest mountains on the earth, rising more than twenty-two feet above the highest peaks" (Genesis 7:11,19-20).

This passage can be interpreted at least two ways. One is that the Flood covered the highest mountains of Planet Earth. This interpretation comes from translating the Hebrew word *erets* as "earth" or "world," meaning worldwide. However, *erets* can also be translated as "country" and "land," which refer to limited land areas. So scholars have differed on the extensiveness of the Flood.

Some point to the Psalms as another indication that the Flood was not global. The psalmist describes the third day of creation, when God separated the land from the sea:

> At your command, the water fled; at the sound of your thunder, it hurried away. Mountains rose and valleys sank to the level you decreed. Then you set a boundary for the seas, so they would never again cover the earth (Psalm 104:7-9).

This, according to some scholars, tells us that God did send the Flood but not over all the earth since Scripture seems to indicate the world would never again be covered entirely by water as it was in the beginning of creation.

If, however, the Flood was global as some geologists claim, the land masses themselves would have undergone tremendous changes. Rocks would have bounced and cracked in the turbulence, disintegrating into gravel and sand. Enormous seas of mud and rocks would have swirled upstream and raced downstream and overtaken plant and animal remains, dragging them along.

As the waters calmed, these sediments would have slowly settled again. Dissolved chemicals would have formed in thick layers at various times and places. This means thick sedimentary layers would have been formed all over the world. Under the great forces of a worldwide cataclysmic flood, they would have formed into fossil-bearing sedimentary rock.

This scenario does not account adequately for everything we find in the geological record. But scattered fossils and gigantic fossil beds of marine invertebrates and plant formations are located around the world, in all climates and all altitudes. There are fossils in Death Valley in California, the lowest elevation in North America. There are fossils on the tops of high mountain ranges, in tropical jungles, in the polar regions. The presence of fossils, and often of large deposits, in almost every area of the world is evidence that points to the universality of the Flood.

While the evidence of fossils in different areas of the world does suggest a global flood, some still raise difficult questions like these:

- If the Flood was global, how do you explain the receding of the water? How did so much water drain away or evaporate in such a short period of time?
- How could plants, trees, and other vegetation survive salt water from the oceans?
- How could many of the marine life survive the mingling of salt and fresh water?

These and other questions lead some to believe that the Flood was very extensive and destroyed those who God wanted killed, but that it was not global.

Whether the Flood was restricted to a local but wide area of the earth, or was on a global scale, will continue to be debated. But clearly there was a flood that accomplished God's purpose.

Additionally, an extensive flood is written about in practically every ancient culture.

- The Babylonian Gilgamesh epic (1900 BC) tells of a Noah-like character named Utnapishtim who was told by Ea, the god of wisdom, to build a ship because a flood was coming.[15]
- In Asia, Flood stories are found in the folklore of remote tribes on the Indian peninsula, including those of the Kamars, those in Kashmir, and in Assam. In a Chinese tradition, Fah-He escaped from the Flood with his wife, three sons, and three daughters, from whom the entire population of the modern world was descended.[16]
- In Australia and the Pacific, the Australian aborigines have

Flood stories that say that God sent a flood as judgment on man's wickedness. The Hawaiians say that a long time after the first man, Kumu-Honua, all of mankind became completely wicked. The only righteous man was Nu-u, who was saved from the Flood that inundated the land. God left the rainbow as a token of his forgiveness of Nu-u and his family.[17]

- In the Americas, Alaskans tell the story that the "father" of their tribe was warned by a vision that a flood would destroy all life on the earth. He built a raft upon which he was able to save his family and all the animals.[18]
- In Europe, the ancient Druids taught that in judgment a great fire split the earth so that all of the seas swept over the earth and killed all life except for one wise man, his family, and the animals he had gathered in his barge.[19]
- In Africa: Plato recorded a statement of an Egyptian priest that the gods purified the earth by covering it with a flood. In the Sudan, some natives call Lake Chad *Bahar el Nuh*, the Lake of Noah.[20]

The parallels between the many stories from practically every culture are amazing. They generally agree that 1) there was some provision made for rescue (an ark, barge, or similar vessel); 2) living things were destroyed by water; 3) only a few were saved through divine intervention; 4) the Flood was judgment against the man's wickedness; 5) animals were often saved with the few humans, and birds were often used by the humans to report the end of the Flood; 6) the vessel came to rest on a mountaintop, or the people were saved on a mountaintop.[21] The fact that the biblical account of a flood, whether local or global, is shared by so many cultures is added evidence that the Flood was indeed a cataclysmic event as described in Genesis.

Passage:

God said, "Never again will I curse the ground because of humans, even though every inclination of the human heart is evil from childhood. And never again will I destroy all living creatures, as I have done" (Genesis 8:21 NIV).

Difficulty: Isn't God's promise to never again "destroy all living creatures" in contradiction to what it says in the New Testament—that the heavens and earth and all living on the earth will be destroyed by fire?

Explanation: The apostle Peter states "the day of the Lord will come as unexpectedly as a thief. Then the heavens will pass away with a terrible noise, and the very elements themselves will disappear in fire, and the earth and everything on it will be found to deserve judgment" (2 Peter 3:10). But this is not a contradiction of Genesis 8:21.

In Genesis God said he would not destroy "all living creatures, as I have done" (Genesis 8:21 NIV). In other words, God would not destroy all of life in the same manner as a flood. This point is further made in the next chapter when God makes this promise—a covenant—and says rainbows will be a reminder of his promise. "Never again will the floodwaters destroy all life. When I see the rainbow in the clouds, I will remember the eternal covenant between God and every creature on earth" (Genesis 9:15-16).

Passage:

All animals of the earth...will look on you with fear and terror. I have placed them in your power. I have given them to you for food, just as I have given you grain and vegetables (Genesis 9:2-3).

Difficulty: Did God change his mind on what humans could eat?

Explanation: In Genesis 1 God gave Adam and Eve "every seed-bearing plant throughout the earth and all the fruit trees for [their] food" (Genesis 1:29). Originally it seems the first couple was vegetarians. But after God sent the Flood he told Noah and his family to repopulate the earth and instructs them to use animals for food. The straightforward way of reading the command in Genesis 9:2-3 seems to be that God changed his dietary menu for human beings from strictly vegetarian to include fish and meat. If so, then this is an example of progressive revelation. This is where later commands by God supersede earlier ones.

But this is not the only way to take this passage. There *may* have actually been meat eating before the Flood. Philosopher Paul Copan gives a few reasons to think the command to eat meat was not actually new.[22] For one, God tells human beings to "rule over the fish of the sea." What could this mean apart from permission to eat them? Further, Abel kept sheep, which were presumably to eat (Genesis 4:2-4). And Noah distinguished between "clean" and "unclean" animals (7:2), signifying that animals were eaten prior to the Flood. Henri Blocher suggests there is not a progression from prohibition of meat eating (Genesis 1) to permission (Genesis 9). He considers the shift *stylistic* rather than substantive. In other words, Genesis 1 does not mention that meat can be eaten (although it permits it) to suggest the perfect harmony in creation. Genesis 9 mentions it as an indication that the harmony has been shattered.[23]

Passage:

If anyone takes a human life, that person's life will also be taken by human hands. For God made human beings in his own image (Genesis 9:6).

Difficulty: Does Scripture provide our modern society with the justification for capital punishment?

Explanation: As humans we were created in God's own image. This in and of itself establishes the dignity, value, and worth of all human life. God desired from the beginning that we honor one another and life itself. God said, "Honor your father and mother...you must not murder...you must not commit adultery...you must not steal...you must not testify falsely...you must not covet your neighbor's wife" (Deuteronomy 5:16-21). From God's interaction with Adam and Eve, Noah, Abraham, Moses, and the early church, it was understood and taught that life was sacred at every stage. Promoting social justice, taking care of the poor, and defending human rights find their basis in each of us and our governmental bodies by the fact that we are created in God's image with value, dignity, and worth.

The Levitical laws given to the children of Israel established guidelines and a rule of law for that society to function with a measure of order and justice. The law of retaliation called for a penalty that matched the crime.

The law of retaliation, also referenced to as "an eye for an eye, a tooth for a tooth," was established to limit the punishment to the severity of the crime itself. Rather than vengeance determining or escalating the level of punishment for the lawbreaker, the punishment was not to be any more severe than the original injury.

In our American justice system an established authority provides remedies and sanctions for crimes against people, property, and the state in a similar manner. There are civil and criminal cases with different law violations—for example, infractions such as a minor traffic violation, littering, jaywalking, and so on; misdemeanors such as disorderly conduct, petty theft, and so on; and, felonies such as grand theft, kidnapping, and homicide. And for killing someone (homicides) there are various levels, such as involuntary manslaughter, murder in the first degree, murder in the second degree, and so on. And all the penalties for these various types of offenses are designed to, in a sense, match the severity of the crime.

Scripture does give us guidelines and principles to establish a fair and equitable justice system for modern society. And the apostle Paul made it clear that governing authorities are there to exact justice. "Everyone must submit to governing authorities. For all authority comes from God, and those in positions of authority have been placed there by God...They are God's servants, sent for the very purpose of punishing those who do what is wrong" (Romans 13:1,4).

But does that mean that it is justified for a society to take a person's life for the crime of murder? Some would say that the Scripture cited above gives governing authorities the power and right to fairly judge, condemn, and execute a murderer. Others would say that Jesus promoted a "law of mercy and forgiveness" that trumps an "eye for an eye" legal system of justice.

There has been honest debate on both sides of the capital punishment issue for years. So many truth-seeking Christians have held to differing views on this subject.

Passage:

The sons of Noah who came out of the boat with their father were Shem, Ham, and Japheth. (Ham is the father of Canaan.) From these three sons of Noah came all the people who now populate the earth...Ham, the father of Canaan, saw that his father [Noah] was naked and went outside and told his brothers...When Noah woke up from his stupor, he learned what Ham, his youngest son, had done. Then he cursed Canaan, the son of Ham. "May Canaan be cursed! May he be the lowest servants to his relatives" (Genesis 9:18,22,24-25).

Difficulty: Since the descendants of Ham settled in Africa, haven't some people claimed that this Scripture shows that God cursed the African people into slavery?

Explanation: It is true that for many years there were those who claimed God cursed the descendants of Ham, Noah's son, for telling his older brothers he found his father naked after a night of drinking wine. The curse was that "he be the lowest of servants to his relatives" (Genesis 9:25). And since the descendants of Ham were thought to be Africans, it was logical to conclude that God had condemned all generations of Africans into slavery. In fact, many people during the 1700 and 1800s and beyond used those verses to justify the enslavement of Africans in America.

However, this is a gross misinterpretation and misunderstanding of the biblical narrative. First, God never cursed Ham for what he did; it was Noah who made the curse. And Noah didn't curse his son Ham, but rather Ham's son Canaan. "May Canaan be cursed!" Noah said. "May the LORD, the God of Shem, be blessed, and may Canaan be his servant" (Genesis 9:25-26). It was more egregious to curse a man's son than to curse the father so Noah leveled his curse at Ham's son, Canaan.

It is true that at least two sons of Ham, Cush and Mizraim, settled in Africa (see Genesis 10:6-20). But Canaan's descendants settled just east of the Mediterranean Sea, in an area that later became known as the land of Canaan—present-day Israel (see Genesis 10:15-19). So it is absurd to claim God cursed a race to slavery based upon a complete misinterpretation of passages in Genesis. Yet for many years people justified their own racist views toward black Africans and African-Americans upon this twisting of Scripture.

Passage:

> At one time all the people of the world spoke the same language and used the same words...they said, "Come, let's build a great city for ourselves with a tower that reaches into the sky. This will make us famous and keep us from being scattered all over the world"...
>
> [But the Lord said,] "Let's go down and confuse the people with different languages"...In that way, the LORD scattered them all over the world, and they stopped building the city (Genesis 11:1,4,7-8).

Difficulty: Is the Tower of Babel story confirmed by any historical evidence other than that of the Bible?

Explanation: Sumerian literature refers to a time in history when there was a single language. Archaeology has also uncovered evidence that Ur-Nammu, King of Ur from about 2044 to 2007 BC, built a great *ziggurat* (temple tower) as an act of worship to the moon god

Nanna. A *stele* (monument) about five feet across and ten feet high reveals Ur-Nammu's activities. One artifact panel shows the king setting out with a mortar basket to begin construction of the great tower, thus showing his allegiance to the gods as he takes his place as a humble workman.[24]

Another clay tablet states that the erection of the tower offended the gods, so they threw down what the men had built, scattered them abroad, and made their speech strange. These descriptions are remarkably similar to the Genesis record of the Tower of Babel.

Passage:

The LORD came down to look at the city and the tower the people were building (Genesis 11:5).

Difficulty: How could God "come down" to the earth prior to him taking on human form in the person of Jesus?

Explanation: Prior to the incarnation—God taking on human flesh in the person of Jesus—he did in fact make his presence known. Adam and Eve "heard the sound of the LORD God as he was walking in the garden in the cool of the day" (Genesis 3:8 NIV). God appeared to Abraham (Genesis 17:1 and Genesis 18:1), Jacob (Genesis 32:1), and Moses (Exodus 3:2).

These appearances or manifestations of God are called *theophanies*. It is when God makes himself tangible to the human senses, as when Job was able to hear God in the wind (Job 38:1), or when God appeared to Moses in the burning bush. But in a more restrictive sense God has "come down" and made himself visible in the form of a man, like he did with Abraham and Jacob. Some scholars believe certain appearances of God were the pre-incarnate Christ. Other possible pre-incarnate appearances include the meeting between Joshua and the "Commander of the LORD's army" (Joshua 5:13-15) and the fourth man "like a son of the gods" who was with Shadrach, Meshach, and Abednego in the fiery furnace (Daniel 3:23-25). But in any case God did make appearances in tangible form prior to the appearance of the God-man Jesus.

Passage:

That night [Lot's daughters] got him drunk with wine, and the older daughter went in and had intercourse with her father. He was unaware of her lying down or getting up (Genesis 19:33).

Difficulty: Is incest condoned under certain circumstances?

Explanation: Lot's daughters faced what they saw as a dilemma. There were no men left in the area where they were living, other than their father. So they decided to get Lot drunk and have sex with him while he was in a drunken stupor. They said, "That way we will preserve our family line through our father" (Genesis 19:32).

In the culture of the time, not having children to preserve the family line was a disgrace. But this does not mean that the Bible condones incest, because God would later give direct commands against it (see Deuteronomy 27:22 and Leviticus 18:6-18).

The Bible is the revealed truth of God, but it is also a record of history. It tells the unvarnished story that includes lies, hatred, jealousy, murder, incest, adultery, idolatry, and so on. In many cases these sins and atrocities are told without necessarily making a specific judgment on them at the time. This doesn't mean God condones them; it simply means these acts are recorded as a matter of the narrative. We can conclude that these acts are wrong from other passages of Scripture.

Passage:

While living there [in Gerar] as a foreigner, Abraham introduced his wife, Sarah, by saying, "She is my sister" (Genesis 20:1-2).

Difficulty: Clearly Abraham lied, so does God sometimes condone lying?

Explanation: Abraham did lie, but why did he do it? He feared for the safety of his wife so he intentionally gave a false statement.

When faced with an ethical dilemma of telling the truth or lying to protect someone we love, does a greater good outweigh the lesser good? Does this make Abraham's lie the loving thing to do? Other biblical examples of deception to protect someone are these:

- Israel's spies would have been killed if Rahab had revealed their hiding place to inquiring soldiers. So she lied to protect them (see Joshua 2). Rahab is later held up as a model of faith in Hebrews 11.
- The queen commands that all God's prophets be killed. But Obadiah defies her and hides 100 of them. Obadiah was doing the greater good even though he deceived the queen (see 1 Kings 18).

God's commands are not situational yet there do appear to be situations when love for God and others would dictate that one could choose a greater good over a lesser obligation to the law. In other words, we live in a fallen world where moral duties sometimes come into conflict. In those situations we must choose the higher duty.

Adultery is always wrong as such. Murder is never right in itself. Lying is objectively wrong. However, when our obligation to the law overlaps with an obligation to unselfishly protecting the needs of another, our duty to the lower could be suspended in view of our responsibility to the higher. For example, imagine you see a young woman running in distress followed by a man who says, "Where did that girl go? I want to rape her." Do you have the obligation to tell him the truth? Of course not. The loving thing to do is to protect the girl by misleading the potential rapist.

Scripture does seem to identify greater and lesser goods. Jesus spoke of "more important aspects of the law" (Matthew 23:23). Justice and mercy appear to have greater weight than tithing on the scale of God's values, although the law required both (Matthew 23:23). Helping someone in need, such as the work of feeding the hungry or healing the sick, seemed to be more important to Jesus than not keeping the strict observance of the Sabbath (Matthew 12:1-5).

The two great commands of Jesus to love God and others may reveal greater and lesser goods. Love for God is a greater good than love for people when that "love" for another diverts our true devotion away from God (Matthew 10:37). Our love for God could lead us to disobey the government if it commands us to sin, but our love for country shouldn't lead us to disobey God. Love for family seems to take precedence over love for strangers (1 Timothy 5:8). Providing for believers appears to be a greater good over providing for unbelievers (Galatians 6:10).

Choosing between greater or lesser goods is not necessarily easy to do, nor are there clear-cut commands in Scripture for how to do it. However, the basis for determining greater and lesser goods is the greatest of all goods—God himself. And since he has not directly spoken to each situation we might find ourselves in, we must identify universal objective goodness in his law, which is written on our consciences (Romans 2:14-16), and in his Son who is revealed in the Bible. The Word of God is our best criterion for measuring greater and lesser goods. And we must always act in faith according to our consciences.

The value of an act, then, should be established by how Christlike or Godlike it is and if we can do that act in good faith. And ethical priorities should then be determined by how near or far they are from God's love as found in his Word and in the life of his Son, Jesus.

Passage:

"Abraham!" God called. "Yes," he replied. "Here I am." "Take your son, your only son—yes, Isaac, whom you love so much—and go to the Land of Moriah. Go and sacrifice him as a burnt offering on one of the mountains, which I will show you" (Genesis 22:1-2).

Difficulty: Does God condone human sacrifices?

Explanation: At the time of this event, Abraham's pagan neighbors sacrificed their children to their gods. On the surface it appears that God used his authority over Abraham and commanded him to do something that violated God's own standard of morality. How do you explain this apparent contradiction?

First, it is clear in other passages of Scripture that God is opposed to human sacrifices. "Do not permit any of your children to be offered as a sacrifice to Molech, for you must not bring shame on the name of your God. I am the LORD" (Leviticus 18:21). Repeatedly he made it clear human sacrifices were forbidden (see Leviticus 20:23 and Deuteronomy 12:31; 18:10). It is actually clear from the text that God's point is that he does *not* want child sacrifice. This is why the passage begins by saying that "God tested Abraham" (Genesis 22:1).

So why would God command Abraham to sacrifice his son Isaac? In verse 1 of Genesis 22 it says "God tested Abraham's faith." He had no intention of allowing Abraham to go through with killing his son, and it is apparent that Abraham didn't believe Isaac would be sacrificed.

It took Abraham, his son, and two servants three days to travel to Moriah where he was to offer the sacrifice. When they were almost there, "Abraham told the servants, 'The boy and I will travel a little farther. We will worship there, and then we will come right back'" (Genesis 22:5). Abraham didn't say, "We will worship and *I* will come right back." He included his son in the return trip and said, "We will come right back." Abraham obviously believed God would somehow intervene. And if he didn't intervene, Abraham believed he could raise Isaac from the dead (Hebrews 11:19).

This is further reinforced when Isaac asked about the sheep that was supposed to be sacrificed, which they did not have. "'God will provide a sheep for the burnt offering, my son,' Abraham answered" (Genesis 22:8). And God did. When Abraham was about to sacrifice Isaac on the altar, God stopped him and instead provided a "ram caught by its horns in a thicket" (Genesis 22:13). God didn't condone human sacrifices, yet he wanted Abraham to demonstrate that he would live out the commandment to "love the LORD your God with all your heart, all your soul, and all your strength" (Deuteronomy 6:5).

Passage:

Take your son, your only son—yes, Isaac, whom you love so much—and go to the land of Moriah (Genesis 22:2).

Difficulty: How could Isaac be Abraham's "only son" when Ishmael was clearly his son before Isaac?

Explanation: Many years before Sarah had Isaac, Abraham had Ishmael with Sarah's Egyptian servant, Hagar—by Sarah's insistence (see Genesis 16). Sarah didn't believe she could have children and so she arranged for Abraham to have a child through Hagar. But that clearly wasn't God's original plan.

God came to Abraham and told him he would have a special son that would be the recipient of God's covenant with him. "You will name him Isaac," God said, "and I will confirm my covenant with him and his descendants as an everlasting covenant" (Genesis 17:19). From God's perspective this was Abraham's only son with whom he would confirm this covenant. God would later tell Abraham, "Isaac is the son through whom your descendants will be counted" (Genesis 21:12). The other sons of Abraham were by human arrangements, first with Sarah's servant and later with concubines. But Isaac was Abraham's only *promised* son, the only son that would be blessed by God's eternal covenant.

This didn't mean that Ishmael wasn't a blessed son of Abraham. Because God did bless him. God told Abraham, "As for Ishmael, I will bless him also, just as you have asked" (Genesis 17:20), and "I will also make a nation of the descendants of Hagar's son because he is your son, too" (Genesis 21:13). Yet Isaac was the only covenant son.

Passage:

Abraham picked up the knife to kill his son as a sacrifice. At that moment the angel of the LORD called to him from heaven, "Abraham, Abraham!" "Yes," Abraham replied. "Here I am!" "Don't lay a hand on the boy!" the angel said. "Do not hurt him in any way, for now I know that you truly fear God" (Genesis 22:10-12).

Difficulty: If God is omniscient (all-knowing) then why didn't he know in advance that Abraham would obey him?

Explanation: Did God know what Abraham would do? Does he have exhaustive foreknowledge? Or does he learn things over time? Some take the position that God's knowledge grows over time, what is sometimes referred to as *dynamic omniscience*.

During the reign of King Josiah, the people of Judah turned away from God just like Israel. And God said of Israel, "I thought, 'After she [Israel] has done all this, she will return to me.' But she did not return" (Jeremiah 3:7). The Scripture seems to be saying that God thought if Israel turned away from him, she would return. But she didn't. So does that mean he really didn't know the future?

When Judas brought Roman soldiers at night to arrest Jesus, notice what Jesus does and says: "He stepped forward to meet them. 'Who are you looking for?' he said" (John 18:4). So did Jesus, the Son of God, not have foreknowledge of who they were looking for? If we just focus on what Jesus asked, it appears Jesus lacked foreknowledge. But when we read the passage of verse 4 in its entirety, we get another picture. "Jesus fully realized all that was going to happen to him, so he stepped forward to meet them. 'Who are you looking for?' he asked" (John 18:4). It becomes clear that Jesus wasn't asking the questions for himself but for those around him.

God wasn't surprised by Israel not returning to him in Jeremiah 3. He was communicating to Josiah in conversational style in order to make a point for Josiah's benefit. And when God said to Abraham, "For now I know that you truly fear God" (Genesis 22:12), it wasn't because God didn't know what Abraham was going to do. It was to affirm to Abraham that God knew that he really loved him.

Throughout Scripture God is revealed as the all-knowing God. "I am God, and there is none like me. Only I can tell you the future before it even happens. Everything I plan will come to pass, for I do whatever I wish" (Isaiah 46:10). King David said, "O LORD, you have examined my heart and know everything about me...You know what I am going to say even before I say it, LORD...such knowledge is too wonderful for me, too great for me to understand" (Psalm 139:1,4,6). God is omniscient and yet communicates in terms we all can understand.

Passage:

Abraham married another wife, whose name was Keturah (Genesis 25:1).

Difficulty: Why is Abraham's wife called his wife in Genesis 25 yet is called a concubine in 1 Chronicles 1:32?

Explanation: In 1 Chronicles 1:32 it lists the descendants of Abraham. And in so doing it identifies Keturah as Abraham's concubine rather than referring to her as his wife. This is not actually a contradiction.

The Hebrew word for wife used in Genesis is *ishsah,* which is normally the word for "woman." And woman would be the appropriate translation here since verse 6 says that "Abraham gave everything he owned to his son Isaac. But before he died, he gave gifts to the sons of his concubines..." (Genesis 25:6). This would include Keturah. So the appropriate translation would be "Abraham married another woman as his concubine."

Passage:

Jacob named the place Peniel (which means "face of God"), for he said, "I have seen God face to face, yet my life has been spared" (Genesis 32:30).

Difficulty: Doesn't this passage contradict the point in Exodus 33:20 that no one can see God and live?

Explanation: The Scripture reveals that, "God is Spirit, so those who worship him must worship him in spirit and in truth" (John 4:24). God is not a physical or material being like us. He does not have a physical face. He of course revealed himself in human form in the person of Jesus, yet the essence of God is Spirit.

God did tell Moses, "You may not look directly at my face, for no one may see me and live" (Exodus 33:20). That is because we as mortal beings could not withstand the full force of God's awesome power, overwhelming holiness, and intense glory. The essence of God's majestic greatness is too much for our physical beings to endure in our fallen state. Yet he is a "God who is passionate about his relationship with [us]" (Exodus 34:14 NLT). That is why when Moses would go before God he would speak to him "face to face, as one speaks to a friend" (Exodus 33:11).

God told the children of Israel that he revealed himself to prophets in dreams and in visions, but not with Moses. "I speak to him face to face, clearly, and not in riddles!" (Numbers 12:8). In the Hebrew culture and language of the time, the phrase "face to face" figuratively means God spoke up-close and personal with Moses. The same is true of Jacob. He experienced God intimately and described it as a "face to face" encounter. That is what God wants—he wants us to know him personally and "worship him in spirit and in truth" (John 4:24).

Passage:

These are the names of the descendants of Israel—the sons of Jacob—who went to Egypt (Genesis 46:8).

Difficulty: Genesis 46 goes on to list the twelve tribes of Israel, yet in other passages there seems to be fourteen. Why the discrepancy?

Explanation: Jacob only had 12 sons and their descendants make up the 12 tribes of Israel. But in Numbers 26, which records the sons of Israel, it leaves out Levi and Joseph. Add those two back into the list and there are 14. How is this reconciled?

First, Levi was not given an inheritance of the land because the sons of Levi became the priests. Second, to compensate for this Jacob granted Joseph an extra portion. So in Numbers 26 it lists Joseph's two sons, Ephraim and Manasseh, as tribes instead of Joseph.

So the discrepancy is resolved when we delete Levi from the list and substitute Ephraim and Manasseh for Joseph.

Difficult Verses *from* *the* Book *of* Exodus

Passage:

Pharaoh called in his own wise men and sorcerers, and these Egyptian magicians did the same thing with their magic (Exodus 7:11).

Difficulty: How could Pharaoh's magicians use occult practices to duplicate the miracles performed by God through Moses and Aaron?

Explanation: While these magicians could have been aided by demonic powers, most scholars believe they used sleight of hand and magical tricks to try to duplicate God's miracles. With each duplication by his magicians Pharaoh meant to discredit Moses and his God. But at some point the miracles God performed through Moses and Aaron went beyond the "powers" of the magicians. When the dust turned to gnats they couldn't duplicate it (see Exodus 8:18). They admitted, "This is the finger of God" (Exodus 8:19). From that point on the magicians couldn't replicate the plagues of flies, the death of the livestock, boils, hailstorm, locusts, and so on.

Passage and Difficulty: Exodus 12:17—Is this the same Passover meal or Last Supper that Jesus celebrated just prior to his crucifixion? If so, what is its significance today?

Explanation: See Luke 22:7-8.

Passage:

The people of Israel walked through the middle of the sea on dry ground, with walls of water on each side (Exodus 14:22).

Difficulty: Isn't it highly improbable that some 2 million

Israelites could cross the Red Sea in less than 24 hours? Wasn't this the Sea of Reeds they crossed and not the big miracle people make it out to be?

Explanation: There is not a consensus among scholars as to where exactly the Israelites crossed the Red Sea. Some point out that the Exodus 3:18 reference to the Red Sea is the Hebrew *yam suph*, which translates as "Sea of Reeds." That is why some skeptics say the Israelites then made their way through a marsh, not a literal body of water.

This of course raises a number of questions. Scripture states that "the LORD opened up a path through the water" (Exodus 14:21), not through reeds. Then the people "walked through the middle of the sea on dry ground, with walls of water on each side!" (Exodus 14:22), not walls of reeds. And then God told Moses that when he raises his hand "the waters will rush back and cover the Egyptians" (Exodus 14:26). When that happened none of the Egyptians survived. Scripture states they were drowned by water rather than reeds causing them to get lost.

With that said, the geographical location of the "Sea of Reeds" is still in question. The children of Israel were camped "by Pi-hahiroth between Migdol and the sea" (Exodus 14:1-2). The Gulf of Suez is much farther south of that point. Some scholars believe the water crossing could have been north of the Suez through Lake Ballah, Lake Timsah, or the Great Bitter Lake. In any case these were large bodies of water. But could some 2 million people get across any one of these bodies of water in 24 hours? These great lakes were no more than some 15 miles wide. Even if the Israelites crossed at the northern part of the Gulf of Suez it would have been no more than 30 to 35 miles wide. That would have posed no problem for a mass of people to get across in a 24-hour period.

Passage and Difficulty: Exodus 20:5—If it is wrong to get jealous, then why does God get jealous?

Explanation: See Exodus 34:14.

Passage:

In six days the Lord made the heavens, the earth, the sea, and everything in them; but on the seventh day he rested. That is why the Lord blessed the Sabbath day and set it apart as holy (Exodus 20:11).

Difficulty: Since God commanded that the seventh day be set aside to observe the Sabbath, why do most Christians observe it on the first day of the week?

Explanation: Keeping the Sabbath holy and resting on the seventh day was a special commandment between God and Israel. God said, "It is a permanent sign of my covenant with the people of Israel" (Exodus 31:17). For the Jewish people the Sabbath was a holy festival and they were to "remember that you were once slaves in Egypt, but the Lord your God brought you out with his strong and powerful arm. That is why the Lord your God has commanded you to rest on the Sabbath day" (Deuteronomy 5:15).

Every one of the Ten Commandments was repeated in the New Testament except for the observance of the Sabbath. And Jesus shook up the Jewish leaders with his views on the Sabbath. When Jesus was walking through some grain fields on the Sabbath and his disciples broke off the heads of the grain and ate them, the Pharisees criticized them and Jesus for breaking the Sabbath. "Jesus said to them, 'The Sabbath was made to meet the needs of people, and not people to meet the requirements of the Sabbath. So the Son of Man is Lord, even over the Sabbath'" (Mark 2:27).

The Sabbath was a special day, set apart as holy—a time to rest and worship God. Yet during the first century the Jewish leaders had made the laws of Moses as a narrow and binding set of rules to follow—including the law about the Sabbath. Jesus was correcting that perspective and announcing that he was Lord over the Sabbath and it was for our benefit.

The early Christians were feeling the lingering effects of the strict observance of the Jewish festival celebrations, including the Sabbath.

Paul addressed this when he wrote to the church in Colosse, "Don't let anyone condemn you for what you eat or drink, or for not celebrating certain holy days or new moon ceremonies or Sabbaths. For these rules are only shadows of the reality yet to come. And Christ himself is that reality" (Colossians 2:16-17).

These believers were feeling the pressure to continue to observe the Jewish Sabbath as their forefathers had done. Yet the early church followers of Jesus were worshipping with each other on the "Lord's Day" (Revelation 1:10), which was the first day of the week—as opposed to the last day of the week. In fact, for years the first-century church observed both the Jewish Sabbath and the "Lord's Day." They began worshipping together on Sunday primarily because Jesus rose on the first day of the week (Matthew 28:1) and Jesus appeared to his followers more than once on the first day of the week (John 20:26). This then became a pattern (see Acts 20:7 and 1 Corinthians 16:2). From that time forward Christians observed the set-aside day of rest on the first day of each week.

Passage:

> Suppose two men are fighting, and in the process they accidently strike a pregnant woman so she gives birth prematurely…if there is further injury, the punishment must match the injury: a life for a life, an eye for an eye, a tooth for a tooth (Exodus 21:22,23-24).

> **Difficulty:** Does this mean the Bible considers a fetus as a human being and therefore calls for punishment upon anyone who brings harm to the fetus?

Explanation: When God gave Moses the Ten Commandments he included a prohibition of murdering another person (see Exodus 20:13). God places a very high value on life.

This passage seems to indicate that if a woman gives birth prematurely yet the baby is unharmed then only a fine is appropriate. On the other hand, if the child (or the mother) dies then the offender must pay with his life. Killing an unborn baby carried the same penalty as killing a child who was born—even if the injury was accidental. This passage demonstrates a powerful point: If God requires such a harsh punishment for the *inadvertent* death of an unborn child, how much more harshly must he judge a *purposeful* abortion!

Some pro-choice advocates have contended with the above interpretation, since the death of the baby results in a fine, whereas the death of the mother requires the life of the offender. Therefore, it is often argued, the fetus is merely potential human life and is not deserving of the same level of legal rights as an adult person.

This interpretation, however, has two core problems. First, the normal Hebrew word for "miscarriage" is not used here. Rather, the word for "premature birth" has the connotation of live birth. The baby was not killed in this passage, just born prematurely. Therefore there is no precedent for considering the unborn baby to have less value than the mother. Second, even if this passage referred to a miscarriage, it is still not a sufficient defense for abortion—because the injury in question was accidental, not intentional (as abortion is).

Passage and Difficulty: Exodus 23:16—Is this the same Festival as Pentecost when the Holy Spirit was poured out on the church in the first century? If so, what is its significance today?

Explanation: See Luke 24:49.

Passage:

When the LORD finished speaking with Moses on Mount Sinai, he gave him the two stone tablets inscribed with the terms of the covenant, written by the finger of God (Exodus 31:18).

Difficulty: Does God have literal hands and fingers with which to write?

Explanation: It seems clear in this scripture that God has fingers. In other passages it refers to God's "right hand" (Exodus 15:6), "everlasting arms" (Deuteronomy 33:27), and "the eyes of the LORD" (Psalm 33:18 NIV). So is this evidence that God has a physical body like ours? Not really. The Bible teaches us that God is Spirit and does not have a physical or material form.

Jesus made it clear that "God is Spirit, so those who worship him must worship him in Spirit and in truth" (John 4:24). When Jesus appeared to his followers after his resurrection they were frightened because they thought they were seeing a spirit. Jesus then said, "A spirit does not have flesh and bones as you see that I have" (Luke 24:39 NASB). So if God is Spirit without physical parts, why does the Bible refer to his fingers, arms, eyes, and so on?

Referring to God having physical parts is a figure of speech, and God refers to himself in that way because he is "passionate about his relationship with [us]" (Exodus 34:14 NLT). He wants to reveal himself to us in ways that allow us to relate to him. In Exodus 15 we learn that his "right hand" is glorious in power, and in Deuteronomy 33 we discover his "arms" are always there as our refuge. These figures of speech reflect his direct involvement in our lives.

And in Exodus 31 when it states the Ten Commandments were "written by the finger of God," it is a clear indicator that he was directly involved in giving us his Word. The Bible also says that he "will cover you with his feathers" and "shelter you with his wings" (Psalm 91:4), but we don't think of him looking like a bird. Again, this is not to be taken literally, but he is painting us a picture that shows he is involved in our lives as our protector. No, God doesn't have animal or human parts, but he does want to relate intimately to us, so his Word describes him in ways we can better relate to him.

Passage:

> [Moses said to God,] "Turn away from your fierce anger. Change your mind about this terrible disaster you have threatened against your people! Remember your servants Abraham, Isaac and Jacob"...So the Lord changed his mind about the terrible disaster he had threatened to bring on his people (Exodus 32:12-14).

Difficulty: God is supposed to be unchanging, but doesn't this passage make it clear that God changed his mind?

Explanation: One of the characteristics of God is that he is immutable—he is by nature constant, unwavering, and secure and can always be counted on to be right and do right. Samuel told Saul that "he who is the Glory of Israel will not lie, nor will he change his mind, for he is not human that he should change his mind!" (1 Samuel 15:29).

Yet it seems clear that Abraham's pleas caused God to change his mind. God is unchanging, yet he seems to change his position. Isn't this somewhat contradictory?

The very essence and character of God is that he is perfectly holy (Isaiah 54:5), just (Revelation 16:5), and right (Psalm 119:137). What God cannot do is go against who he is. He will reward virtue and will not tolerate wrong (see Habakkuk 1:13). Yet this does not mean that all of God's responses to his creation are without conditions. Many of his promises and judgments have either an expressed or implied condition.

When God was about to send judgment on Sodom and Gomorrah, Abraham interceded on behalf of his nephew Lot who lived in the city (see Genesis 18:16-33). And because of Abraham, God would have changed his mind if he could have found ten righteous people in the city. It seems clear that God's judgment was conditional.

God spoke through his prophet Jeremiah and explained how his judgment and blessing were conditioned upon Israel's response. God said,

> If I announce that a certain nation or kingdom is to be uprooted, torn down, and destroyed, but then that nation

> renounces its evil ways, I will not destroy it as I had planned. And if I announce that I will plant and build up a certain nation or kingdom, but then that nation turns to evil and refuses to obey me, I will not bless it as I said I would (Jeremiah 18:7-10).

God changes his response to people and nations conditioned upon their response to him. He created a beautiful world along with humans and said it "was good." He had a relationship with the first human couple. But when they disobeyed him, he reversed course and separated from them. This change in how he responds to individuals and nations doesn't contradict his immutability—it rather affirms it. If he would have accepted human evil and said, "Well, humans will be humans, and I'll just give them a pass," then he would be denying himself. He is a God of rightness, holiness, and justice. His response to sin is consistent with his immutability and righteous nature.

God changing his position isn't a sign of indecisiveness, as it is with us. It is not even an indication he doesn't know in advance he is going to change (see *Explanation* of Genesis 22:12). Rather God often changes how he responds to us based on our response to him. As sinners, born in sin, we are under his judgment. He is unchanging in his position on that for he is "pure and cannot stand the sight of evil" (Habakkuk 1:13). So we find ourselves doomed and separated from him. Yet he reverses course and changes his mind toward us when we place our trust in the atoning death and resurrection of his Son, Jesus Christ. God's response may change based on how individuals respond while at the same time he will always remain true to his holiness, justice, and mercy. There is nothing inconsistent or contradictory with his changing his mind toward us. We should expect that from a relational and perfectly holy God.

Passage:

> You must worship no other gods, for the LORD, whose very name is Jealous, is a God who is jealous about his relationship with you (Exodus 34:14).

Difficulty: If it is wrong to get jealous then why does God get jealous?

Explanation: There is a kind of jealousy that is right and a kind of jealousy that is wrong. While this may seem to be contradictory, it makes sense when we understand the two different meanings for *jealous.*

In 1 Corinthians it says, "You are still controlled by your sinful nature. You are jealous of one another and quarrel with each other" (1 Corinthians 3:3). It is clearly wrong to be selfishly possessive and contentious toward those who have something you want, and the apostle Paul was pointing this out. Yet in the very next letter Paul wrote to the Corinthians he said, "I am jealous for you with the jealousy of God himself" (2 Corinthians 11:2). Paul was concerned that their "pure and undivided devotion to Christ will be corrupted" (verse 3) and so he was jealous like God is jealous. Obviously, Paul isn't condemning the jealousy of God. So what kind of jealousy does God have that isn't wrong?

The Bible on a number of occasions states that God is jealous. In the second of the Ten Commandments God gave to Moses, he said, "I, the LORD your God, am a jealous God" (Exodus 20:5). Joshua also told the children of Israel that their God was "a holy and jealous God" (Joshua 24:19). These two words "jealous God" in the Hebrew are *el qanna*, which denotes passion and zeal. The word *jealous* in English is generally used in a negative sense. But here in the Hebrew it is used in a passionate, caring manner most often in connection with the marriage relationship. God considered the children of Israel his marriage partner and he wanted them to love him as a wife would devote herself exclusively to her husband. That is why he said they were to worship no other but him. He wants to be loved with a pure and passionate love reserved only for him.

As relational beings we can relate to wanting to be loved exclusively. How would you feel if someone said that he or she truly loved you and then cheated on you? It's not wrong to feel bad about someone cheating on you, is it? Isn't it natural to want to be number one in someone's life? We were relationally created to have someone focus their love and attention on only us. We were designed to jealously want another to exclusively love us.

Of course that kind of jealousy can turn ugly. A person can react to a cheating husband or wife in a wrong manner. The feelings of betrayal (which aren't wrong in and of themselves) can prompt resentment and hatred and manifest themselves in any number of selfish acts.

But with God being perfectly good and holy, his jealousy is not inappropriately selfish. He knows that when we love him exclusively, with all our heart, soul, and strength, it allows us to experience the joy and meaning we are looking for in life. And when he allows us to feel negative consequences for not loving him exclusively, he is disciplining us out of love. He wants us to experience all the joy that comes with putting him first in our lives. So it is by no means wrong for him to jealously want our exclusive love and devotion. In fact, his jealous love is a model for us to follow.

Difficult Verses *from* *the* Book *of* Leviticus

Passage:

Lay your hand on the animal's head, and the LORD will accept its death in your place to purify you, making you right with him (Leviticus 1:4).

Difficulty: How did the sacrifice of animals rather than Christ purify people in the Old Testament and grant them forgiveness by God?

Explanation: Those living in Old Testament times sacrificed animals, but that was a temporary substitute that pointed to the Messiah who would sacrifice himself for them. "Jesus did this once for all," the Scripture states, "when he offered himself as the sacrifice for the people's sins" (Hebrews 7:27).

Just as Christ's death and resurrection reach forward in time to raise us from spiritual death into a right relationship with God, so they also reach back in time to deliver all those born before Jesus. The apostle Paul said that Jesus' "sacrifice shows that God was being fair when he held back and did not punish those who sinned in times past, for he was looking ahead and including them in what he would do in this present time" (Romans 3:25-26).

In other words, those living prior to Jesus got credit for his sacrifice even before he died for them. It's like today when we buy something on credit—we get to use the merchandise or service even though, technically, we haven't paid for it yet. That is what the Scriptures mean when they say that Abraham "believed the LORD, and he credited it to him as righteousness" (Genesis 15:6 NIV). Abraham had salvation applied to him even though the final transaction by Jesus had not yet been completed.

Jesus' perfect sacrifice solves the sin and death problem for all those who believe in God's provision—past, present, and future. The sacrificial system of the Old Testament simply pointed to Christ as God's provision. All those who have died, all of us who are still living, and all those who will come after us are saved by faith through the death and resurrection of Jesus Christ.

Passage:

Aaron's sons Nadab and Abihu put coals of fire in their incense burners and sprinkled incense over them. In this way, they disobeyed the LORD by burning before him the wrong kind of fire, different than he had commanded. So fire blazed forth from the LORD's presence and burned them up, and they died there before the LORD (Leviticus 10:1-2).

Difficulty: Isn't this killing by God a severe punishment for an apparent slight deviation from his command?

Explanation: It is not clear exactly what Nadab and Abihu's violation was. The "wrong kind of fire" may have been coals that came from some pagan worship, or perhaps they simply had not prepared the incense exactly as God had instructed. He had given very specific instructions on preparing the incense (see Exodus 30:34-38). Whatever they did, three things were clear: 1) They knew how God wanted the incense and fire to be; 2) they deliberately went against his command; and 3) he will not allow a defilement of his holiness.

These men were not ignorant of what was required of them. As priests who represented the people to God, they were aware that he held them to an exceptionally high standard. They knew they were directly violating his commands. They committed the sin of arrogance and self-sovereignty. It was as if they were thumbing their noses at God and saying, "We know you have all these silly rules about who you are and how we are supposed to approach you, but we don't think we have to do things your way. We can do things our way and you should accept us on our terms."

When Aaron's two sons were killed, Moses told his brother that this is what God meant when he said, "Among those who approach me I will be proved holy; in the sight of all the people I will be honored" (Leviticus 10:3 NIV).

Second Samuel records another incident when God was not honored. It was a time when King David had the ark of God transported to Jerusalem. A man named Uzzah simply reached out his hand to steady the ark to keep it from falling off the cart. And "the LORD's anger was aroused against Uzzah, and God struck him dead because of this" (2 Samuel 6:7).

Again, on the surface it might appear that God is overreacting. But not so. The Israelites had repeatedly been told how to carry the ark of God (Exodus 25:10-15; Numbers 4:15; 7:7-9; Deuteronomy 10:8). The ark represented God's presence and no one was to touch or experience the presence of God without going through purification rituals, making sacrifices, and approaching God in the most reverent of ways. This was the responsibility of the priests.

Uzzah disregarded all of that and brought insult to God. It showed, like the sons of Aaron, an arrogance and disrespect for their relationship with him. We don't get to dictate how we are to have a relationship with him. It is the other way around. He sets the terms of relationships. The question is whether we will follow it or not.

If God is anything he is holy. It is the attribute of his repeated most commonly in Scripture. And it is his holiness, his righteousness, his absolute purity that makes all of life beautiful, perfect, and good. God didn't want to leave the slightest impression that having a relationship with him is anything except on the basis of holiness. And when the two priests profaned his holy place in his holy presence and King David insulted God's honor in the way the Ark was carried, God's righteous anger communicated a righteous purpose: that a holy God is passionate about having a *right* relationship with his holy people.

God doesn't want any of us to miss the point that happiness and joy, true love and friendship, peace and satisfaction, and goodness and fulfillment come from one place and only one place—living in right relationship with him. And his holiness is his condition for that relationship. That is why he went to such lengths to deal with our sin problem.

Holiness isn't natural for any of us because we all have a sin problem. It wasn't natural for the children of Israel either. But God needed for them to understand that only those made holy could enjoy all the benefits of a relationship with him. That is why he made such a big deal of the clean and unclean rituals, and the sacrificial system being performed precisely as he had instructed. And that is why the eventual coming of the perfect and holy "Lamb of God who takes away the sin [the unholy] of the world!" (John 1:29) was such a big deal. God required holiness then and he still requires it now. He has mercifully made a way for each of us to be made holy before him through each of us trusting in the sacrificial death and resurrection of his Son.

> **Passage:**
>
> The hyrax chews the cud but does not have split hooves, so it is unclean. The hare chews the cud but does not have split hooves, so it is unclean (Leviticus 11:5-6).
>
> **Difficulty:** Isn't the Bible incorrect in saying the rock badger (hyrax) and rabbit (hare) chew their cud, when we know today that is not true?

Explanation: First, it is important to note that God gave Israel certain purity regulations, including eating restrictions to distinguish Israel as his people apart from other nations. Complying with these purity regulations established a spiritual state of worthiness for the children of Israel to come in contact with a holy God. So it was necessary for them to readily know what was clean and unclean and what to do if they violated these regulations.

It is true that the hyrax or rock badger and the hare or rabbit do not chew their cud as cows do. Chewing the cud simply means that the animal regurgitates previously swallowed food back into its mouth and chews it again. However, both the rock badger and rabbit chew their food with their jaws rotating in such a fashion that it appears as though they are chewing their cud. Calling these animals cud chewers is a functional description rather than a technical designation.

Passage:

These are the instructions regarding land animals, birds, marine creatures, and animals that scurry along the ground. By these instructions you will know what is unclean and clean, and which animals may be eaten and which may not be eaten (Leviticus 11:46-47).

Difficulty: Leviticus and a lot of the Old Testament are full of instructions and laws on eating, purifications, and sacrifices that are strange and antiquated to us today. How can we know which ones are binding on us?

Explanation: First, it is important to realize that neither the Old nor the New Testament was written to people living in the twenty-first century. The Old Testament audience was the children of Israel living under the Mosaic covenant, and the New Testament was written to Jews and Gentiles in the first century. But that doesn't mean the truth of Scripture isn't relevant to or binding on us today (see "How to Use This Handbook" on page 9 and throughout).

The Bible was written within certain historical contexts, all quite different from ours today. But even though the words of Scripture may not have been written specifically *to* us, that doesn't mean they weren't written *for* us. Scripture is God's universal and relevant truth, which is applicable to all people, in all places, for all times. The Old Testament messages transcend history, cultures, customs, languages, and time lines. So to interpret what God is saying to us in the twenty-first century we must first identify the universal truths of Scripture that were applicable in ancient times in order to understand how the truth applies to us today.

The Old Testament is rich with truth that is relevant to us today. God made a promise to Abraham—a covenant—that included his raising up a nation, and through Abraham's descendants he would send a Savior, the Redeemer of the world. And the Old Testament is the story of God's faithful and loving relationship with his people, the children of Israel. And so it is understandable that certain promises, conditions, and instructions to Israel would not apply to everyone.

But to understand how the truth of the Old Testament applies universally and to Christians today we must also interpret it within the context of the New Testament. The apostle Paul said,

> Why then, was the law given? It was given alongside the promise to show people their sin. But the law was designed to last only until the coming of the child who was promised [Jesus]...The law was our guardian until Christ came; it protected us until we could be made right with God through faith. And now that the way of faith has come, we no longer need the law as our guardian (Galatians 3:19,24-25).

Jesus made it clear that *he* was the context for interpreting the Old Testament. He said, "Don't misunderstand why I have come. I did not come to abolish the law of Moses or the writings of the prophets. No, I came to accomplish their purpose" (Matthew 5:17). He actually fulfilled many of the ceremonial laws of Moses and satisfied God's justice in dealing with our sin.

For example, the law required for Israel to be clean prior to offering sacrifices before God. The instructions as to what to eat, how to be cleansed when one comes in contact with something that is unclean, how to offer sacrifices, and so on, were all pictures of what Christ would eventually do to make us clean and right before God. He became our sacrificial lamb to deal with our sin and satisfy God's holy and just nature.

The same can be said about what is known as Israel's *civil laws*. Throughout the first five books of the Old Testament the children of Israel were not only given the Ten Commandments (the moral law), but specifics on how God's law was to be enforced within their nation. In Leviticus and throughout the Old Testament we find very specific things that God commanded his people to do, as well as how to do them, when to do them, and the consequences for disobedience and remedies to follow. These laws were given specifically to the Hebrew people while they were under the Mosaic covenant. A question we need to ask ourselves in determining whether an Old Testament command applies to us today is, what is the basis for *why* the command was given? By answering that question we can determine if there is a moral reason for the command or a ceremonial reason, Jewish civil reason, and so on.

For example, the Hebrew people were commanded not to weave two fabrics together. There is nothing inherently immoral about weaving two fabrics together, but God gave the commands to his people so they would have a daily reminder, even in the clothes they wore, that God desired them to be a holy nation set apart from the pagans.

When Old Testament commands are rooted in God's character we can also know they somehow apply to us today. His commands against murder stem from his being the author of life. Commands against deceit and stealing come out of his nature, which is true. Laws of fidelity and against immorality are rooted in a God who is pure. These truths are from his very nature and are given for all people for all time.

Also when commands are rooted in God's creation, they are applicable universally. We are to protect the innocent and treat everyone with dignity because humans were made in God's image. God created male and female and designed them to live united in marriage. Civil rights, how we are to treat different races, and the definition of marriage then find their roots in God's creation.

And certainly the *moral law* of the Old Testament, often referred to as the Ten Commandments, reflects God's character and universal truth to all of us. Each of the Ten Commandments is repeated in the New Testament, except observance of the Sabbath day. And that one is in effect repeated in the truth that as Christ's body, the church, we are to love each other and worship together. The writer of the book of Hebrews said, "Let us not neglect our meeting together, as some people do, but encourage one another" (Hebrews 10:25). So certainly the moral law of the Old Testament is binding on and applicable to us today.

When we read the Old Testament we must understand God's truth within the historical context of the children of Israel. And when we do, it becomes clear how God's relevant truth is to be applied in our personal lives and the life of the twenty-first-century world.

Passage:

By these instructions you will know what is unclean and clean…(Leviticus 12:47). [And Leviticus chapters 11–15.]

Difficulty: Why does God seem obsessed with cleanliness?

Explanation: God isn't obsessed so much with what is clean and unclean but what is holy and unholy (see *Explanation* on Leviticus 10:1-2). And to prepare the children of Israel to be a holy people, he had them follow strict instructions of what was clean and unclean—for example, things that could and could not be eaten; rules regarding menstrual periods, circumcision, skin rashes and diseases, contaminated clothing, bodily discharges, and so on.

The things that were declared unclean were not sinful per se, but rather represented a state of unworthiness to come in contact with the holy. When God's people followed the instructions for what was clean, they and the things made clean then acquired the potential for becoming holy. All the regulations regarding purity or cleansing were a constant reminder to Israel that they were called to be a dedicated (a separate) people in relationship with a holy God.

Later the apostle Peter would come to understand how God altered the purification laws for the early church (see Acts 10:9-33). And Paul would issue a call to all believers in Christ that paralleled God's call to the children of Israel to be his holy people:

> God knew his people in advance, and he chose them to become like his Son…and having chosen them, he called them to come to him. And having called them, he gave them right standing with himself. And having given them right standing, he gave them his glory (Romans 8:29-30).

Passage:

When a garment has a mark of leprosy in it, whether it is a wool garment or a linen garment...it is a leprous mark and shall be shown to the priest (Leviticus 13:47,49 NASB).

Difficulty: Isn't the Bible in error by indicating that leprosy infects clothing, when medical science has shown it is an infectious disease caused by bacterium and does not infect clothes?

Explanation: This passage is not referring to what we know today as leprosy, or Hansen's disease, which is caused by bacterium. The word in Hebrew, *tsaraath*, translated in some versions as leprosy, is a broad term that includes skin rashes, burns, abnormal baldness, mildew, and molds.

During the rainy season in Israel mildew and molds were commonplace and could trigger allergic reactions that would pose a health risk. These health regulations were to protect the Israelites. This passage was simply pointing out that if mold or mildew was found on wool, linen, or leather, the people were to report it to the priest. The New Living Translation more idiomatically renders verse 47 as "Now suppose mildew contaminates some woolen or linen clothing" (Leviticus 13:47).

Passage and Difficulty: Leviticus 19:17-18—Is this command to love self a selfish love?

Explanation: See Matthew 22:37-39.

Passage:

Anyone who dishonors father or mother must be put to death. Such a person is guilty of a capital offense (Leviticus 20:9).

Difficulty: Isn't this penalty to kill a disobedient child extreme?

Explanation: Children were stoned for disobeying their parents during the time Moses led Israel. People were also put to death for offenses including adultery, incest, and homosexuality.

Some people categorize the laws of the Old Testament into the moral law, the civil law, and the ceremonial law. Within these distinctions it is acknowledged that the moral law would be binding on us today. Israel's societal structure was governed by the civil law and laws dealing with sacrifices and ritual cleansing, which are considered nonbinding on Christians today. But this categorization can be misleading.

"All Scripture is inspired by God and is useful to teach us..." (2 Timothy 3:16). The civil and ceremonial laws in Leviticus and Deuteronomy can give us insight and understanding both into God and into how he wanted his people to honor and fear (respect) him for who he was. So while the command to stone stubborn and rebellious children does not apply today, we can learn something as to why God gave Israel such commands.

Deuteronomy 21 provides us with greater detail as to why a child would be stoned for parental disobedience. "Suppose a man has a stubborn and rebellious son who will not obey his father or his mother, even though they discipline him" (Deuteronomy 21:18). This is not referring to a boy who pulled his sister's hair or tracked mud in from outside after his mother told him repeatedly to wipe his feet. This is a delinquent boy who has been rebellious, insubordinate, and repeatedly refuses to honor his parents even though they have tried again and again to correct him. In verse 20 the boy is called "a glutton and a drunkard."

Once the parents had done everything they could do to "tame" their wild and unruly child with no results, then they were to take the boy to the "elders as they hold court at the town gate" (verse 19). At that point the matter was out of the hands of the parents. It was the men of the town who exacted the penalty on the boy. "In this way," the law states, "you will purge this evil from among you, and all Israel will hear it and be afraid" (verse 21). And remember, anyone who continued to dishonor his father and mother did so with full knowledge of what the consequences would be.

God had made a covenant with Israel. They were his people and he gave them the law for their good. Each family was to pass on God's laws to the next generation. This rebellious son would no doubt squander his parent's inheritance and not pass on a godly heritage to any children he had. This severe punishment was God's way of instilling a healthy fear in Israel that would help them remain true to the teachings and ways of their forefathers. Had Israel taken these commands to heart, they could have avoided the harsh consequences that came after they fully abandoned God (2 Kings 17 and 25).

Passage:

You may purchase male and female slaves from among the nations around you. You may also purchase the children of temporary residents who live among you, including those who have been born in your land. You may treat them as your property (Leviticus 25:44-45).

Difficulty: Does the Bible condone or at least allow for the owning of slaves?

Explanation: This Old Testament passage of course raises the question of the legitimacy of owning slaves. The New Testament position on slavery is also in question, with the apostle Paul saying, "Slaves, obey your earthly masters with deep respect and fear. Serve them sincerely as you would serve Christ" (Ephesians 6:5). Slavery was common during Jesus' lifetime and in the period of the first-century church. It is estimated that during the first century AD, 85 to 90 percent of the population of Rome consisted of slaves.[25] So does Scripture accept slavery as a norm and condone the owning of slaves?

In the Old Testament

The concept of slavery or servitude was put into perspective by the laws God gave Israel. It allowed for someone who was in deep debt to "sell" themselves into employment with another. This was essentially a contractual agreement to work off debt. "If one of your fellow Israelites falls into poverty and is forced to sell himself to you, do not treat him as a slave. Treat him instead as a hired worker or a temporary resident who lives with you, and he will serve you only until the year of Jubilee" (Leviticus 25:39-40).

This arrangement was similar to what took place in early colonial America. People who couldn't afford the costly fares to travel to America would contract themselves out to others until they paid back the price of the fare. These were indentured servants. Only in Israel every seven years all debts were cancelled (Deuteronomy 15:1-3). This provision was a guarantee that indentured servanthood would not be institutionalized or abused.

Slavery was common in the ancient Near East. And foreign slaves would run away from their masters. God had commands to Israel for this: "If slaves should escape from their masters and take refuge with you, you must not hand them over to their masters. Let them live among you in any town they choose, and do not oppress them" (Deuteronomy 23:15-16).

Israel was permitted to "purchase male and female slaves from among the nations around [them]" (Leviticus 25:44). However, they were given strict guidelines on how these foreign servants would be treated.

> Do not take advantage of foreigners who live among you in your land. Treat them like native-born Israelites, and love them as you love yourselves. Remember that you were once foreigners [slaves] living in the land of Egypt. I am the LORD your God (Leviticus 19:33-34).

These "slaves" were treated more as employees by Israel and not as property to be mistreated. "You must not mistreat or oppress foreigners in any way. Remember, you yourselves were once foreigners in the land of Egypt" (Exodus 22:21). This constant reminder by God of what it felt like to be oppressed in Egyptian slavery was an attempt to remind them of the need to treat everyone with human dignity.

Slaves in Israel had a high degree of status, rights, and protection unheard of in the ancient Near East. Scholars universally recognize this fact. Slaves were included in religious life, were granted a weekly Sabbath rest (that is, had a day off), had to be set free if bodily harm was inflicted on them, and had the opportunity for freedom every seven years.[26]

In the New Testament

Some have suggested that Jesus and the apostles were tolerant of Roman slavery. Not so. While it would have been a serious offense to actively challenge Rome on the slavery issue, the apostles nevertheless made it known that slavery was unacceptable.

The apostle Paul addressed slaves. "Are you a slave? Don't let that worry you—but if you get a chance to be free, take it. And remember, if you were a slave when the Lord called you, you are now free in the Lord" (1 Corinthians 7:21-22). Paul encouraged slaves to break free of their slavery and certainly gave them the high status of human dignity as being "free in the Lord." He said there were "no longer Jew or Gentile, slave or free, male and female. For you are all one in Christ" (Galatians 3:28).

When Paul put together a list of terrible sins, he included in it "slave traders." He said the law was for the lawless—those who defiled what was holy and murderers. He identifies these as "people who are sexually immoral, or who practice homosexuality, or are slave traders, liars, promise breakers..." (1 Timothy 1:10). He made no bones about condemning those who trafficked in slavery.

And finally, Jesus made his position known when he read from Isaiah 61 in the synagogue at the beginning of his earthly ministry. He was declaring himself as the one who Isaiah was prophesying about. "He has sent me," Jesus said, "to proclaim that captives will be released, that the blind will see, that the oppressed will be set free, and that the time of the Lord's favor has come" (Luke 4:18-19). The very mission of Jesus was to free all those who are physically and spiritually enslaved. In God's kingdom there is no slavery or oppression.

(For more on slavery in the Bible see chapter 11 of the book *Is God Just a Human Invention?* by Sean McDowell and Jonathan Morrow, described in the back pages of this book.)

Difficult Verses *from* *the* Book *of* Numbers

Passage:
A year after Israel's departure from Egypt, the LORD spoke to Moses in the Tabernacle in the wilderness of Sinai (Numbers 1:1).

Difficulty: Critics say Numbers was written centuries after Moses died. So how could Moses have written the book of Numbers?

Explanation: Jewish and Christian tradition recognizes that Moses wrote Numbers as well as the rest of the first five books of the Old Testament (the Pentateuch). The date of his writings is believed to be during the Bronze Age (1500s–1200s BC).

However, since the mid-1800s critical scholars have contended that the Pentateuch was a collection of writings from numerous sources by different groups of people gathered together between 850 BC and 445 BC. This view is referred to as the *documentary hypothesis*. According to this notion the books previously ascribed to Moses were actually collected over time and not edited until the 400 BC time frame. This would of course preclude Moses from being the author since this is hundreds of years after his death.

There are many reasons the documentary hypothesis fails to be credible. (Extensive documentation of the evidence for Mosaic authorship of the Pentateuch is provided in Josh McDowell, *The New Evidence That Demands a Verdict*, chapters 13 and 17–21.) Here we will simply cite two of the dozens of reasons the documentary hypothesis is questionable.

First, the hypothesis fails to satisfactorily answer why Israel was monotheistic (worshipping one God) in a totally polytheistic context. The critics assume the writers of the biblical text borrowed their religious ideas from pagan predecessors. But since the rest of the known world was polytheistic and idol worshippers, where did Israel's monotheism come from? That certainly wasn't borrowed from the pagans.

Secondly, there are continuing archaeological finds that give credibility to the Hebrew text and its Mosaic authorship. These finds contradict the assumption that the Pentateuch was written hundreds of years after Moses. For example, in 1986 archaeologists in Jerusalem discovered a biblical text older than the Dead Sea Scrolls. Part of the text of Numbers 6:24-26 was engraved on two small silver amulets. Gabriel Barkay of Tel Aviv University placed the date of these during the First Temple period, between 960 BC and 586 BC.

Critics also argue that the name *Yahweh* was not used before 500 to 400 BC. If true this would preclude Moses authoring the Pentateuch. But the silver amulets contained the name *Yahweh* and were dated before 586 BC, calling into question the assumption the Pentateuch was not written by Moses nor even in Moses' time.[27]

The critics further claim that the Hebrew moral code was too advanced to have been developed by 1200 BC. They say such an advanced social structure would have had to been closer to the 800s BC. Yet archaeology has uncovered the Code of Hammurabi dating prior to 1200 BC. These Akkadian laws paralleled the laws of Moses, establishing that such advanced moral codes did in fact exist during Moses' time.[28]

The documentary hypothesis also assumes that certain difficult expressions and passages from Leviticus would not have been used as early as 1200 BC; therefore the Pentateuch had to have been written much later. The ancient references were those like "whole burnt offering" (*kalil*), "peace offering" (*shelamin*), and "guilt offering" (*asham*). Yet archaeologists uncovered the Ras Shamra tablets (1400 BC), which contained a large amount of Ugaritic literature. And

> many of the technical sacrificial terms of Leviticus were discovered in far-removed Canaanite-speaking Ugarit dating at 1400 BC...These terms were already current in Palestine at the time of Moses and the conquest, and that whole line of reasoning which made out terminology of the Levitical cultures to be late, is devoid of foundation.[29]

These findings and many others are evidence that supports the view that Moses indeed wrote Numbers and the whole of the Pentateuch.

Passage and Difficulty: Numbers 2:2—Isn't it a contradiction to cite the Tabernacle as inside the camp (Numbers 2), yet outside the camp (Numbers 12)?

Explanation: See Numbers 12:4.

Passage:

List all the men between the ages of thirty and fifty who are eligible to serve in the Tabernacle (Numbers 4:3).

Difficulty: How do we account for the apparent discrepancy in the lower age limit for men serving in the Tabernacle in Numbers 4 (30 years) and Numbers 8 (25 years)?

Explanation: At first glance it appears that these two passages make a contradictory statement regarding the age of those serving in the Tabernacle. But upon closer review we see that they are referencing two different types of service.

Numbers 4 is listing the service or duties "related to the most sacred object" (Numbers 4:4). The word in Hebrew to describe this service is *melakah*, referring to the "business or occupation" of the Tabernacle. This was for those 30 and over and up to 50 years of age.

In Numbers 8 it refers to the service done in the Tabernacle with a different Hebrew root: *abodah*, which has the sense of "work" or "labor." These younger men from ages 25 to 29 were most likely considered unofficial "workers" or apprentices. And this therefore would account for the stated age difference.

Passage and Difficulty: Numbers 8:24—How do you account for the apparent age discrepancy of men serving in the Tabernacle in Numbers 8 (25 years) and Numbers 4 (30 years)?

Explanation: See Numbers 4:3.

Passage:

Immediately the LORD called to Moses, Aaron, and Miriam and said, "Go out to the Tabernacle, all three of you!" So the three of them went to the Tabernacle (Numbers 12:4).

Difficulty: Isn't it a contradiction to cite the Tabernacle as outside the camp (Numbers 12), yet inside the camp (Numbers 2)?

Explanation: Some people may cite passages like this to discredit the Bible, claiming it is full of contradictions and discrepancies. Regarding the Tabernacle, it is actually an answer of "both-and."

In Numbers 2 it states that the "Israelites are to camp around the Tent of Meeting [Tabernacle]" (Numbers 2:2 NIV). In other words the Tabernacle was positioned in the middle of the encampment and the Israelites camped around it. So the Tabernacle was inside the camp. But if you were in your campsite or tent you would in fact have to leave your tent and "go out to the Tabernacle…" (Numbers 12:4). So the Tabernacle was *both* inside the camp *and* yet outside each individual's camping area.

Difficult Verses *from* *the* Book *of* Deuteronomy

Passage:

> There will be no poor among you, since the LORD will surely bless you in the land which the LORD your God is giving you as an inheritance to possess (Deuteronomy 15:4 NASB).

> **Difficulty:** Isn't it contradictory to say, "There will be no poor among you" in verse 4 and at the same time say, "The poor will never cease to be in the land" in verse 11?

Explanation: Upon closer examination of this passage we see that there is no contradiction. The next verse says,

> You will receive this blessing if you are careful to obey all the commandments of the LORD...if there are any poor Israelites in your towns when you arrive in the land...do not be hard-hearted or tightfisted toward them. Instead be generous and lend them whatever they need (Deuteronomy 15:5,7-8).

First, there was a condition to the notion that no poor would be among them. And of course there wouldn't be as long as they were not tightfisted and gave to those in need. Secondly, in verse 11, it is simply stating that there will always be people in need, yet if the Israelites would respond to those people as God commanded, the needs of the poor would be met. Reading all of verse 11 makes that point clear: "There will always be some in the land who are poor. That is why I am commanding you to share freely with the poor and with other Israelites in need" (Deuteronomy 15:11).

With the proper context of this passage we then can interpret it to mean: "There should be no poor among you as long as you continue to give generously to those who are in need—and there will always be those who come on hard times, but you can be there to help them."

Passage:

I will raise up a prophet from among their countrymen, and I will put My words in his mouth, and he shall speak to them all that I command him (Deuteronomy 18:18 NASB).

Difficulty: Is this passage a prophecy of the coming of Muhammad?

Explanation: Muslims believe this passage is fulfilled in Muhammad, who is the prophet God raised up (see Sura 7:157 of the Koran). But God's promise to Moses was that he would raise up a prophet among "their countrymen," which is referring to the countrymen of Israel—not Ishmael, from whom the Arab nations came. Other translations, like the NLT, render the verse "I will raise up a prophet like you from among their fellow Israelites" (Deuteronomy 18:18).

This passage is referring to Jesus, and he fulfilled it perfectly. He said, "I do nothing on my own but say only what the Father taught me" (John 8:28). "The Father who sent me has commanded me what to say and how to say it" (John 12:49). Deuteronomy 18 prophesies that God will raise up a prophet among the Israelites. Jesus was one of them (see Matthew 1:1-17), and he was the mouthpiece of his Father God as indicated in John 8 and 12.

Passage:

You must completely destroy the Hittites, Amorites, Canaanites, Perizzites, Hivites, and Jebusites, just as the Lord your God has commanded you (Deuteronomy 20:17).

Difficulty: How could a loving God order the mass killing of an entire group of people?

Explanation: God did order that the inhabitants of the land of

Canaan be wiped out. Scripture records that "Joshua conquered the whole region...He completely destroyed everyone in the land, leaving no survivors, just as the LORD, the God of Israel, had commanded" (Joshua 10:40). But does this make God a genocidal killer who in anger wipes out entire races of people?

It should be noted that any killing by God in the Old Testament was not arbitrary. God was motivated by moral concerns, not race. So this was actually *not* genocide. Mass murder is not within God's nature. In Scripture we discover that God is merciful and loving (Psalm 103:8), holy and righteous (Psalm 145:17 and Revelation 3:7), and fair and just (Psalm 119:137-138). He does not rush to judgment; he is "slow to get angry and filled with unfailing love" (Psalm 103:8). But he will "judge the world with justice, and the nation with his truth" (Psalm 96:13). It is not in his nature to be unjust.

God could not be a perfect and loving God without equally being a just God who judges perfectly. To act differently would be less than who he is.

There is a reason why God commanded that an entire people be destroyed. Moses told the children of Israel that "God will drive these nations out ahead of you only because of their wickedness, and to fulfill the oath he swore to your ancestors Abraham, Isaac, and Jacob" (Deuteronomy 9:5). Removing the Canaanites from the land that was promised to Abraham wasn't because of anything the children of Israel did or because they were living true to God—they were not. The land was to go to them because God promised it to Abraham. Additionally, the Canaanites were destroyed because of their wickedness.

The Canaanite people were idolaters. They engaged in incest, temple prostitution, adultery, homosexuality, and bestiality. They molested children and sacrificed children alive up to four years old. They were a depraved people. Yet God was patient and he extended mercy to them even in their despicable sin. The people of Canaan were given over 400 years to repent of their wicked ways (Genesis 15:16). God had nothing against them as a people. He did, however, take issue with their depraved and evil behavior.

Yet God was willing to save those within Canaan that were righteous. In fact he saved Rahab in Jericho because she was a righteous individual. God does eventually bring judgment upon all that are unrepentant of their sin. And the people of Canaan were no different. This does not make God genocidal; it simply reflects his holy justice and righteous judgment. And keep in mind—he brought the very same judgment against his chosen people when they committed the same sins (see 2 Kings 17 and 25). (For a more exhaustive treatment of this see chapter 13, "Is God a Genocidal Bully?" in the book *Is God Just a Human Invention?* by Sean McDowell and Jonathan Morrow, described in the back of this book.)

Passage and Difficulty: Deuteronomy 21:18-21—Isn't the killing of a child for disobedience extreme?

Explanation: See Leviticus 20:9.

Passage:

If a man happens to meet a virgin who is not pledged to be married and rapes her and they are discovered, he shall pay the girl's father fifty shekels of silver. He must marry the girl, for he has violated her. He can never divorce her as long as he lives (Deuteronomy 22:28-29 NIV).

Difficulty: It appears the Bible doesn't consider rape a serious offense. Why does a man who rapes a virgin only have to pay her father some money and then marry the woman he violated instead of being severely punished?

Explanation: These verses not only seem to say the man who violates the young woman must pay the father, but the woman must become the wife of the rapist. Naturally rape victims want nothing to do with their attacker. It would be torture to end up having to live with their violator! But upon closer look at this passage within context we see that is not a proper interpretation of those verses.

God is utterly opposed to rape. It is a heinous violation of another person. In Deuteronomy 25:25, it describes a man who meets an engaged woman and "he rapes her"; then the Scripture says, "The man must die. Do nothing to the young woman."

The Hebrew word in verse 25 that is translated "rape" in English is *chazaq* which means "to strongly seize or force." When a man forces himself on a woman sexually the civil law of Israel called for the man to pay for the crime with his life.

But in verses 28-29 it is describing another situation. Here a man meets a virgin who is not engaged to be married and he doesn't rape her: rather he seduces her. The Hebrew word that the NIV translates "rape" is actually the word *tapas*, which means "seize by manipulation." That is why other translations render the verse, "Suppose a man has intercourse with a young woman who is a virgin but is not engaged to be married" (Deuteronomy 22:28).

This passage is explaining a situation in which a young Jewish man goes out with a young available Jewish girl. His hormones get the best of him and he makes a move on his girlfriend. She probably says to her overheated boyfriend, "What if Daddy finds out what we're doing?" He disregards her warnings, persists, and she gives in. Notice the verse says "*They* are discovered" not "*He* is discovered." Both of these unmarried people are discovered in consensual sex. They are both responsible for their sexual escapade.

This same situation is dealt with in Exodus when it says, "If a man seduces a virgin who is not engaged to anyone and has sex with her, he must pay the customary bride price and marry her" (Exodus 22:16). The requirement for the man to marry the girl was in many respects a protection for the young woman. In that day a young unmarried woman who was involved sexually was shunned by the community. It would be very difficult to find a man who would marry a girl that was not a virgin. So to require the "passionate lover" to take her for his wife provided an economic security for her future.

The Historical Books
Joshua–Esther

Difficult Verses *from* *the* Book *of* Joshua

Passage and Difficulty: Joshua 2:4-5—Clearly Rahab lied, so does God sometimes condone lying?

Explanation: See Genesis 20:1-2.

Passage:

When the people heard the sound of ram's horns, they shouted as loud as they could. Suddenly, the walls of Jericho collapsed, and the Israelites charged straight into the town and captured it (Joshua 6:20).

Difficulty: Have archaeologists been unable to verify the biblical account of the destruction of Jericho?

Explanation: During the late nineteenth and mid-twentieth centuries, teams of archaeologists excavated the area in and around where the city of Jericho was located. But they could not match the data that is recorded in Joshua concerning its destruction.

However, in 1990, professor Bryant G. Wood presented evidence in the *Biblical Archaeology Review* that did in fact match the biblical account of Jericho's fall. His detailed investigation showed that after the walls had fallen the city was burned (Joshua 6:24); the collapsed walls did allow Joshua's army to invade the city (Joshua 6:20); the attack had occurred in the spring (Joshua 2:6; 3:15; 5:10); those in the city didn't have time to escape with their grain and food (Joshua 6:1); and those that were left in the city didn't consume their stored food because the invasion was so short (Joshua 6:15). Overall the archaeological evidence confirms the historical record provided to us in the book of Joshua. Archaeologist Joel Kramer has confirmed these same findings, and more, in his recent series *Bible Expedition: Jericho Unearthed*.[1]

Passage and Difficulty: Joshua 6:21—How could God order the mass killing of the entire inhabitants of a city?

Explanation: See Deuteronomy 20:17.

Passage:

On the day the LORD gave the Israelites victory over the Amorites, Joshua prayed to the LORD in front of all the people of Israel. He said, "Let the sun stand still over Gibeon, and the moon over the valley of Aijalon." So the sun stood still and the moon stayed in place until the nation of Israel had defeated its enemies (Joshua 10:12-13).

Difficulty: Isn't the Bible in error to say the "sun stood still" when we know that if the sun stayed in place the earth would have had to stop rotating rather than calling for the sun to stop?

Explanation: Some point out that the Bible seems to reflect a lack of scientific knowledge; its writers didn't realize that the earth rotates to create our day and night. But in the twenty-first century, while we all know how our days and nights occur, we still talk of the "sunrise" and the "sunset." This is just part of our observational language. We say the "sun sinks into the west" because that certainly is what it looks like from our vantage point. Yet we know that is not technically or scientifically true.

Did the author of Joshua know that the earth rotated once every 24 hours and that is what created the days and nights? It is actually immaterial. Because the observational language that was used is no more inaccurate than what we use today.

Passage:

Deborah, the wife of Lappidoth, was a prophet who was judging Israel at the time. She would sit under the Palm of Deborah, between Ramah and Bethel in the hill country of Ephraim, and the Israelites would go to her for judgment (Judges 4:4-5).

Difficulty: Did God allow women to be prophets and judges?

Explanation: Some believe because women were created from man and were to be his helper, they do not qualify as a spokesperson for God (see *Explanation* of Genesis 2:18,21-23). Additionally some people make the point that God forbade women from teaching men or having authority over men in the early church (see *Explanation* of 1 Timothy 2:11-12).

However, as explained in Genesis 2 and 1 Timothy 2 it is clear that God does not disqualify women from being his spokespersons. While scholars and various Christian leaders hold differing views on this subject, it is quite clear that Deborah was both a prophet and a judge.

Deborah fulfilled both a judicial and military role implied in the title "judge." And she did speak in the name of God (Judges 4:6). Additionally the Bible records that God appointed Miriam, Moses' sister, as a prophet (Exodus 15:20-21). Huldah was a prophet who equally spoke on behalf of God (2 Kings 22:14-20). It is quite apparent that God considered women as able and fit leaders to judge and speak on his behalf.

Passage:

When Sisera fell asleep from exhaustion, Jael quietly crept up to him with a hammer and tent peg in her hand. Then she drove the tent peg through his temple and into the ground, and so he died (Judges 4:21).

Difficulty: Does God condone assassinations?

Explanation: The Bible records violence, murder, rape, incest, and all types of brutality. But this does not mean God approves of such behavior.

We must recognize that we live in a world of violence that is caused not by God, but by humans. Every newspaper and online news source around the globe today is full of headlines and stories of greed, distrust, robberies, conflicts, killings, war, destruction, and death. And these things have existed ever since Adam and Eve were driven from the Garden of Eden. Jesus explains it is not outside circumstances that causes such evil violence in the world; rather, "from the heart come evil thoughts, murder, adultery, all sexual immorality, theft, lying and slander" (Matthew 15:19). Violence in this world isn't a sociological, economic, or even pathological problem; it is a spiritual or heart problem. Sin and humans' propensity to be self-centered are at the heart of selfish, violent acts.

Yet God, who is the antithesis of sin and self-centeredness, at times engages in violence because he is the ultimate protector of the innocent and judge of the unrighteous. And it is true that Jael's assassination of Sisera is praised in the song of Deborah (Judges 5:25-27). Evil people are eventually punished, and Sisera was an enemy of Israel. If he had not been killed he most certainly would have brutalized the Israelites as he had in the past. So God does at times initiate violence to accomplish his will.

It's important to realize that Judges is more graphic than other biblical books because of its theme: *People rejected God and all of them did whatever seemed right in their own eyes* (Judges 21:25). The people rejected God and personally experienced the misery of living in sin. The graphic violence reveals their rebellious hearts and the results of pursuing evil. For a more comprehensive treatment of why God uses violence see *Explanation* of 2 Kings 19:35 and Deuteronomy 20:17.

Difficult Verses *from the* Book *of* Ruth

Passage:

A man from Bethlehem in Judah left his home and went to live in the country of Moab, taking his wife and two sons with him. The man's name was Elimelech and his wife was Naomi...Then Elimelech died, and Naomi was left with her two sons. The two sons married Moabite women (Ruth 1:1-4).

Difficulty: Didn't Naomi's sons violate the laws of Moses by marrying Moabite women?

Explanation: The Mosaic law stated that "no Ammonite or Moabite or any of their descendants for ten generations may be admitted to the assembly of the LORD" (Deuteronomy 23:3). Technically it was not a violation to marry an Ammonite or Moabite—however, they were prohibited from attending the worship gatherings.

The Scripture doesn't comment on the wisdom of Naomi's sons marrying outside of the Israelite family. Obviously it would not be ideal or preferred to marry a woman who was barred from worshipping with them. But the two sons did not technically violate the laws of Moses simply by marrying Moabite women.

Passage:

After Boaz had finished eating and drinking and was in good spirits, he lay down at the far end of the pile of grain and went to sleep. Then Ruth came quietly, uncovered his feet, and lay down (Ruth 3:7).

Difficulty: Wasn't Ruth wrong for sleeping (having sex) with Boaz to obligate him to marry her?

Explanation: The biblical narrative explains that Naomi instructed

Ruth to "take a bath and put on perfume and dress in your nicest clothes..." (Ruth 3:3) and then go lay down with Boaz. Then once Boaz woke up Ruth said to him, "Spread the corner of your covering over me, for you are my family redeemer" (verse 9).

Some suggest that when Ruth lay down with Boaz and uncovered his feet she was asking him to have sexual intercourse with her. That way Boaz would be obligated to her. But uncovering of the feet was not sexual in nature. Rather it was a customary practice to show submission. Ruth did this as a symbol of her being in subjection to Boaz and demonstrating the cultural willingness to be his wife.

When Ruth asked Boaz to spread the corner of his covering, literally translated "wing," she was seeking his protection and refuge . None of the conduct of Ruth or Boaz indicated there was any sexual involvement between the two.

Difficult Verses *from* *the* Books *of* 1 & 2 Samuel

Passage:

> "Give us a king to judge us like the other nations have." Samuel was displeased with their request and went to the LORD for guidance. "Do everything they say to you," the LORD replied, "for it is me they are rejecting, not you. They don't want me to be their king any longer" (1 Samuel 8:5-7).

Difficulty: Why did God establish guidelines for a king yet condemn having a king in this passage?

Explanation: God did provide Israel with guidelines for a king to rule (see Deuteronomy 17:14-20). A king was to provide a visible representation of God ruling over his people. God ultimately wanted his people to see him as their leader and guide and to trust and worship him alone. But Israel no longer saw God as their leader. They envied other nations and wanted "a king to judge us like all the other nations have" (1 Samuel 8:5).

It wasn't a king to rule the people that God objected to, it was the fact they wanted a king for the *wrong* reasons. They had rejected God and wanted to be a powerful nation in their own strength. And that is why both Samuel and God were displeased.

God knew there would be disastrous consequences if they rejected him and chose to have an earthly king. Samuel warned that a king would enslave some of the young people, institute heavy taxes on grain and livestock, and make many more people work for him (see 1 Samuel 8:11-17). And this is exactly what happened (see 1 Samuel 14:52; 15:1; 1 Kings 21:5-16; and 2 Chronicles 2:17-18).

Passage:

> The Philistines gathered together to fight with Israel, thirty thousand chariots and six thousand horsemen, and people as the sand which is on the seashore in multitude. And they

came up and encamped in Michmash, east of Beth Aven (1 Samuel 13:5 NKJV).

Difficulty: Could the Bible be in error by reporting 30,000 chariots for only 6000 chariot drivers?

Explanation: When conservative Christian theologians say the Bible is without error (inerrant) they mean that, when all the facts are known, the Scriptures as they were penned by the authors in the original writings—called the *autographa*—and as properly interpreted will be shown to be true and not false in all they affirm. However, scribes that copied the Hebrew text could and did make copying errors.

In 1 Samuel some translations, like the New King James Bible, get their rendering from the Masoretic Hebrew and Septuagint (Greek) texts, which set the number of chariots at 30,000 and 6000 chariot drivers. But it is reasonable to ask why the Philistines would have 30,000 chariots for 6000 charioteers.

The Syriac (Aramaic) version, some versions of the Septuagint, and one Greek translation render the chariot count at 3000. That number seems more credible, and so more recent translations like the New International Version and New Living Translation put the figure at 3000 chariots. It is most likely that a scribe copying this verse miswrote the number. And once this was done, all the subsequent manuscripts that were copied from the altered one carried that error forward.

Passage and Difficulty: 1 Samuel 15:2-3—How could a loving God order the mass killing of an entire group of people?

Explanation: See Deuteronomy 20:17.

Passage:

David triumphed over the Philistine with only a sling and a stone, for he had no sword. Then David ran over and

> pulled Goliath's sword from its sheath. David used it to kill him and cut off his head (1 Samuel 17:50-51).

> **Difficulty:** Did David actually kill Goliath, or was it Elhanan as it is recorded in 2 Samuel 21:19?

Explanation: Here in 1 Samuel 17 it recounts David being the person who killed the Philistine Goliath. But in 2 Samuel 21:19 (in such versions as the NASB) it says that Elhanan killed Goliath. This is an apparent contradiction. Because in 1 Chronicles 20:5 it clearly says Elhanan "killed Lahmi, the brother of Goliath of Gath" (NASB). This points to a likely error made by a copyist in 2 Samuel 21:19, who left out the words "the brother of" in the Masoretic text. Most more recent translations like the New International Version and New Living Translation add the words "the brother of."

> **Passage and Difficulty:** 2 Samuel 6:6-7—Isn't this a severe punishment for an apparent slight deviation from God's command not to touch the ark?

Explanation: See Leviticus 10:1-2.

> **Passage:**
>
> You made a great name for yourself when you redeemed your people from Egypt. You performed awesome miracles and drove out the nations and gods that stood in their way (2 Samuel 7:23).

> **Difficulty:** Is God out to make a great name for himself? This doesn't seem to align with his being humble and other-focused.

Explanation: King David spoke of how God delivered Israel out of

Egypt "to defend the honor of his name and to demonstrate his mighty power" (Psalm 106:8). Is God obsessed with self-praise and boasting of power and achievements as some critics claim? Some would then say Scripture paints a picture of a prideful, not humble, God.

Pride is essentially an inflated view of ourselves. Humility is a reflection of a realistic assessment of ourselves, including our weaknesses and our strengths. A humble person doesn't try to take credit for something he or she doesn't deserve, but a prideful person does.

God is far from prideful. The descriptions of God in the Bible reflect an all-powerful (Psalm 147:5), all-knowing (Isaiah 46:9-10), eternal God (Isaiah 40:28) who is everywhere-present (Jeremiah 23:23-24)—a God who is perfect and holy (Isaiah 54:5) and cannot tolerate sin (Habakkuk 1:13), yet is compassionate, merciful, and just (Psalm 103:8). This God was rejected by disobedient humans yet he took on the lowly form of humanity to die that they might live. We are the prideful ones, the ones who want to make a name for ourselves. He is the one who humbled himself to save us.

God does not have an inflated view of himself—he *is* the Almighty. As ancient theologians often said, God is the *summum bonum*—the highest good. He takes no praise that he is undeserving of—he is deserving of all praise. He humbled himself to restore a relationship with humans because he is in fact other-focused.

Passage:

David captured from him 1,700 charioteers and 20,000 foot soldiers (2 Samuel 8:4).

Difficulty: Why is the number of chariots and horsemen that David captured recorded differently in 1 Chronicles 18:4?

Explanation: In 1 Chronicles 18:4 it recounts the same story but says David captured 1000 chariots, 7000 charioteers, and 20,000 foot soldiers. The Septuagint and Dead Sea scrolls agree with 1 Chronicles

18:4 as the correct number. Most likely the error in 2 Samuel occurred through incorrect copying.

Passage:

David confessed to Nathan, "I have sinned against the LORD" (2 Samuel 12:13).

Difficulty: Why did David say that his sin was against the Lord when it appears it was primarily against Bathsheba and Uriah?

Explanation: This does at first seem strange for David to say. And he makes the point that his sin is exclusively against God even more strongly when he says, "Against you, and you alone, have I sinned; I have done what is evil in your sight" (Psalm 51:4). So how could he say that when he had just committed adultery with Bathsheba and committed murder by having her husband, Uriah, sent to the front lines of the battle to be killed?

Those of course were sins. But they were not the primary and first sins of David in this situation. His first sin was against God. And this is true for all of our sins. Our sins are foremost against God—the Creator and Judge of the universe—and yet also against people.

Scripture tells us that God had anointed David and saved his life from Saul. He had been with him to empower him as a young man in killing Goliath. He had been David's provider and protector from the very beginning. David had consistently placed his faith and trust in him, and that is what made him such a powerful man of God.

But in this situation David's faith and trust in God wavered. He no longer depended on God to give him what he thought he needed. Rather David selfishly took what didn't belong to him. Listen to what God said to David:

> I gave you your master's house and his wives and the kingdoms of Israel and Judah. And if that had not been enough,

> I would have given you much, much more. Why, then, have you despised the word of the Lord and done this horrible deed? (2 Samuel 12:8-9).

God was providing David everything he needed physically, emotionally, and relationally, in his good timing. And if David had needed more, he would have given him much more. But what did David do? He didn't trust in God's timing; instead he took matters in his own hands. He doubted that God would give him all he needed when he thought he needed it. That was his primary sin—a lack of trust in God to meet his needs. All the other offenses cascaded down from that primary lack of trust in God's timing as his provider and protector.

David learned a valuable lesson. He saw his sin for what it was—not entrusting all of his life to God's hands. Psalm 145 is a testimony of David's transformation. It is full of describing God as his provider and protector. He discovered that "the eyes of all look to [God] in hope; you give them their food as they need it. When you open your hand, you satisfy the hunger and thirst of every living thing" (Psalm 145:15-16). If David would have lived that out before, he would have resisted the sexual temptation and trusted in God's provisions.

Passage and Difficulty: 2 Samuel 21:19—Why does this passage say Elhanan killed Goliath when 1 Samuel 17:50-51 says David killed Goliath?

Explanation: See 1 Samuel 17:50-51.

Difficult Verses *from* *the* Books *of* 1 & 2 Kings

Passage:

Solomon had 40,000 stalls of horses for his chariots, and 12,000 horsemen (1 Kings 4:26 NASB).

Difficulty: Why does 1 Kings 4 say Solomon had 40,000 horse stalls, but 2 Chronicles 9 says he had only 4000 horse stalls?

Explanation: Yes, in 2 Chronicles 9:25 some manuscripts read that Solomon had 4000 horse stalls for the 1400 chariots he owned, as described in 1 Kings 10:26 and 2 Chronicles 1:14. But in 1 Kings 4 other copied manuscripts say "40,000 stalls of horses." Clearly Solomon didn't need 40,000 stalls to accommodate 1400 chariots. This was obviously the result of an overworked and perhaps sleepy scribe copying down 40,000 instead of 4000. This is an understandable and easily corrected human error.

Passage:

King Solomon levied forced laborers from all Israel; and the forced laborers numbered 30,000 men (1 Kings 5:13 NASB).

Difficulty: Doesn't this verse that says Solomon made forced laborers of the Israelites contradict 1 Kings 9:21, where it says he did not force them into labor?

Explanation: This apparent contradiction is cleared up with an understanding of the words used here. The words "forced laborers" are not accurately translated in 1 Kings 5:13. The Hebrew word *hammas* is a "labor force," not forced labor or a slave labor force. The NLT translates the verse more accurately: "Solomon conscripted a labor force of 30,000 men from all Israel" (1 Kings 5:13).

In 1 Kings 9:21 the Hebrew word *mas-obed* is used and is translated "slave, or forced, labor." So "Solomon did not conscript any of the Israelites for forced labor" (1 Kings 9:22). He did draft them to form a labor force but not as slave labor. With the correct understanding of the words used there is no contradiction in these passages.

Passage and Difficulty: 1 Kings 11:1—If polygamy is wrong, why doesn't the Bible speak out more against it?

Explanation: See Genesis 4:19.

Passage and Difficulty: 1 Kings 18:4—Obadiah went against the queen and deceptively hid the prophets—so does God sometimes condone deception?

Explanation: See Genesis 20:1-2.

Passage:

Elisha left Jericho and went up to Bethel. As he was walking along the road, a group of boys from the town began mocking and making fun of him. "Go away, baldy!" they chanted. "Go away, baldy!" Elisha turned around and looked at them, and he cursed them in the name of the Lord. Then two bears came out of the woods and mauled forty-two of them (2 Kings 2:23-24).

Difficulty: Shouldn't a man of God like Elisha control his temper? Why would he curse some boys just for being boys, and why would God honor the curse and have bears attack the boys?

Explanation: On the surface this appears as though the prophet Elisha overreacts to some harmless teasing by some schoolboys. But upon a closer look this is not the case.

The boys in question are not small schoolchildren, as the King James translation suggests. The words in the Hebrew here can either be translated "young boys" or "older teenagers." The location is suspect for schoolboys to be at play. These "boys" showed up in the hills outside of town. Young boys wouldn't be out roaming the hills in a pack of at least 42. This was more of a roving gang than an innocent group of children.

It is not unreasonable to assume Elisha's life was in danger. This gang was probably going to taunt him, rob him, and rough him up.

Verbal insults in the Old Testament were taken seriously. That is even true today in the Middle East. Insulting a king, ruler, or a leader was met with severe punishment. Leadership and authority demanded respect, and parents along with local communities taught their children to honor those in authority.

If the parents of these young men or community leaders had witnessed just the verbal insults that were made toward Elisha, action would have been taken. The young men would have faced a stiff penalty. But no one was around to either protect Elisha from harm or teach this gang a lesson in respect—except for God.

When Elisha cursed or rebuked the gang, two bears came out of the woods to conduct a lesson in respect. While these boys may have had trouble showing respect for the authority of God's prophet, they learned to respect the authority of bears. These bears didn't kill them, but 42 of the boys didn't soon forget what happens when you insult God's anointed leader.

Passage and Difficulty: 2 Kings 8:26—Why does this passage say Ahaziah was 22 years old but in 2 Chronicles it says he was 42 years old?

Explanation: See 2 Chronicles 22:2.

Passage:

That night the angel of the LORD went out to the Assyrian camp and killed 185,000 Assyrian soldiers. When the surviving Assyrians woke up the next morning, they found corpses everywhere (2 Kings 19:35).

Difficulty: If God is merciful and loving, why does he commit mass killings?

Explanation: It is true that God is merciful and loving (Psalm 103:8). But God is also fair and just. "O LORD, you are righteous, and your regulations are fair. Your laws are perfect and completely trustworthy" (Psalm 119:137-138). "He is the Rock," Scripture states, "his deeds are perfect. Everything he does is just and fair. He is a faithful God who does no wrong; how just and upright he is!" (Deuteronomy 32:4).

So whenever God commits acts of violence he does so out of a perfect sense of justice. He does not punish out of sinful vengeance. God is the antithesis of sin and self-centeredness. When he at times engages in violence, he is doing so as the ultimate protector of the innocent and judge of the unrighteous. Yes, God killed 185,000 Assyrians. But he was killing soldiers who were attempting to capture Jerusalem and destroy Judah. The Assyrian army under King Sennacherib had already destroyed Israel and was ready to annihilate the people of God.

Assyria was a cruel, aggressive nation that had brutally tortured and killed innocent men, women, and children. The evil Assyrian king, Sennacherib, mocked God in his reply to Judah. "What god of any nation has ever been able to save its people from my power? So what makes you think that the LORD can rescue Jerusalem from me?...Don't let your God, in whom you trust, deceive you with promises that Jerusalem will not be captured by the king of Assyria" (2 Kings 18:35; 19:10).

A heathen empire that murdered the innocent and mocked the true God deserved punishment. The Righteous Judge of the universe came to the defense of his people being unjustly treated. God does use violence to defend, protect, and bring deserved judgment on evildoers. He said of the king of Assyria, "For my own honor and for the sake of my servant David, I will defend this city and protect it" (2 Kings 19:34).

We should not think less of God for defending the righteous and judging the unrighteous. He is our hero for coming to the aid of the oppressed. What was he to do when his holiness, justice, and power were challenged by Satan? Should he have stood by and not fought against rebellion and evil? No, it was right and just for God to resort to violence to cast Satan from heaven. And it is right and just for him to continue that war until he conquers Satan, all evil, and death so that one day there will be eternal peace (see Revelation 12–21).

God is a merciful and loving God, "slow to get angry and filled with unfailing love" (Psalm 103:8), yet he will not stand by and let evil go unjudged. "He is coming to judge the earth," the Bible says. "He will judge the world with justice, and the nations with his truth" (Psalm 96:13). He is just, and he at times uses violence to execute perfect justice. The prophet Isaiah referred to him as the "Prince of Peace" and said his government of peace would never end. And he predicted that peace would be achieved by a war that would end all wars. "He will rule with fairness and justice from the throne of his ancestor David for all eternity. The passionate commitment of the LORD of Heaven's Armies will make this happen!" (Isaiah 9:7).

Difficult Verses *from* *the* Books *of* 1 & 2 Chronicles

Passage and Difficulty: 1 Chronicles 1:32—Why is Abraham's concubine called concubine in 1 Chronicles yet is called his wife in Genesis 25?

Explanation: See Genesis 25:1.

Passage:

All Israel was listed in the genealogical records in *The Book of the Kings of Israel* (1 Chronicles 9:1).

Difficulty: Are books missing from the Old Testament?

Explanation: The writers of the Old and New Testaments referenced various source documents. The apostle Paul quoted from philosophers and poets of his time (Acts 17:28 and Titus 1:12). *The Book of the Kings of Israel* is one such source document, which the writers of Kings and Chronicles used. In fact this book is referenced 17 times in 1 and 2 Kings. Yet at some point *The Book of the Kings of Israel* was lost. This doesn't mean an inspired book of the Bible was lost. It simply means the inspired writers of the Bible used source documents that at some point in time were lost. For more on why certain books were left out of the official Scriptures see *Explanation* of Jude 14.

Passage and Difficulty: 1 Chronicles 18:4—Why is the number of chariots and horsemen David captured as recorded in 1 Chronicles 18 not the same as recorded in 2 Samuel 8?

Explanation: See 2 Samuel 8:4.

Passage and Difficulty: 2 Chronicles 9:25—Why does this passage say Solomon had 4000 horse stalls but in 1 Kings 4 it says he had 40,000 horse stalls?

Explanation: See 1 Kings 4:26.

Passage:

Forty and two years old was Ahaziah when he began to reign, and he reigned one year in Jerusalem (2 Chronicles 22:2 KJV).

Difficulty: Why does 2 Chronicles 22 say Ahaziah was 42 years old when he began to reign, and yet in 2 Kings 8 it says he was 22 years old?

Explanation: Yes, 2 Kings 8:26 says Ahaziah was 22, which contradicts what 2 Chronicles records about his age. But Ahaziah could not have been 42 at the time or he would have been older than his father. We see in 2 Kings 8:17 that Ahaziah's father, Joram, was 32 when he became king and he died 8 years later at the age of 40. So Ahaziah could not have been king when he was 42. This was a clear case of a copying error. Ahaziah was 22 as reported in 2 Kings 8:26.

Difficult Verses *from* *the* Book *of* Ezra

Passage:

Let us now make a covenant with our God to divorce our pagan wives and to send them away with their children (Ezra 10:3).

Difficulty: Why did God require the Jewish men to divorce their unbelieving wives, while the apostle Paul (1 Corinthians 7:12) said a man shouldn't divorce his wife just because she is an unbeliever?

Explanation: It should be noted that people rarely consider divorce the best option. The best option is that two people love and enjoy each other for a lifetime. The prophet Malachi spoke on behalf of God when he said,

> Didn't the Lord make you one with your wife? In body and spirit you are his. And what does he want? Godly children from your union. So guard your heart; remain loyal to the wife of your youth [your first wife]. "For I hate divorce!" says the Lord, the God of Israel (Malachi 2:15-16).

Yet the men of Israel were told to divorce the pagan unbelieving wives and for good reason. Ezra the priest said, "By marrying pagan women, you have increased Israel's guilt" (Ezra 10:10). He called it a sin. God had told Israel before and specifically Solomon not to marry pagan wives "because they will turn your hearts to their gods" (1 Kings 11:2). But this was by no means a blanket endorsement of divorce.

When Jesus was asked about divorce in general he said, "Moses permitted divorce only as a concession to your hard hearts, but it was not what God had originally intended" (Matthew 19:8). Divorce was not part of the original design yet, when in the case of Israel the pagan wives were leading the men away from God, they were told to divorce them. This is certainly not ideal, but Ezra saw it as the way to make the best of a bad situation.

Paul on the other hand is saying if the unbelieving wife is willing to stay in the marriage, perhaps she will be brought to God by the believing husband or vice versa. "Don't you wives realize that your husbands might be saved because of you? And don't you husbands realize your wives might be saved because of you?" (1 Corinthians 7:16).

In Ezra's time pagan women were causing the men of Israel to turn away from God. Paul was not addressing that type of situation. He was admonishing a believing husband or wife to be a godly influence on an unbelieving spouse. "But," Paul said, "if the husband or wife who isn't a believer insists on leaving, let them go" (1 Corinthians 7:15). The passage of Ezra 10 and 1 Corinthians 7 are dealing with two completely different situations that require different instructions.

Difficult Verses *from* *the* Book *of* Nehemiah

Passage:

When Sanballat, Tobiah, and Geshem the Arab heard of our plan, they scoffed contemptuously (Nehemiah 2:19).

Difficulty: Why was the name of the city official Geshem the Arab spelled differently in Nehemiah 6:6?

Explanation: Some critics would cite the variant spelling of Geshem as Gashmu in Nehemiah 6:6 as an error and contradiction in Scripture. This is simply a difference in the form of proper names in the Hebrew and Arabic languages. The Hebrew version of the name is in Nehemiah 2:9, while the Arabic version is given in 6:6 (NASB).

Difficult Verses *from* *the* Book *of* Esther

Passage:

These events happened in the days of King Xerxes, who reigned over 127 provinces stretching from India to Ethiopia (Esther 1:1).

Difficulty: Why do some critics consider the book of Esther fiction rather than a true historical narrative?

Explanation: Critics suggest that the book of Esther is fiction primarily for these reasons: 1) Esther would have never been chosen as queen since she was not Persian; 2) it is implausible that the Jews slaughtered 75,000 of the enemy in one day; and 3) there is no historical record of the events in Esther documented outside of the book of Esther itself.

First, the facts are that outside sources such as the Greek historians Herodotus and Ctesias as well as Persian records do confirm the biblical accuracy of Esther. Second, monarchs do not generally oppose the killing of their enemies. So the Jews could very well have slaughtered thousands. It is conceded that it may not have been 75,000. The Hebrew word translated thousands can also refer to an extended family or lineage. So it is possible that Esther 9:16 can be translated "They gained relief from all their enemies, killing 75 of their extended families who hated them." This is perhaps more plausible.

Lastly, Esther hid her identity as a Jew long after she became queen. There is no reason she would not have been thought of as a Persian. Additionally, the book reflects authentic Persian names and customs, which further reinforces that Esther is an authentic and accurate historical narrative.

Passage:

The king loved Esther more than any of the other young women. He was so delighted with her that he set the royal crown on her head and declared her queen instead of Vashti (Esther 2:17).

Difficulty: While the book of Esther may present an interesting story, it never mentions the name of God—so how can it be considered Scripture?

Explanation: It is true that God is not mentioned in the book of Esther, but God's sovereign control is clearly seen protecting his people. The book demonstrates that God uses both believers and unbelievers to accomplish his will. The prophet Isaiah quotes God as saying, "Everything I plan will come to pass, for I do whatever I wish. I will call a swift bird of prey from the east—a leader from a distant land to come and do my bidding. I have said what I would do, and I will do it" (Isaiah 46:10-11). The book of Esther illustrates how God moves in the affairs of men and nations to accomplish his sovereign will.

Poetry and Wisdom

Job–Song of Songs

Difficult Verses *from* *the* Book *of* Job

Passage:

Do you still want to argue with the Almighty? You are God's critic, but do you have the answers? (Job 40:2).

Difficulty: Why does God not want us to ask him hard questions about what he does or doesn't do?

Explanation: It is not that God doesn't want us to ask questions. Jesus wasn't put off when his disciples and followers asked whether he was the Messiah, and when the time would come to restore God's kingdom (see Matthew 11:3 and Acts 1:6).

Seeking information to gain an understanding of what God is doing is no problem, but questioning his judgment or motives is another matter. For example, there are some things in life that just don't make sense—like tragedies and great human suffering. And on some issues God remains silent. This is not because he couldn't explain them to us because he could, but sometimes he chooses not to. To question his judgment about things we humans know so little about and then argue with God about it is what is in question here in the book of Job.

What Job seemed to be doing was not simply asking God some tough questions—he was questioning the integrity of God and his perfect justice. "Will you discredit my justice," God asked, "and condemn me just to prove you are right?" (Job 40:8). God objects to our questioning his love, mercy, and perfect justice. He wants us to trust that he knows what he is doing even though we don't understand why he allows bad things to happen to good people.

The prophet Habakkuk had questions too when people were suffering and injustice was everywhere. His question to God was, "How long, O Lord, must I call for help? But you do not listen!... The wicked far outnumber the righteous, so that justice has become perverted" (Habakkuk 1:2,4).

But God did answer: "I am doing something in your own day, something you wouldn't believe even if someone told you about it"

(Habakkuk 2:5). And while God didn't really give him an answer for how he planned to resolve things, he did give him an answer. In effect he says, "Don't focus on the details of my plan—focus on me as a person and trust that I know what I'm doing."

God told Habakkuk,

> These things I plan won't happen right away. Slowly, steadily, surely, the time approaches when the vision will be fulfilled. If it seems slow, wait patiently, for it will surely take place. It will not be delayed. Look at the proud! They trust in themselves, and their lives are crooked; but the righteous will live by their faith (Habakkuk 2:3-4 NLT).

Job eventually got the same message. He responded to God like this: "You asked, 'Who is this that questions my wisdom with such ignorance?' It is I—and I was talking about things I knew nothing about, things far too wonderful for me...I had only heard about you before, but now I have seen you with my own eyes" (Job 42:3,5).

In the end Job had faith in the God he came to know personally. And in the end we can do the same. On questions God does not provide us answers we must "live by faith" and put our trust in a God who is loving and merciful and will eventually bring justice to an unjust world.

Difficult Verses *from* *the* Book *of* Psalms

Passage:

Answer me when I call to you, O God who declares me innocent (Psalm 4:1).

Difficulty: Are all the psalms written by King David?

Explanation: Actually, many composers contributed to the collection of poems and songs that we call the Psalms. King David had a major influence on this book. Seventy-three psalms are somehow identified with David—either he wrote them or they were written to him or composed in honor of him. The other psalms were written by the sons of Korah (Psalms 42–49, 84–85, 87), Asaph (Psalms 50, 73–83), Solomon (Psalms 72, 127), Herman (Psalm 88), Ethan (Psalm 89), and Moses (Psalm 90).

Passage and Difficulty: Psalm 13:1-2—Why does God seem to abandon us in our trouble?

Explanation: See Matthew 27:46.

Passage and Difficulty: Psalm 51:4—Why did David say his sin was only against God when it was also against Bathsheba and Uriah?

Explanation: See 2 Samuel 12:13.

Passage:

You do not desire a sacrifice, or I would offer one. You do not want a burnt offering (Psalm 51:16).

Difficulty: Why does David say God would not be pleased with sacrifices, when sacrifices are what provided for his and our forgiveness?

Explanation: Sacrifices given in the Old Testament and the final and perfect sacrifice of Jesus were needed for the forgiveness of sin and a right relationship with God. But he doesn't want us to try to earn forgiveness by our own acts of sacrifice. He does not want us to have a self-condemning spirit or beat ourselves up to try to appease him. David went on to say in the next verse, "The sacrifice you desire is a broken spirit. You will not reject a broken and repentant heart, O God" (Psalm 51:17).

God wants us to be broken and sorry for our sins, but he also wants us to realize that any penance or sacrifices on our part don't win us his forgiveness. No amount of acts of contrition or obedience to a set of laws grants us his forgiveness. "Can we boast...that we have done anything to be accepted by God? No, because our acquittal is not based on obeying the law. It is based on faith" (Romans 3:27). Our faith in Jesus as our perfect sacrifice is what provides us forgiveness and brings us into right relationship with God.

Passage:

He has removed our sins as far from us as the east is from the west (Psalm 103:12).

Difficulty: What does it mean to remove our sins as far as the east is from the west?

Explanation: In this verse King David was describing the complete, total, and absolute nature of God's forgiveness of our sins. We all deserve punishment for our sins, but David states that "[God] does not punish us for all our sins; he does not deal harshly with us, as we deserve. For his unfailing love toward those who fear him is as great as the height of the heavens above the earth" (Psalm 103:10-11). Then he goes on to say how far our sins are removed from us.

But why did he say "as far from us as the east is from the west" rather than "as far as the north is from the south"? "From east to west" is a Hebrew expression for infinity. While you can measure the north from the south (there is a North Pole and a South Pole), you cannot measure the distance from the east to the west. If you go east or if you travel west, you will go on for eternity. It is like saying your sins have been obliterated. You could travel through all eternity and never find a trace of them to condemn you before God. Because "the LORD is compassionate and merciful, slow to get angry and filled with unfailing love" (Psalm 103:8), your sins have vanished forever because his forgiveness is infinitely absolute.

Difficult Verses *from* *the* Book *of* Proverbs

Passage:

The Lord made me at the beginning of His creation, before His works of long ago (Proverbs 8:22 HCSB).

Difficulty: Some, namely the Jehovah's Witnesses, say this passage refers to Jesus. Does this then mean Jesus was a created being rather than God's co-existing eternal Son?

Explanation: Jehovah's Witnesses (JWs) do use this passage to contend that Jesus is a created being and not part of the Godhead. They also use a passage in Colossians to do the same (see *Explanation* of Colossians 1:15).

Since Paul said that "Christ is the power of God and the wisdom of God" (1 Corinthians 1:24), the JWs assert that this Proverbs passage is referring to Jesus. The basis for their notion that "wisdom" or "Jesus" was created is deduced from the word *made*—that is, "The Lord made me" (Proverbs 8:22).

The Hebrew word translated "made" here is *qanah,* which actually means "to possess," not "to create" or "make." Even if this passage was referring to Jesus, the verse is saying, "The Lord possessed me, or I was part of God, at the beginning of his creation."

However, it is far more likely, judging from the context, that Solomon wasn't describing the Son of God but rather a personification of wisdom. In this common poetic technique, an abstract idea is described as if it were a person. So Solomon is making a personification of the virtue of wisdom to make his point. This does not of course detract from the truth that Jesus is the wisdom of God, because he does personify wisdom perfectly. The apostle Paul said that in him "lie hidden all the treasures of wisdom and knowledge" (Colossians 2:3).

Passage:

Train up a child in the way he should go, and when he is old he will not depart from it (Proverbs 22:6 NKJV).

Difficulty: Is there a guarantee that if you train a child correctly he or she will always remain true to your teachings?

Explanation: No matter how many instructions are given to a child or how good the instructions are, he or she has individual choices to make. So there are no guarantees about what a child will do once adulthood is reached. Yet this particular proverb is often misunderstood to mean that if we saturate our kids with church, the Bible, Christian fellowship, and religious teaching, they will grow up Christian and never depart from the true faith.

Although those types of efforts by a parent are good, that is not the focus of this verse. The phrase "the way he [or she] should go" refers not to a religious path, but to the child's own way—his or her natural leaning or bent. The key word in the phrase is translated "bend" in two of the psalms—it refers to the bending of an archer's bow. In biblical days, archers made their own bows to fit their own strength and unique characteristics. A person could shoot an arrow well only with his own personal bow.

A note on Proverbs 22:6 in the *Ryrie Study Bible* explains that "the way he should go" means according to "the child's habits and interests. The instruction must take into account his individuality and inclinations, his personality, the unique way God created him, and must be in keeping with his physical and mental development."[1] We've all known of successful parents who pushed their sons or daughters to follow in their footsteps, even when their child had a natural bent in another direction. This approach rarely works out. But when we seek to understand our children's "bent"—their natural talents and unique individuality—and encourage them in that direction, we can see positive and lasting results that endure for a lifetime.

Passage:

These are more proverbs of Solomon, compiled by the men of Hezekiah king of Judah (Proverbs 25:1 NIV).

Difficulty: Does this mean that Solomon didn't write all of Proverbs?

Explanation: During the reign of King Hezekiah his advisors collected the writings of Solomon to form Proverbs. Solomon "composed some 3,000 proverbs and wrote 1,005 songs" (1 Kings 4:32), which is more than the book of Proverbs contains. So the men working under Hezekiah simply collected portions of them and probably transcribed them word for word to create the book of Proverbs.

Passage:

Alcohol is for the dying, and wine for those in bitter distress. Let them drink to forget their poverty and remember their troubles no more (Proverbs 31:6-7).

Difficulty: Doesn't this passage encourage alcoholic drinking so a person will forget their troubles?

Explanation: Solomon speaks out against the abuse of alcohol when he says, "Wine produces mockers; alcohol leads to brawls. Those led astray by drink cannot be wise" (Proverbs 20:1). And in the verses prior to endorsing alcohol in Proverbs 31 he says, "Rulers should not crave alcohol. For if they drink, they may forget the law and not give justice to the oppressed" (Proverbs 31:4-5).

With that as a context Solomon shares how alcohol can be used. Wine was often used for medicinal purposes prior to modern medicine. Paul encouraged Timothy to use it that way (see 1 Timothy 5:23).

The alcohol in wine also numbs the senses. Solomon was saying that the rulers needed clear minds to rule justly. That would certainly apply today for people on the job, operating machinery, or driving cars. But for the dying and those suffering a loss or experiencing a tragedy, Solomon encouraged a sedative.

Scripture does speak against the abuse of alcoholic drink on numerous occasions (see Proverbs 23:29-35; 1 Corinthians 5:11; Ephesians 5:18). Drunkenness is what causes a person to be out of control physically and it is what impairs judgment. For more on the scriptural position on the use of alcohol see *Explanation* of John 2:9-10.

Difficult Verses *from* *the* Book *of* Ecclesiastes

Passage:

These are the words of the Teacher, King David's son [Solomon] who ruled in Jerusalem. "Everything is meaningless," says the Teacher, "completely meaningless!" (Ecclesiastes 1:1-2).

Difficulty: Why does this passage say, "Everything is meaningless" when we know that isn't true?

Explanation: This phrase "everything is meaningless" is in fact the theme of the book of Ecclesiastes. Solomon constantly says that life and all of reality is *hebel*, the Hebrew word for "mist, vapor, breath." It is used figuratively to indicate something is transitory, worthless, futile, or meaningless.

Throughout the entire book Solomon takes us on a journey for meaning and purpose. He points out that life is short and there is futility in wisdom (great learning), pleasure, work, political power, and wealth. And at the end of the journey he contends that we will find nothing but an existence without meaning and then we die.

"That's the whole story," Solomon says. "Here now is my final conclusion: Fear God and obey his commands, for this is everyone's duty. God will judge us for everything we do, including every secret thing, whether good or bad" (Ecclesiastes 12:13-14). In other words, all of life is worthless and without meaning in the end without God. The wise counsel of Solomon is that the "fear of the LORD is the foundation of true knowledge, but fools despise wisdom and discipline...For the LORD grants wisdom! From his mouth comes knowledge and understanding...Then you will understand what is right, just and fair, and you will find the right way to go. For wisdom will enter your heart, and knowledge will fill you with joy" (Proverbs 1:7; 2:6,9-10).

Solomon concludes that "everything is meaningless" outside of a life that fears God—being in awe of him—knowing him and living to love and please him. For at the end of this short life we will give an account before him. And those that have feared him and lived wisely will be rewarded accordingly.

Difficult Verses *from* *the* Book *of* Song of Songs

Passage:
Like a lily among thistles is my darling among young women. Like the finest apple tree in the orchard is my lover among other young men. I sit in his delightful shade and taste his delicious fruit (Song of Songs 2:2-3).

Difficulty: Isn't this entire book violating sexual morality by portraying two unmarried lovers engaging in sensuous sex?

Explanation: There is no question the Song of Songs describes sensuous longings and implies physical sex. And since the romantic interludes do not explicitly describe a married couple, some conclude it is portraying two unmarried lovers.

However, various passages do suggest this is about a marriage relationship between a man and a woman. "You have captured my heart," the lover says, "my treasure, my bride" (Song of Songs 4:9). Throughout chapter 4 and the beginning of 5 he refers to her repeatedly as "my bride." Also, when you place this book within the context of the Hebrew Scriptures it is clear this is referring to a couple within a married relationship. The Law of Moses made it clear that any sexual involvement outside the bounds of marriage was adultery (Exodus 20:14).

The Prophets
Isaiah–Malachi

Passage:

All right then, the Lord himself will give you the sign. Look! The virgin will conceive a child! She will call him Immanuel (which means "God is with us") (Isaiah 7:14).

Difficulty: This verse is commonly used to refer to Jesus as virgin born, but isn't it merely referring to the natural birth of King Hezekiah?

Explanation: Conservative scholars say the prophet Isaiah foretold that Jesus would be born of a virgin seven centuries before the event took place. However, critics point out that the New Testament writer "misquotes" the word *virgin* from Isaiah 7. The Hebrew word used in Isaiah 7:14 is *almah,* meaning "young woman." Yet in Matthew 1:23 the Greek translation of the Old Testament is quoted using the word *parthenos,* meaning "virgin." Critics say that Matthew is twisting what Isaiah was saying.

Truth is, the Hebrew word *almah* can mean either "young woman" or "virgin," even though there is a specific word for *virgin* in Hebrew. However, because of the word's traditional usage, readers of Isaiah's time understood that he did mean a virgin would conceive. And that is why the Jewish scholars over 200 years before Jesus was born rendered the Hebrew word *almah* as the Greek word for *virgin* when translating Isaiah 7:14 for the Septuagint. Matthew wasn't twisting things at all—he was quoting the Greek translation, considered both then and now to be accurate in translating Isaiah. Jesus accepted the Septuagint translation of the Hebrew text and quoted frequently from it. For additional clarification on the quotation of Isaiah 7 in Matthew 1 see *Explanation* of Matthew 1:23.

Passage:

I form the light, and create darkness: I make peace, and create evil: I the LORD do all these things (Isaiah 45:7 KJV).

Difficulty: Did God create evil?

Explanation: Scripture reveals a God who is perfectly holy (Isaiah 54:5 and Revelation 4:8), just (Revelation 16:5), and right (Psalm 119:137). "The LORD is just! He is my rock! There is no evil in him" (Psalm 92:15). The very nature of God is holy and right and therefore nothing he creates could ever be morally evil. So how is it that Isaiah says that he created evil?

The word for *evil* in the Hebrew is *ra* and does not necessarily denote a moral evil. It can also be translated "calamity, bad or disaster." The New International Version translates the verse as "I bring prosperity and create disaster" (Isaiah 45:7). God can create disasters, but because he is perfectly holy he cannot create evil.

But Scripture clearly states that God created everything (see John 1:1-3 and Colossians 1:15-17). And if we accept that evil is a reality, how can we say he didn't create it? The answer lies in the fact that evil is not a thing or substance or entity to be created. Rather, evil is the corruption of a good thing that God did in fact make.

God made humans and it was good. This is repeated multiple times in Genesis 1. He gave humans the power of free will, and that was good as well. This means he gave them the choice to believe that he was the arbiter of right and wrong and that he knew what was best for them when he said not to eat of a certain fruit—and that was good. When the first humans believed he did *not* know what was best for them—which was the corrupting of a particular good thing—evil was then born.

Evil then is not a substance or an entity, but the corruption of that which is good. This means that evil is parasitic upon good. Evil depends upon the existence of good in a way good does not depend upon evil. Thus, while there can be good without evil, there cannot be evil without the existence of goodness. Just as the concept of "bentness" requires "straightness," the existence of evil requires that good be previously in existence.

Evil became a reality when there was 1) a rejection of what God said was true and worthy of obedience, and 2) an act in opposition to his command. He wanted humans to trust and obey him. In fact, he designed all of us to live fulfilled and meaningful lives by worshipping him and living in right relationship with him. And when the choice was made to cease trusting in him and following his ways, evil became a reality.

Difficult Verses *from* *the* Book *of* Jeremiah

Passage:

I knew you before I formed you in your mother's womb. Before you were born I set you apart and appointed you as my prophet to the nations (Jeremiah 1:5).

Difficulty: Does this verse support the idea of reincarnation?

Explanation: There are those who believe that a person's soul preexists before he or she is placed into a body. They use this verse to demonstrate that God knew Jeremiah as a soul before he was placed into a physical body. However, the words "I knew you" in the Hebrew do not support the idea of a preexistent soul.

The word *know* in the Hebrew is *yada,* which denotes an intimate knowledge or relationship of commitment. Place that within the context of "I set you apart and appointed you" before you were born, it then more accurately refers to a prenatal intimacy and commitment God is making. In other words, God preordained Jeremiah for a special ministry.

King David says that God "watched me as I was being formed in utter seclusion...in the dark of the womb...You saw me before I was born. Every day of my life was recorded in your book. Every moment was laid out before a single day had passed" (Psalm 139:15-16). This shows God's foreknowledge, that he knew all about us as a fetus growing inside our mother's womb. God was aware of our pre-birth existence and what we would eventually do after birth, but this doesn't mean we were pre-existent souls waiting to be incarnated into a body. This has to do with God's amazing foreknowledge—"Only I can tell you the future before it even happens" (Isaiah 46:10)—and his preordaining or setting individuals apart for service even before they are born.

Passage and Difficulty: Jeremiah 3:7—If God is omniscient—"all-knowing"—then why didn't he know in advance that Judah would not return to him?

Explanation: See Genesis 22:10-12.

Passage and Difficulty: Jeremiah 18:5-10—God is supposed to be unchanging, but doesn't this passage make it clear that he changes his mind?

Explanation: See Exodus 32:12-14.

Difficult Verses *from the* Book *of* Lamentations

Passage:

Tenderhearted women have cooked their own children. They have eaten them to survive the siege (Lamentations 4:10).

Difficulty: Why would a loving God allow such suffering on the part of his creation?

Explanation: Lamentations depicts the horrific and tragic destruction of Jerusalem by the Babylonian army. It is emotionally wrenching in its description of human suffering, with starving mothers eating their own babies in an attempt to survive. This raises the question, "If God is good, and he is, why would he allow such emotional and physical devastation on his creation, especially on his chosen people?" In fact in numerous cases throughout Scripture, God gets angry and actually causes suffering as it is recorded in Lamentations. For more on why God's anger causes pain and suffering on his creation, see *Explanation* of Zephaniah 2:2.

In this explanation we will focus more on why God would allow suffering of humans in the first place. Various scholars have different answers: It is God's punishment for sin; it is a test of faith; it is God's means of redemption; it is a huge mystery and we shouldn't question God's doings. Yet the question of suffering and God's role in it appears to be a valid one that deserves a response. Volumes have been written about this, but perhaps the following brief discussion will at least provide some perspective.

First, it is doubtful there is any logical explanation that somehow satisfies the profound emotional cry for a solution to the horrific problem of pain and suffering. So it is highly improbable that reason and philosophical discourse can fully answer the cries of the heart. But this does not mean that one should not think deeply about it. All things considered, Christian scholars believe a biblical worldview provides the most intellectually satisfying and emotionally fulfilling response to the problem of suffering and why God allows it.

From the very beginning, God has given humans created in his image the power of free choice or free will. From a human perspective there was a great risk in his doing this—humans might choose their own way and not his. And of course they did. That might not sound that earth-shattering on the surface, but it is.

If you accept the premise that "whatever is good and perfect comes down to us from God" (James 1:16), then you probably accept the notion that experiencing a life of joy, peace, gentleness, beauty, kindness, love, and all that is called good depends upon and is the result of being in relationship with God and living in accordance with his ways. So then, if a finite human created to be in relationship with God chooses against that relationship, what is the alternative? The alternative is a life without joy, peace, love, goodness, and so on: a life the opposite of God's—resulting in a life of pain and suffering.

The following is a feeble illustration of how free choice can cause suffering, but imagine that the very first family of fish were intelligent beings with eternal souls. Of course as fish they were designed to live in water with gills that breathed "good oxygen" from Lake Paradise. But what if this first fish couple chose to "live" outside their perfect home of Lake Paradise? As we know, this would be a tragic mistake. Fish are not designed to breathe the open air because that is "bad oxygen" for them. And if they do they will experience pain and suffering.

But because these particular fish have eternal souls they experience the suffering of a "living death." And what about all the offspring of these fish? The "living death" experience is passed to every new fish born outside of Lake Paradise. Is this tragedy the fault of the fish creator? Or is the suffering a result of the first fish that chose to live contrary to their design and outside of the Paradise in relationship with their Maker?

Granted, this illustration doesn't answer all the difficult details of why suffering happens. But perhaps it helps to remember that an infinite Creator, who is perfect, holy, and good, created humans to enjoy life in relationship with him. God gave the first couple a very good thing—the power to choose between unselfishly loving him and believing that he knew what was best (a very good thing)...or selfishly loving themselves and believing *they* knew what was best (a very bad thing). What he wanted was for finite humans to trust that he (the infinite God) knew what was best for them (finite humans). He wanted them to unselfishly put him first and learn that his way of living was the way of joy, peace, and goodness. If the first couple had followed that way, they would have avoided pain and suffering.

To a degree, it is possible to craft a theological or philosophical answer for why there is suffering and why free choice has in effect allowed it. Yet in many respects the intensity of human suffering is simply too emotionally overwhelming for reason or logic to provide a thoroughly satisfying answer. And actually, the Bible by and large doesn't directly address the question of why there is suffering. However, from the first book of Genesis to the last book of Revelation it does tell us what God is doing about it. *He has not ignored suffering; he is working to bring an end to it.*

When humans chose to reject God and his ways it did bring immeasurable pain and suffering to them. But it wasn't only humanity that suffered. God did not at all have an impersonal response to suffering. He suffered as well, for the Bible says, "It broke his heart" (Genesis 6:6). While it is true that he is "slow to get angry and filled with unfailing love" (Psalm 103:8), he does get angry. He is angry that death has separated him from the children he created. He is angry with his archenemy, the devil, who holds the power of death. And he is angry that sin and death have brought such anguish on his creation.

But in his holy anger and unfailing love he has taken action. Long ago he promised Abraham that through his descendants he would provide a final solution to sin, suffering, pain, and death. He promised the children of Abraham that "he will remove the cloud of gloom, the shadow of death that hangs over the earth. He will swallow up death forever! The Sovereign LORD will wipe away all tears. He will remove forever all insults and mockery against his land and people" (Isaiah 25:7-8).

God's solution to all suffering meant that he would take the form of a human and also suffer. Jesus would experience the full weight of human suffering—that is, hunger, betrayal, rejection, loneliness, and the torturous death of crucifixion. So in a real sense God knows what it is to suffer, and he sympathizes with us (see Hebrews 2:18; 4:15).

But he did not leave it there. Jesus' death would be an atoning sacrifice for sin, and he would rise again to reclaim fallen humans from the power of death and from the power of his ancient enemy, the devil himself. The following passages chronicle his plan to abolish sin and suffering.

> All who belong to Christ will be raised when he comes back. After that the end will come, when he will turn the Kingdom over to God the Father, having destroyed every ruler and power. For Christ must reign until he humbles all his enemies beneath his feet. And the last enemy to be destroyed is death (1 Corinthians 15:23-26).

> The Son of God appeared for this purpose, to destroy the works of the devil (1 John 3:8 NASB).

> When all things are under his authority, the Son will put himself under God's authority, so that God, who gave his Son authority over all things, will be utterly supreme over everything everywhere (1 Corinthians 15:28).

> Look, God's home is now among his people! He will live with them, and they will be his people. God himself will be with them. He will wipe every tear from their eyes, and there will be no more death or sorrow or crying or pain (Revelation 21:3-4).

God of course knew that we humans would not trust that he knew what was best for us and would choose our own way. But if love was to be genuine it had to be of our own choosing. He was willing to allow us to choose, even if it brought him and his creation great pain to redeem us back to him.

Difficult Verses *from* *the* Book *of* Ezekiel

Passage:

I will bring King Nebuchadnezzar of Babylon against Tyre...They will plunder all your riches and merchandise and break down your walls (Ezekiel 26:7,12).

Difficulty: Doesn't this passage that says Nebuchadnezzar plundered all the riches of Tyre contradict Ezekiel 29:18, which says he didn't plunder Tyre?

Explanation: Ezekiel 29 seems to contradict Ezekiel 26 when it says, "Yet Nebuchadnezzar and his army won no plunder to compensate them for all their work" (Ezekiel 29:18). This apparent contradiction is cleared up when we realize that Ezekiel was prophesying that God would "bring many nations against you, like the waves of the sea crashing against your shoreline. They will destroy the walls of Tyre and tear down its towers" (Ezekiel 26:3-4). Nebuchadnezzar was just one among many that would come up against Israel to destroy her. He would plunder part of Israel, but it would take others to plunder her totally.

In Ezekiel 26:15-21 the fall of the island city of Tyre is prophesied. Nebuchadnezzar did defeat and plunder the coastal cities (Ezekiel 26:12). But he couldn't capture and plunder the island city so he was rewarded with the land of Egypt (Ezekiel 29:18-19).

It was around 587 BC that Ezekiel prophesied about Tyre's total destruction, but it would take over 250 years before it fully happened. Around 332 BC Alexander the Great finally obliterated Tyre. The total desolation Ezekiel said would take place came at last, and the city was never rebuilt.

Passage:

In a vision from God he took me to the land of Israel and set me down on a very high mountain. From there I could see toward the south what appeared to be a city (Ezekiel 40:2).

Difficulty: Is Ezekiel's vision in chapters 40–48 prophesying a literal millennial reign, or is this referring to Christ becoming the all-sufficient atoning sacrifice for sin?

Explanation: The book of Ezekiel is full of visions that led up to and followed the fall of Jerusalem in 586 BC. His final vision from chapters 40–48 reflects the same message as the entire book: God will bring his people back to him and redeem them to holiness so he can once again live among them. His glory then will transform the land and his people and the Temple will never again be defiled.

Ezekiel sees this Temple in detail. He describes a time when sacrifices will once again be offered in it, and a life-giving river will flow through it that will heal the nations.

Scholars generally fall into two camps on the interpretation of these chapters. There are those who subscribe to a more literal translation. They believe Ezekiel is predicting the fulfillment of Revelation 20, in which Jesus returns to earth for a millennial reign. This is a time when Israel recognizes Jesus as the Messiah and re-establishes the sacrificial system as a memorial or a covenant of remembrance of his own sacrificial offering of redemption. This view is said to be supported by Old Testament passages such as Genesis 12:1-3 and Isaiah 59:20-21, in which God established an eternal covenant with Abraham and a Redeemer is prophesied to come to Jerusalem in order to purchase back his people. Those who hold this view also point to Romans 9 and 12 and Revelation 20 as New Testament passages that refer to a literal reign of Christ over Israel. And finally, the dimensions and measurements for the Temple that Ezekiel saw are said to be too precise and detailed not to be interpreted literally.

Other scholars interpret Ezekiel's vision of the Temple as a theological statement described through the lens of an architectural plan. They point out that the plans for construction lack specifics of materials and are not considered physically buildable. Rather this new Temple, they say, finds its fulfillment in Jesus becoming the all-sufficient atoning sacrifice for sin and thereby abolishing the Old Testament sacrificial system and priesthood. All of this is replaced with Christ becoming our High Priest, as described in Hebrews chapters 8–10. In this view Israel's calling to be a kingdom of priests is fulfilled in Christ's body, the church, and in the sending of the Holy Spirit as described in Ephesians 1:5, Galatians 5:16, and 2 Peter 2:9.

Both views are held by learned scholars who simply disagree on the interpretation of Ezekiel's vision. For more on the millennial reign of Christ see *Explanation* of Revelation 1:1.

Passage:

All these things did happen to King Nebuchadnezzar. Twelve months later he was taking a walk on the flat roof of the royal palace in Babylon. As he looked out across the city, he said, "Look at this great city of Babylon! By my own mighty power, I have built this beautiful city as my royal residence to display my majestic splendor" (Daniel 4:28-30).

Difficulty: Is there proof outside of the Bible to answer critics who say that King Nebuchadnezzar II of Babylon never existed?

Explanation: The city of Babylon had magnificent walls of royal blue ceramic tile, gold-colored artwork of dragons and lions, the famous Hanging Gardens, and the exotic Ishtar Gate that the king ordered to be built. But was there really a King Nebuchadnezzar who built it all?

King Nebuchadnezzar II was said to have lived and reigned over Babylon from 605 to 565 BC. And confirmation of his existence has been made by archaeologists who uncovered evidence near present-day Hillah, Babylon Province, Iraq, about 55 miles south of Baghdad.

Numerous fragments of bricks with remains of white-glazed cuneiform characters have been found that belong to a building inscription of Nebuchadnezzar II at the Ishtar Gate. Archaeologists claim there is no doubt that the text refers to the construction of the gate. The text was restored by comparing it with another complete inscription found on a limestone block, which gives three excerpts of the main inscription of the King: "I, Nebuchadnezzar, laid the foundation of the gates...I magnificently adorned them with luxurious splendor for all mankind to behold in awe."[1]

Passage:

Many years later King Belshazzar gave a great feast for 1,000 of his nobles, and he drank wine with them (Daniel 5:1).

Difficulty: Are critics correct to say that King Belshazzar was just a legendary figure and never existed?

Explanation: It is true that Belshazzar was not listed in any extra-biblical Babylonian king list. Greek historians also did not record his existence. However, archaeologists then discovered the Cylinder of Nabonidus while excavating in southern Iraq at the Temple of Shamash.

King Nabonidus's inscription chronicles his stay in Tema and the fall of Babylon (539 BC). More importantly, this discovery listed former Babylonian kings. And Belshazzar was listed as king and firstborn son of King Nabonidus.

Difficult Verses *from* *the* Book *of* Hosea

Passage:

When the LORD first began speaking to Israel through Hosea, he said to him, "Go and marry a prostitute, so that some of her children will be conceived in prostitution" (Hosea 1:2).

Difficulty: Would God really command someone to marry a prostitute?

Explanation: Many, including some in the early centuries of the church, could not believe God would have a person marry a prostitute. So some have considered the entire book of Hosea an allegory in which Gomer represented Israel and Hosea represented God. But the rest of verse 2 explains why God gave the command: "This will illustrate how Israel has acted like a prostitute by turning against the LORD and worshiping other gods" (Hosea 2:2).

Many today believe that Hosea's marriage to Gomer was a real one. Some suggest that Gomer may not have been promiscuous when he married her, although she was predisposed to be unfaithful. Therefore, they say, Hosea didn't marry a prostitute, but his wife became one after they were married. Others disagree and believe Hosea did in fact marry a prostitute. While marrying a prostitute may seem extreme, it certainly does provide a vivid and powerful illustration to what extent God will go to redeem us. For more on the meaning of the book of Hosea see *Explanation* of Zephaniah 2:2 and Matthew 9:12-13.

Passage and Difficulty: Hosea 6:6—What does it mean that God wants us to "show love, not offer sacrifices"? Jesus quoted this verse to reveal a significant truth.

Explanation: See Matthew 9:12-13.

Passage and Difficulty: Hosea 11:1—Isn't this verse being misquoted by Matthew when he says it refers to Jesus?

Explanation: See Matthew 1:23.

Difficult Verses *from* *the* Book *of* Joel

Passage:

Sound the alarm in Jerusalem! Raise the battle cry on my holy mountain! Let everyone tremble in fear because the day of the LORD is upon us (Joel 2:1).

Difficulty: Why does Joel prophesy that the "day of the LORD is upon us," when it has taken hundreds and thousands of years to fulfill, with some prophesies yet to be fulfilled?

Explanation: The phrase "the day of the LORD" is a central focus of Joel. It can be referring to the judgment of Israel in their rebellion against God or a joyous day of deliverance when Israel turns back to him and their rule is re-established. Yet the judgment of God continued for years after Joel's prophecies. And the prophecy of the coming of God's Spirit didn't happen until after Jesus' ascension hundreds of years after Joel had prophesied it (Joel 2:28-29). And some believe there are still prophecies yet to be fulfilled (Joel 2:30-32; 3:1-21). So how could Joel say the "day of the LORD is upon us"?

The phrase is not referring to the timing of "the day" but of its certainty. In other words timing is not the issue—that is not what is relevant. Rather God's promises of judgment, redemption, and restoration are what are relevant.

Peter made this same point. He wrote of people scoffing at the delay of Christ's return to fulfill his promises of "the day of the LORD." But Peter says,

> You must not forget this one thing, dear friends: A day is like a thousand years to the Lord, and a thousand years is like a day. The Lord isn't really being slow about his promise, as some people think. No, he is being patient for your sake. He does not want anyone to be destroyed, but wants

> everyone to repent. But the day of the Lord will come as unexpectedly as a thief (2 Peter 3:8-10).

And since the "day of the Lord" is still upon us—it is still certain to come. The timing of its fulfillment isn't as important as its inevitability.

Difficult Verses *from* *the* Book *of* Amos

Passage:

This is what the LORD says: "The people of Israel have sinned again and again, and I will not let them go unpunished! They sell honorable people for silver and poor people for a pair of sandals. They trample helpless people in the dust and shove the oppressed out of the way" (Amos 2:6-7).

Difficulty: Are God and his followers truly concerned about social justice?

Explanation: To some, the God of the Old Testament and Christianity in general are not concerned about social justice in the world. They see Christianity as an evil empire imposing its will on the masses and threatening to suppress the free expressions of humanity.

Although there are those past and present who, under the banner of Christianity, have waged war, enslaved people, and otherwise brought disgrace on the name of Christ, this is only a small, sad corner of the whole picture. Here in Amos, God is outraged at the social injustice perpetrated by Israel. And it can be demonstrated that it is the compassion of Jesus and those following in his steps that has fostered social justice and provided more positive contributions to society in general than any other force in history.

Atheists and other detractors of Christianity fail to point out that it is the human propensity to be self-centered that has brought such misery and suffering upon the masses. Christianity is actually the antidote to this propensity, for it is the message and power of Christ that addresses the core problem of self-centeredness.

Greed, corruption, abuse of power, and a basic disregard for others spring from self-centeredness. Left unchecked, human nature will always revert to self-serving ways that seek to gain at another's expense. On the opposite side of the equation, making the interest and care of others as important as your own creates goodwill and harmony and meets human needs. This is at the center of Jesus' teaching—it represents the very heart of God. Jesus said, "Do to others whatever you would like them to do to you. This is the essence of all that is taught in the law and the prophets" (Matthew 7:12).

Looking out for the interests of others, especially those in need, is the primary core value of Jesus' teachings and the Scripture in general. The expression used most often to describe Jesus' heart of love was that he was "moved with compassion." When he saw the two blind men he was "moved with compassion." When he saw the leper he was "moved with compassion." When he saw the sick and the hungry he was "moved with compassion" (see Matthew 9:36; 15:32; 20:34; Mark 1:41; 6:34; 8:2). Jesus had a heart of love that moved him to put others first, and it is that Christlike heart that has empowered his followers to change the world for good.

At its core, compassionate Christianity represents a focus on caring for the interest of others. "In humility," Paul said, "value others above yourselves, not looking to your own interests but each of you to the interests of others" (Philippians 2:3-4 NIV). This compassion toward others is a radical message now, and it was certainly so during the time of Christ. Within the Roman Empire during the first century, enslaving others was commonplace. Abortion was rampant. Parents abandoned virtually all babies that were deformed or otherwise unwanted. Women had few rights and were considered the property of their husbands.

Yet during this time James, a disciple of Jesus, made a radical statement: "Pure and genuine religion in the sight of God our Father means caring for orphans and widows in their distress and refusing to let the world corrupt you" (James 2:27). These early Christians rejected the cultural practice of allowing abandoned babies and orphaned children to die on the streets. Instead, they would literally pick them up and adopt them into their own homes. What caused them to do this? It was the "moved with compassion" heart of their Lord being lived out in their lives. Early Christians believed that everyone—including the poor, the homeless, the handicapped, the sick—was made in the image of God and had infinite value, dignity, and worth.

Beyond any shadow of a doubt Christianity has been a powerful force for social justice in our world. It is Jesus' concern for a hurting world that has led his followers to establish protection for infants and the unborn, child-labor laws, separation of church and state, liberty and justice, care for those in need, abolition of slavery in the Western world, and advancements in modern science. They have built universities and hospitals and brought about musical innovations and the advancement of the written word. And those efforts continue today.

Difficult Verses *from* *the* Book *of* Obadiah

Passage:

All you nations will drink and stagger and disappear from history. But Jerusalem will become a refuge for those who escape; it will be a holy place. And the people of Israel will come back to reclaim their inheritance (Obadiah 1:16-17).

Difficulty: Why is God so partial to Israel even though they rejected him over and over? Isn't this a form of racial discrimination by God?

Explanation: The entire book of Obadiah predicts how God will judge those who come against Israel and how Israel will triumph over their enemies. This certainly makes it appear as though God racially discriminates. All throughout history, as recorded in Scripture, God has had a chosen race—Israel.

It is true that in the book of Genesis it tells us God singled out a man named Abram and said,

> Leave your native country, your relatives, and your father's family, and go to the land that I will show you. I will make you into a great nation. I will bless you and make you famous, and you will be a blessing to others. I will bless those who bless you and I will curse those who treat you with contempt. All the families on earth will be blessed through you (Genesis 12:1-3).

But the charges of God being racist are due to misinterpreting and misunderstanding the biblical narrative.

God did make a special covenant with Abraham and his descendants—and for good reason. Before creation God planned to redeem sinful humans, and he would do that by taking on the form of humans through the birth of Jesus. So he identified a people. He gave them his holy Word, the Scripture. He established a sacrificial system with them that would lead to a final remedy for sin and death. He prophesied in his Word that the perfect sacrifice—the Lamb of God—would be born out of the descendants of Abraham (see Matthew 1:1-17). And it was the God-man, Jesus, who came to redeem all who would receive him, both Jew and Gentile.

So God choosing Israel wasn't simply about Israel—it was about his making his name known and offering salvation to the rest of the world. Also he judged Israel as he did other nations (see 2 Kings 17). He was not playing favorites. God is not racist. Whether Jew or Gentile, we all must give an account equally to him.

Difficult Verses *from* *the* Book *of* Jonah

Passage:

The LORD had arranged for a great fish to swallow Jonah. And Jonah was inside the fish for three days and three nights (Jonah 1:17).

Difficulty: Is the story of Jonah being swallowed by a great fish a historical incident or just a fictional parable to teach us a certain truth?

Explanation: Some would say there is a "moral to the story" of Jonah but it's hard to believe it is a real event. It does appear improbable for a person to survive being swallowed by a fish and live to tell about it. But Scripture is full of miraculous events. Jonah's experience is no more miraculous than creation, the parting of the Red Sea, the burning bush, the virgin birth of Christ, or the many miracles Christ performed.

Jonah was a historical figure identified in the historical book of 2 Kings 14:25. Jesus referred to him as a real person in Luke 11:29-30. And Jesus specifically referenced the fact that "Jonah was in the belly of the great fish for three days and three nights" (Matthew 12:40). The story of Jonah and the great fish is presented as a historical account from Scripture, and Jesus, God's Son, relates it to us as a real story.

Difficult Verses *from* *the* Book *of* Micah

Passage:

In the last days, the mountain of the LORD's house will be the highest of all—the most important place on earth. It will be raised above the other hills, and people from all over the world will stream there to worship (Micah 4:1).

Difficulty: Did Micah plagiarize this passage from Isaiah or vice versa?

Explanation: Micah 4:1-5 and Isaiah 2:1-4 are practically the same, almost word for word. Micah and Isaiah were contemporaries beginning and ending their ministries at the same time. They were probably familiar with each other's writings. So did one plagiarize from the other?

Prophets often quoted or interacted with the prophecies of others without identifying the other prophet. Nahum, Habakkuk, Zephaniah, Zechariah, and Hosea all use Isaiah's words in some form or another without mentioning him by name.

The use of the phrase "hammer their swords into plowshares and their spears into pruning hooks" written by Micah and Isaiah is a reversal of what Joel wrote years earlier. He wrote, "Hammer your plowshares into swords and your pruning hooks into spears" (Joel 3:10). A variation of such specific usage of words probably isn't a coincidence. These prophets were well versed in the Hebrew text and could have easily rendered their passages with similar verbiage.

When you consider these men were inspired by God to write what he wanted recorded, it is not strange that their language would be similar. Remember that God did not put people into a trance and use their hands and pens to write out his thoughts and ideas. He chose to use their minds and knowledge to speak his message through them. So it would be natural, since they had read Isaiah, that they would have that knowledge stored in their hearts and minds. God would then use that knowledge to communicate a similar message.

Charging Micah or Isaiah with plagiarism seems harsh. One or the other may have copied the other and so noted it on the side of the manuscript. This note may have been left out during the manuscript copying over the centuries. Or perhaps being contemporaries they didn't feel the need to note that one got it from the other. Either way it seems God wanted to make sure—doubly sure—we got his message.

Difficult Verses *from* *the* Book *of* Nahum

Passage:
The LORD is a jealous God, filled with vengeance and wrath (Nahum 1:2).

Difficulty: What is the reason God is so jealous?

Explanation: In Exodus it says God's "very name is Jealous," and that he "is a God who is jealous about his relationship with you" (Exodus 34:14). (See *Explanation* of Exodus 34:14 on details of why it is not wrong for God to get jealous.) But essentially God's jealousy is not wrong because he by nature is not selfish. He wants us to love him exclusively just like we want someone to love us exclusively.

But it appears God really gets angry when we don't put him first and love him exclusively. Why is that? What is the reason for such a passionate jealousy on God's part that he even gets angry about it when we don't put him first in our lives?

As indicated, God's jealousy and anger aren't like ours, which are selfish. Humans get jealous *of* another and at times lash out in anger. It is in the human nature to be self-centered and think only of self. However, God's jealousy and anger are holy with a holy purpose. He gets jealous *for* us and his holy anger is expressed, in part, to bring us back to loving him exclusively. (Also see *Explanation* of Zephaniah 2:2 and why God gets angry.)

God's entire purpose of redeeming us from a life of sinful self-centeredness is so we can relationally enjoy all that he enjoys. He created us in his image as relational beings and he wants us to experience a Godlike joy. And he is extremely jealous for us to experience that.

Jesus said he came and gave his life "so that [his] joy may be in you and that your joy may be complete" (John 15:11 NIV). He jealously wants us to know what it is like to experience godly love and be in oneness with him and others. The Godhead has experienced an infinite love of oneness beyond comprehension. The Father, Son, and Holy Spirit have eternally existed in relationship with each other. They have forever experienced a circle of relationship that looks out for the best in each other. They have an infinitely deep abiding love that is intent on pleasing the other. And this caring for one another in such passionate and unselfish ways creates infinite joy.

God created each of us to live eternally in his joy. He jealously wants that for us. It is understandable that he is angry that sin has stolen that from us. And he is doing everything within the constraints of our free will to eventually bring us back into perfect relationship with him. In fact, once he has redeemed his lost creation he intends them to live in a perfect world with him where there is nothing but eternal joy. Because once we are ready to enter our eternal home with him he will say, "Well done, good and faithful slave...enter into the joy of your master" (Matthew 25:23 NASB).

The simplicity and purity of enjoying a growing love relationship with God throughout eternity is incomprehensible to our mortal minds. Our ability to love is so limited now in this life, and so is our capacity to experience pure joy. But when these earthly bonds are broken and we have new bodies and are living on a new earth, what then? We can only try to imagine. But we suspect our face-to-face experience of knowing God will grow throughout eternity and our love and joy will expand to contain it.

As we come to increasingly know God's nature of unconditional acceptance, we will experience a secure love beyond measure. As we forever learn of his infinite grace, we will capture the strength and unity of his love. As we constantly explore the humility and servanthood of God's heart, we will come to understand his true greatness. As we continually come to know the true essence of the Triune God with all his infinite devotion, faithfulness, goodness, and holiness, our capacity to love and grow to be like him will expand so we can embrace him more and more.

And all this will enable us to experience an ever-increasing joy throughout the ages of eternity. It will be as if God says to each of us, "I have been so jealous for you to experience my kind of joy. I want my infinite joy as Father, Son, and Holy Spirit to be in you with all its glory so that your joy will be made complete throughout time without end." God loves you passionately and wants you to experience his eternal circle of perfect relationship, and that can't happen unless you put him first in your life. And that is the reason he is so jealous for you.

Difficult Verses *from* *the* Book *of* Habakkuk

Passage and Difficulty: Habakkuk 1:1-2—Why does God allow us to suffer?

Explanation: See Lamentations 4:10 and Matthew 27:46.

Passage:

You are pure and cannot stand the sight of evil (Habakkuk 1:13).

Difficulty: If God cannot stand the sight of evil, how does he tolerate sinful humans?

Explanation: It is true that God is holy and by his very nature of holiness he is unable to have any kind of relationship with those infected by sin. So he doesn't tolerate sinful humans—he can't. Therefore to preserve his holiness and purity he had to separate himself from humans. And that separation between the God of love and life and humanity has caused the death of humans. So God doesn't actually have to tolerate our sin because death (separation from him) solves that problem. But of course that presents humans with a great dilemma.

Since God is life and we are separated from him, it means that once we die physically we are eternally separated from him. And even though he is "rich in mercy" (Ephesians 2:4), he can't overlook our sin problem. The apostle Paul underscored our dilemma when he said we "were dead because of [our] disobedience and [our] many sins" (Ephesians 2:1). And even if God could somehow offer us forgiveness we couldn't even accept the offer. Because dead people can't accept anything—they're dead!

But God came up with a merciful and miraculous plan. Of course he recognized that we are all born dead spiritually and sin has us enslaved. The apostle Paul said, "I am all too human, a slave to sin"

(Romans 7:14). Paul said he was a prisoner to sin and declared, "What a wretched man I am! Who will rescue me from this body that is subject to death?" (Romans 7:24 NIV). He then answers his own question with God's solution to our sin and death: "Thanks be to God, who delivers me through Jesus Christ our Lord" (Romans 7:25 NIV).

"God loved the world so much that he gave his one and only Son" (John 3:16), and in providing such a gift he "made Christ, who never sinned, to be the offering for our sin, so that we could be made right with God through Christ" (2 Corinthians 5:21). It was Jesus, the God-man, who had to be sacrificed, "for only as a human being could he die, and only by dying could he break the power of the devil, who had the power of death" (Hebrews 2:14).

Our freedom from the enslavement of sin and death and the gift of an unhindered relationship with God came through the redeeming act of Christ as our sacrifice. It was "redemption that came by Christ Jesus. God presented Christ as a sacrifice of atonement" (Romans 3:24-25 NIV). And because of him we can be made alive to God.

It is an amazing miracle. Even though the "wages of sin is death" (Romans 6:23), "God paid a ransom [your wages]...And the ransom he paid was not mere gold or silver. It was the precious blood of Christ, the sinless, spotless Lamb of God" (1 Peter 1:18-19). It is Jesus' death on the cross that atones for your sins. He became your sacrifice for sin. His death substitutes for your death, and then his resurrection to life is your resurrection to new life in him. So because of his atoning sacrifice you can be set free, forgiven of your sins, and escape eternal banishment from the presence of God. "Christ...suffered once for sins, the righteous for the unrighteous, to bring you to God" (1 Peter 3:18 NIV).

When we accepted Christ's atoning death as our sacrifice for sin and his resurrection as ours, God in turn "removed our sins as far from us as the east is from the west" (Psalm 103:12). God no longer sees our sinfulness since he is looking at us through Christ. And at that point he doesn't just tolerate us; he adopts us "as his own children. Now we call him, 'Abba, Father.' For his Spirit joins with our spirit to affirm that we are God's children" (Romans 8:15-16).

Difficult Verses *from* *the* Book *of* Zephaniah

Passage:

Act now, before the fierce fury of the LORD falls and the terrible day of the LORD's anger begins (Zephaniah 2:2).

Difficulty: Why does God seem like such an angry God?

Explanation: The term "day of the LORD" or of "the LORD's anger" is repeated by the prophets to signify God's coming judgment. He is a God of judgment and he does get angry. And it may sound strange to say, but one of his qualities is his ability to get angry.

When humans get angry it is usually self-centered. We get ticked when things don't go our way, when someone hurts our feelings, or when someone does something against us. We lash out in anger to get even, to hurt another, or to "settle the score." But God's anger isn't like that.

God's anger is holy, with a holy purpose. Sometimes his anger is measured out to protect the innocent and to bring justice. Scripture states, "He will judge the world with justice, and the nations with his truth" (Psalm 96:13). In anger he will use violence and suffering to execute perfect justice. For a more detailed discussion on his anger to bring justice see *Explanation* of 2 Kings 19:35 and Deuteronomy 20:17.

Another purpose for God's anger is to bring the guilty and disobedient back to him. Notice the context of his anger in Zephaniah. "Gather before judgment begins, before your time to repent is blown away like chaff" (Zephaniah 2:2). When Israel violated their covenant with God and turned their back on him, he got angry. His anger and punishment was temporary and was meant to cause them to seek forgiveness and find restoration so they could once again enjoy his blessing. The pain humans feel from God's anger is also to cause us to turn to him for salvation.

Actually God is "slow to get angry and filled with unfailing love" (Psalm 103:8). It is his unfailing and perfect love that prompts his holy anger so that we would be prompted to repent. He has every right to cut us off as he did the children of Israel who repeatedly disobeyed him. But the prophet Micah declared, "Where is another God like you, who pardons the guilt of the remnant, overlooking the sins of his special people? You will not stay angry with your people forever, because you delight in showing unfailing love" (Micah 7:18).

The righteous motivation behind God's anger is clearly evident in the book of Hosea. God took action when Israel betrayed him. Hosea said to God's people, "You have been unfaithful to your God, hiring yourselves out like prostitutes...So now your harvests will be too small to feed you. There will be no grapes for making new wine. You may no longer stay here in the LORD's land" (Hosea 9:1-3).

And why would God not bless Israel's harvests? He appealed to the self-interest of those he loved. It is as if he was saying, "I'll keep you from fulfilling your self-serving desires until you turn to me out of pure self-preservation."

Notice what God said: "They will eat and still be hungry. They will play the prostitute and gain nothing from it" (Hosea 4:10). Their empty living had a purpose; their hunger would point them back in his direction. He continues, "I will return to my place until they admit their guilt and turn to me. For as soon as trouble comes, they will earnestly search for me" (Hosea 5:15). His motivation for bringing punishment to Israel was to bring them back home.

"I will make you my wife forever," God said, "showing you righteousness and justice, unfailing love and compassion. I will be faithful to you and make you mine, and you will finally know me as the LORD" (Hosea 2:19-20). All throughout his relationship with Israel and the lost and dysfunctional human race, he has shown his love through anger and mercy. What he is after is for his lost creation to be his loving companion. And he will even inflict pain on them until they call out and say...

> Come, let us return to the LORD. He has torn us to pieces; now he will heal us. He has injured us; now he will bandage our wounds. In just a short time he will restore us, so that we may live in his presence. Oh, that we might know the LORD! Let us press on to know him (Hosea 6:1-3).

Difficult Verses *from* *the* Book *of* Zechariah

Passage and Difficulty: Zechariah 11:12-13—Why does Matthew quote this passage yet say it is the prophecy of Jeremiah?

Explanation: See Matthew 27:9-10.

Difficult Verses *from* *the* Book *of* Malachi

Passage:

Should people cheat God? Yet you have cheated me! But you ask, "What do you mean? When did we ever cheat you?" You have cheated me of the tithes and offerings due me (Malachi 3:8).

Difficulty: Does God require that we give him (the church we attend) a tithe or 10 percent of all our income?

Explanation: God commanded Israel to give a tenth, or a tithe, to God. "One tenth of the produce of the land, whether grain from the fields or fruit from the trees, belongs to the LORD" (Leviticus 27:30). Each year the tithe was to be taken to the sanctuary—the designated place of worship (see Deuteronomy 14:22).

The Levites (including the priests) had received no tribal land. And the tithe was to support them. A second tithe was also to be given every third year of the harvest to additionally support the Levites as well as orphans, widows, and foreigners. This additional tenth was to be taken to the nearest town (see Deuteronomy 14:28; 26:12). Additional offerings were also required of the children of Israel.

Some feel this establishes a 10 percent minimum contribution for Christians today to pay to their local church. Others contend that this was a financial requirement for Israel and point out that it didn't amount to a minimum of 10 percent but rather 13⅓ percent average annually (10 percent every year as a national tithe plus 10 percent every three years in addition as a local tithe—13⅓ percent average per year).

Others say Jesus' standard of giving was different. "You cannot become my disciple," Jesus said, "without giving up everything you own" (Luke 14:33). In 1 Chronicles it says, "Everything in the heavens and on earth is yours, O LORD, and this is your kingdom" (1 Chronicles 29:11). This view considers that God owns everything and to be a Jesus follower we must relinquish our right of selfish ownership and become a faithful steward. This makes Christians stewards of what God allows each of them to "possess." And so how much a Christian actually gives to the local church or charitable organizations depends on how God leads them to give out of *his* 100 percent they are stewards over.

While there may not be a consensus on how the Old Testament concept of tithing is to be applied today, most see the necessity of supporting the work of the local church and charitable groups financially. And a 10 percent gifting of one's income to the church is considered a minimal baseline by many.

The Gospels/Narratives
Matthew–Acts

Passage:

This is the record of the ancestors of Jesus the Messiah, a descendant of David and of Abraham:...All those listed above include fourteen generations from Abraham to David, fourteen from David to Babylonian exile, and fourteen from the Babylonian exile to the Messiah (Matthew 1:1-17).

Difficulty: Why does Matthew's detailed family line from Abraham through King David to Jesus so radically differ from the Luke 3:23-38 account of Jesus' ancestry?

Explanation: At first glance, we may get the impression that both accounts are tracing the family line of Jesus through his legal father, Joseph, in which case there is an obvious contradiction. It is confusing because Matthew 1:16 indicates Jacob is Joseph's father, while Luke 3:23 says that Heli is the father of Joseph.

A plausible solution is to recognize that Matthew is giving us Joseph's family line, but Luke is tracing the genealogy of Mary. The reason that Mary is not mentioned in Luke 3 is probably because she has already been designated the mother of Jesus in several instances.

The usual practice of a Jewish genealogy is to give the name of the father, grandfather, and so on, of the person in view. Luke follows this pattern, and does not mention the name of Mary, but the name of the legal father. However, Luke makes it clear that Joseph is not, in reality, the father of Jesus, since Jesus had been virgin born (see Luke 1:26-35).

Luke is no doubt tracing the roots of Jesus through his mother, Mary, who was a descendant of Heli, and so on. Joseph's name is mentioned, according to the common practice, but he is portrayed as the *supposed* father of Jesus, and God as the actual father.

Additionally the reason two genealogies are even given could be that one (Luke's) demonstrates Jesus' connection to all humanity since it traces his roots to Adam. And the other (Matthew's) shows he is the rightful heir to King David's throne and is the continuing fulfillment of God's promises to Abraham. This emphasizes Jesus as both the Messiah to the Jews and the Savior of the entire human race.

Passage:

> Look! The virgin will conceive a child! She will give birth to a son, and they will call him Immanuel, which means "God is with us" (Matthew 1:23).

Difficulty: Isn't Matthew misquoting Isaiah 7:14, because wasn't the child who was born actually Hezekiah, who became king of Israel?

Explanation: Yes, Matthew quotes Isaiah 7 and claims it was prophesied that Jesus was to be born of a virgin and would be called Immanuel. And critics do point out that a full reading of chapter 7 of Isaiah seems to more likely refer to the birth of Hezekiah, who became a godly king of Israel. For how Isaiah uses the term *virgin* see *Explanation* of Isaiah 7:14.

Some accuse writers of the New Testament of twisting and taking Old Testament passages like this out of context to teach their brand of Christianity. They say writers of the Gospels and the epistles seemed to take liberties with the Old Testament text to establish a whole new religion of their own.

Another example is in Matthew 2. Mary and Joseph fled into Egypt with baby Jesus to escape Herod's decree that infant boys in the Bethlehem area under the age of two be killed. Matthew then wrote,

> This fulfilled what the Lord had spoken through the prophet: "I called my Son out of Egypt"...Herod's brutal action fulfilled what God had spoken through the prophet Jeremiah: "A cry was heard in Ramah—weeping and great mourning. Rachel weeps for her children, refusing to be comforted, for they are dead" (Matthew 2:15,17-18).

Matthew is quoting first Hosea the prophet, who said that when Israel was a child, God loved him and "called my son out of Egypt" (Hosea 11:1). We all know that God did in fact call his people out of Egypt. Yet Matthew claims this was a prophecy about Joseph and Mary taking Jesus to Egypt and later bringing him back. Matthew quotes Jeremiah about Rachel weeping over her dead children and claims it was referring to first-century mothers weeping after Herod had the infant boys in Bethlehem killed. Critics claim, again, that Matthew is grossly twisting and misinterpreting Hosea and Jeremiah.

What critics overlook is that Jesus came to fulfill God's promise to Israel and provide a means for all of God's lost children to be redeemed. This means the many prophecies and promises to Israel were foreshadows of Jesus' plan to bring Israel and his church into his eternal kingdom.

Jesus came to establish his kingdom, and it was he who said, "Don't misunderstand why I have come. I did not come to abolish the law of Moses or the writings of the prophets. No, I came to accomplish their purpose" (Matthew 5:17). He was the realization of all the prophets and the law taught. He was the fulfillment of God's message to Israel, and therefore we must understand the Old Testament in light of him.

So Matthew and other writers of the New Testament weren't twisting the Old Testament passages or taking them out of context. Rather, they were understanding them as God had inspired his writers to understand them—Israel was God's means of bringing salvation to the world, and Jesus was the literal fulfillment of his masterful and merciful plan. Jesus was the true Son called out of Egypt, the son Israel was unable to be. This was not a misinterpretation of Hosea 11:1. Isaiah did predict a child would be born to deliver Israel. Hezekiah was only a temporary salvation to God's people. God revealed through Matthew that Jesus was the permanent salvation not only for Israel but for the whole world. New Testament writers like Matthew did not misquote the Old Testament passages; they simply gave them the Christocentric context that God intended.

Passage and Difficulty: Matthew 2:15-18—Isn't Matthew misquoting Hosea and Jeremiah to say they were prophesying about Jesus?

Explanation: See Matthew 1:23.

Passage and Difficulty: Matthew 5:3—Why is Matthew's account of Jesus' sermon (Matthew 5:3-12) different from Luke's account (Luke 6:20-23)?

Explanation: See Luke 6:20.

Passage and Difficulty: Matthew 5:22—Why is it so wrong to call someone a fool?

Explanation: See Matthew 23:17.

Passage:

Do not judge, or you too will be judged (Matthew 7:1 NIV).

Difficulty: Is it true that Jesus taught that none of us has the right to judge another person?

Explanation: This verse is one of the most commonly misused verses in the Bible. Many people feel this verse says we are prohibited from judging others. Yet when we place Jesus' statement within context we discover what he really meant.

Matthew 7:1 is part of Jesus' Sermon on the Mount, which is recorded beginning in Matthew 5.

Jesus' sermon begins with a statement about those who enter the kingdom of God (Matthew 5:3). He is continually calling people to the kingdom throughout his sermon. So any interpretation of what he said needs to be set within the context of his kingdom message. Given that context, Jesus is presenting an ethic to his disciples to follow. He is sharing his kingdom view of how to think, be, and live in this world—his worldview. And in this passage he says we are not to judge for a reason.

The context is Jesus ushering his kingdom in, with him as the Righteous King, the Perfect Standard, the Judge of all. God said, "It is mine to avenge; I will repay" (Deuteronomy 32:35 NIV). He told Israel to "not seek revenge or bear a grudge" (Leviticus 19:18). Why? Because judgment belongs to the Righteous Judge. When a person condemns another he or she in effect presumes to determine who can and cannot be forgiven by God. And doing so usurps God's rightful position as Judge.

But this does not mean we must abandon our moral sensibilities as Christ-followers and take no moral stand. Note what Jesus says next. "The standard you use in judging is the standard by which you will be judged" (Matthew 7:2). So now it is becoming clear that we are to judge, but we must be careful which standard we use. It is not our standard of judgment, but his, that is to do the judging. In other words we are to make godly judgment.

Jesus goes on to explain about those who worry about a speck in another person's eye when they have a log in theirs. He asks,

> How can you think of saying to your friend, "Let me help you get rid of that speck in your eye," when you can't see past the log in your own eye? Hypocrite! First get rid of the log in your own eye, then you will see well enough to deal with the speck in your friend's eye (Matthew 7:4-5).

Jesus was not directing his disciples to never judge others—he was emphasizing that their first responsibility was to purify themselves. When God first gave his instructions to Israel he said, "Do not nurse hatred in your heart...Confront people directly so you will not be held guilty for their sin" (Leviticus 19:17). This suggests that it is not wrong to judge and confront the wrong being done; rather, it is wrong to judge while hypocritically harboring ill will toward others and overlooking sin in our own lives.

God is the Righteous Judge. He establishes the standard for judging, not us. Yet he expects his followers to judge rightly. What he is prohibiting here is judging the wrong way. We are not to judge according to our own preferences, for it is God who ultimately judges us all. We are to uphold his standards. We are not to judge while hypocritically overlooking our own sins but to assess others and ourselves with honesty. We are to see things as he sees things. We are not to become dull in our moral discernment, for not everyone values God's standard of truth. When we understand these things, we realize that proper judging is not only allowed; it is our obligation as followers of Christ.

Passage:

[Jesus] said, "Healthy people don't need a doctor—sick people do." Then he added, "Now go and learn the meaning of this Scripture: 'I want you to show mercy, not offer sacrifices.' For I have come to call not those who think they are righteous, but those who know they are sinners" (Matthew 9:12-13).

Difficulty: What was Jesus getting at that the Pharisees didn't understand?

Explanation: Jesus had just called a tax collector by the name of Matthew to follow him. Later that day he was eating with Matthew along with his tax collector colleagues and other "disreputable sinners. But when the Pharisees saw this, they asked his disciples, 'Why does your teacher eat with such scum?'" (Matthew 9:10-11).

Jesus took the initiative and responded to the Pharisees. Matthew 9:12-13 was his response. He tells the "learned" scholars of the day—the "experts" on the Hebrew text to "go and learn the meaning of this Scripture" (Hosea 6:6). Jesus of course had quoted from a book the Pharisees were very familiar with. But it was obvious they did not understand its meaning. In fact on the surface it seems a rather strange answer to the Pharisees, who were critical of Jesus eating with sinners. Just how does Hosea 6:6 make Jesus' point that "healthy people don't need a doctor—sick people do"?

The key word in Hosea 6:6 is the Hebrew word *hesed,* translated "loyalty" in the NASB, "mercy" in the NIV, and "love" in the NLT. It seems odd that three major translations render *hesed* differently. But these different translations are all correct because the word *hesed* does mean "loyal love, unfailing kindness, mercy, and a devotion that is steadfast based on a prior relationship." At first it may seem strange that Jesus would quote Hosea's words about committed love in regard to his eating with sinners. But the entire focus of the book of Hosea clears that up.

God had told Hosea to go out and marry a prostitute to "illustrate how Israel has acted like a prostitute by turning against the LORD and worshiping other gods" (Hosea 1:2). So Hosea married the prostitute Gomer.

Israel, like Gomer and all of us, has been unfaithful to God. We all have become prostitutes going after the things of this world. But Hosea, like God, went after the prostitute and purchased the wayward wife back. "I will make you my wife forever," God said of Israel, "showing you righteousness and justice, unfailing love and compassion. I will be faithful to you and make you mine, and you will finally know me as the LORD" (Hosea 2:19-20). It is clear that all throughout God's relationship with us, the lost and dysfunctional human race, he has shown *hesed* toward us. And it is also clear he wants more than our strict obedience. He wants us to be his loving companion. And he will even inflict pain on us until we call out and say like Israel...

> "Come, let us return to the LORD. He has torn us to pieces; now he will heal us. He has injured us; now he will bandage our wounds. In a short time he will restore us, so that we may live in his presence. Oh, that we might know the LORD! Let us press on to know him"...[now the verse Jesus quoted] "I want you to show love [*hesed*] not offer sacrifices. I want you to know me more than I want burnt offerings" (Hosea 6:1-3,6).

God wants both Israel and us to know him for who he is—the Lord of *hesed*, the God who is by nature faithful, loyal, merciful, and full of compassion. And through an intimate, loving wife-husband relationship he wants us to channel his kind of love toward others. He wants us to show *hesed* to those who are sick and in need of help. This is the meaning of Hosea 6:6.

Jesus was in effect saying to the Pharisees,

> Sure, I'm eating with tax collectors and sinners. What else would you expect me to do? I am the God of *hesed*. I have made a covenant with you to be your God forever, and I am being faithful to my promise by coming as the Lamb of God to atone for your sins and restore you to a companion relationship. And you who are given to the holy Scriptures are to join me in showing *hesed* to all those who are lost and enslaved in their adulterous lives. So don't judge the tax collectors and sinners—join me in my mission of showing *hesed* in order to redeem and restore them to an intimate relationship with me.

God has sent his Son as an atonement for our sins for one reason: He wants us to be his loving companion in this life and forever. We were enslaved to sin (a prostitute), but he purchased us back. He now wants us to join him in showing his kind of love (*hesed*) to those around us.

Passage:

Go and announce to them that the Kingdom of Heaven is near. Heal the sick, raise the dead, cure those with leprosy, and cast out demons. Give as freely as you have received! (Matthew 10:7-8).

Difficulty: Since it is clear Jesus told his disciples to perform miracles, why don't most Christians perform them today?

Explanation: It is clear throughout Scripture that God made himself known through miraculous signs both in the Old Testament and then through those by Jesus himself as recorded in the New Testament. Some scholars view miracles as God authenticating himself to humanity. Jesus did miracles, in part, to prove who he was. He said, "Believe that I am in the Father and the Father is in me. Or at least believe because of the work you have seen me do" (John 14:11).

When the disciples were filled with the Holy Spirit on the day of Pentecost, Peter preached to the people and said, "People of Israel, listen! God publicly endorsed Jesus the Nazarene by doing powerful miracles, wonders, and signs through him, as you well know" (Acts 2:22). Some feel that God used miracles throughout Israel's history, during Jesus' life on earth and the immediate years after his resurrection as a dramatic way to reveal himself to the world. But once the early church was established and Christ's evangelistic mission was embraced by his followers, some say that the time of miraculous signs and wonders came to a close. Just as God's revelation of his truth through the inspiration of Scripture came to a close a few decades after Jesus' ascension, some claim that the time of great miraculous works came to a close. While some will acknowledge that God can and does perform miracles today, they feel he simply isn't displaying himself to the world that way anymore.

Yet others contend that Jesus' directive to his disciples to heal the sick, raise the dead, cast out demons, and so on, is equally a directive to us today. They see the powers granted to Christ's followers on the day of Pentecost as powers God wants us to exercise in today's world. As additional proof that God wants miracles to continue some will point to the Scripture's teaching on the power of prayer: "Are any of you sick?" James asks. "You should call for the elders of the church to come and pray over you, anointing you with oil in the name of the Lord. Such a prayer offered in faith will heal the sick, and the Lord will make you well" (James 5:14-15). Therefore if miracles are not being exercised today, then some say it is because Christians lack faith.

Christians remain divided on how God is using miracles today. There is general agreement among evangelical Christians that God is miraculously transforming people today by bringing them into a relationship with him. But people don't fully agree that God intends to exercise his healing powers today as he has in the past.

Passage and Difficulty: Matthew 12:31-32—What is the blasphemy against the Holy Spirit that is unforgivable?

Explanation: See 1 John 5:16-17.

Passage:

As Jonah was in the belly of the great fish for three days and three nights, so will the Son of Man be in the heart of the earth for three days and three nights (Matthew 12:40).

Difficulty: If Jesus was crucified on Friday and rose on Sunday morning, how could this be considered three days and three nights?

Explanation: To explain this apparent contradiction some people contend that Jesus was crucified on Wednesday. This way, they say Jesus' "three days and three nights" statement is literally fulfilled.

However, Jesus stated that "Passover begins in two days, and the Son of Man will be handed over to be crucified" (Matthew 26:2). Jesus and his disciples celebrated Passover and that evening he was arrested and taken before Caiaphas, the high priest (see Matthew 26:57).

The next day Pilate brought Jesus before the people. "It was now about noon on the day of preparation for the Passover" (John 19:14). This is not referring to the Passover meal—that had occurred the night before. The "day of preparation" was the time to get ready for the Festival of Unleavened Bread on the Sabbath, which would begin at sundown that night.

So Jesus was crucified on that day (Friday). The Jewish leaders asked Pilate to have Jesus' legs broken to hasten his death because they didn't want bodies hanging on the cross over the Sabbath (see John 19:31-32).

But since Jesus was already dead by the time this request could be enforced, he was taken from the cross and buried.

Then "early on Sunday morning, as the new day was dawning, Mary Magdalene and the other Mary went out to visit the tomb" (Matthew 28:1). And by that time Jesus had risen from the dead. So calculating the days, Jesus was crucified in the daytime on Friday, dying before sundown, spent Friday night, all day Saturday, and Saturday night in the grave. He rose sometime before early morning on Sunday. That only accounts for two full nights and two partial and one full days. How can Jesus' statement be accurate?

Under Jewish calculations a period of light and darkness constituted a "day." And any part of a "day" was considered a whole day. So Jesus didn't mean he would be in the tomb 72 hours. The fact that he was dead and buried on part of Friday, all of Saturday, and part of Sunday meant that period was considered three days.

Calculating days in this fashion is borne out in Genesis 42:17; 1 Samuel 30:12-13; Esther 4:16 and 5:1.

Passage:

The Son of Man came not to be served but to serve others and give his life as a ransom for many (Matthew 20:28).

Difficulty: Is it true as some critics point out that Jesus referred to himself as the Son of Man, not the Son of God, because Jesus himself never really claimed to be God?

Explanation: The Jehovah's Witnesses and other critics point to the fact that Jesus referred to himself as the "Son of Man" not the "Son of God." They claim this is an indication that he only claimed to be human, not deity.

While it is true that Jesus referred to himself dozens of times as the "Son of Man," this was far from an admission of being just another human. His use of the words "Son of Man" can be traced back to the book of Daniel. And when Daniel described the "son of man" in a vision, it is far from a reference to a mere human. Daniel prophesied that he saw "a son of man coming with clouds of heaven...He was given authority, honor, and sovereignty over all the nations of the world...His rule is eternal—it will never end. His kingdom will never be destroyed" (Daniel 7:13-14). This is not the description of a mere mortal.

Daniel's "son of man" is a clear reference to a divine figure—the sovereign Lord whose kingdom is eternal. To claim to be the Son of Man would actually be making a claim to divinity. And this is precisely what Jesus was doing.

To reinforce his deity, Jesus also referred to himself as the Son of God, and that assertion did not go unnoticed by the religious leaders of the day. In fact, that claim was the very reason they tried to discredit him and, eventually, the reason they worked to see him put to death: "The Jewish leaders tried all the harder to find a way to kill him. For he not only broke the Sabbath, he called God his Father, thereby making himself equal with God" (John 5:18). Jesus went on to say, "I assure you that the time is coming, indeed it's here now, when the dead will hear my voice—the voice of the Son of God. And those who listen will live" (John 5:25). Jesus made it abundantly clear who he was.

On more than one occasion, Jesus' clear assertion of his own deity caused his fellow Jews to try to stone him. One time he told the Jewish leaders,

> "Your father Abraham rejoiced at the thought of seeing my day; he saw it and was glad." "You are not yet fifty years old," they said to him, "and you have seen Abraham!" "Very truly I tell you," Jesus answered, "before Abraham was born, I am!" At this, they picked up stones to stone him, but Jesus hid himself, slipping away from the temple grounds (John 8:56-59 NIV).

On another occasion, when Jesus said that he was one with the Father, the Jewish leaders again picked up stones to kill him (see John 10:30-31). When Jesus asked why they wanted to kill him, they retorted, "For blasphemy! You, a mere man, claim to be God" (John 10:33).

All that Jesus said and did confirmed his assertion and claim to be

God in the flesh. That is why his followers declared, "You are the Messiah, the Son of the living God" (Matthew 16:16).

(For a more extensive treatment on Jesus' claim to deity and the historical evidences that substantiate his claim, see chapter 18 of *Is God Just a Human Invention?* by Sean McDowell and Jonathan Morrow, described in the back pages of this book.)

Passage:

"You must love the Lord your God with all your heart, all your soul, and all your mind." This is the first and greatest commandment. A second is equally important: "Love your neighbor as yourself" (Matthew 22:37-39).

Difficulty: Is Jesus advocating that we selfishly love ourselves before loving others?

Explanation: Jesus was actually quoting from Leviticus 19:18, which was the cornerstone principle for biblical ethics. A lot of people recognize the value of loving God. But few understand Jesus' reasoning to love others as you love yourself, mainly because it seems self-serving. But being selfish isn't what Jesus was advocating. Being selfish is looking out for number one regardless of how that affects others. What Jesus was saying is that we should love others in the same way we want to be loved—in the same way we want to be thought of and taken care of. Earlier in Matthew Jesus said, "Do to others whatever you would like them to do to you. This is the essence of all that is taught in the law and the prophets" (Matthew 7:12).

Loving others as we love ourselves actually defines a Godlike love. Many of us can explain what love does or doesn't do: Love is patient and kind, it isn't jealous, proud or hurtful. It is like what Paul said, "Love does no wrong to others" (Romans 13:10). But it's another thing to actually define what love is. And what Jesus was doing in Matthew 22 was providing a foundational definition for Godlike love.

When Jesus said we should love others as we love ourselves, he was saying to see others through the grid of how you want to be treated.

Paul put it this way: "In humility value others above yourselves, looking not only to your own interests but each of you to the interest of others" (Philippians 2:4 NIV). He gives a specific application of this as it relates to married couples when he told husbands, "to love their wives as they love their own bodies...No one hates his own body but feeds and cares for it" (Ephesians 5:28-29).

Drawing from these verses and others similar, we can derive a concise definition of a Godlike love. *Love is making the security, happiness, and welfare of another person as important as your own.* This Godlike love—loving others like you love yourself—seeks to protect others from harm and provide for their good. Godlike love is giving and trusting, unselfish and sacrificial, secure and safe, loyal and forever. And because its priority is to protect and provide for the loved one, it will not do things that are harmful to the security, happiness, and welfare of another person. When you love like this you are, as Jesus said, fulfilling "the essence of all that is taught in the law and the prophets" (Matthew 7:12). For more on how a Godlike love is to be experienced between a husband and wife see *Explanation* of Ephesians 5:28.

Passage:

Blind fools! Which is more important—the gold or the Temple that makes the gold sacred? (Matthew 23:17).

Difficulty: Why did Jesus call the Pharisees fools when he prohibits us from calling other people fools?

Explanation: In Matthew Jesus says, "Anyone who says, 'You fool!' will be in danger of the fire of hell" (Matthew 5:22 NIV).

There is a clear distinction in the use of the word *fool* here. It is similar to our use of the word *pig*. We can call the snouted, mud-wallowing animal a pig and that isn't a problem. A pig is a pig, and we are not being mean-spirited when we call it that. But if we call a person a pig it is an insult that generally carries with it a mean-spirited attitude.

In Matthew 5 Jesus is in fact addressing the attitude of the heart reflected in a hateful curse at someone. The word *fool* is not so much the issue but the mean-spirited attitude, and Jesus condemned it.

However, in Matthew 23 Jesus is rightly judging the Pharisees and saying they are being fools as blind leaders of others. Jesus wasn't lashing out in a hateful and mean-spirited manner. He is simply calling those who are hypocritical and disbelieving foolish—and they are.

The apostle Paul did the same when he exclaimed, "Oh, foolish Galatians!" (Galatians 3:1). Paul was pointing out the futility of the Galatians' trying to be perfect "by your own human effort" (Galatians 3:3). He was not lashing out in hatred, but admonishing out of concern. Neither Paul nor Jesus was wrong for the use of the word *fool.* They were right to use it because their attitude, concern, and judgment warranted it.

Passage and Difficulty: Matthew 25:23—What will Christians—the redeemed—be put in charge of in heaven?

Explanation: See Revelation 21:6-7.

Passage:

Peter declared, "Even if everyone else deserts you, I will never desert you." Jesus replied, "I tell you the truth, Peter—this very night, before the rooster crows, you will deny three times that you even know me" (Matthew 26:33-34).

Difficulty: Doesn't this account in Matthew 26 contradict the Mark 14 assertion that Jesus said Peter would deny him before the rooster crows twice, not just once?

Explanation: Mark's account tells us that Jesus said, "Before the rooster crows twice, you will deny three times that you even know me" (Mark 14:30). Verse 68 records Peter's first denial and says, "Just then, a rooster crowed" (Mark 14:68). Then when Peter denied Christ for the second and third time Mark reports "immediately the rooster crowed the second time" (Mark 14:72).

The Gospels of Luke and John give the same basic account as Matthew, making Mark's statements seem contradictory to the rest. This difficulty is not as problematic as it may seem. It is quite reasonable that Jesus made both statements. He told Peter that he would deny him before the rooster crowed, and his denial would occur before it had crowed twice.

What we probably have is Mark recording the story in more detail. This would seem to be the case since Mark very likely wrote his Gospel under the influence of Peter, and it would be natural for Peter to add further detail to this story, seeing that he is one of the main characters.

In all four recorded accounts we have Jesus predicting Peter's denial, with Mark adding further details. A possible full reconstruction would be the following: Jesus reveals to Peter that before the rooster crows, Peter will deny him three times. Peter, as was his way, objects to the idea that he would deny his Lord. Jesus probably in turn repeats his earlier prediction, along with a further note that before the rooster crows twice Peter will deny him three times. (This harmonization fits well with Mark's account in his Gospel.)

The clause "Before the rooster crows, you will deny three times" (Matthew 26:34), is not contradicted by Mark relating that after Peter had denied Jesus the first time, the rooster crowed. When all the facts are considered, Matthew, Luke, and John are not in contradiction with Mark's account.

Passage:

Judas threw the silver coins down in the Temple and went out and hanged himself (Matthew 27:5).

Difficulty: Doesn't Matthew's account of Judas's death contradict the account given in Acts 1?

Explanation: In Acts 1 it says Peter explained that "Judas had bought a field with the money he received for his treachery. Falling headfirst there, his body split open, spilling out all his intestines" (Acts 1:18). Matthew's account and Peter's account are different, but do they necessarily contradict each other?

Matthew does not say that Judas did not fall; neither does Peter say that Judas did not hang himself. This is not a matter of one person calling something black and the other person calling it white. Both accounts can be true and supplement each other.

A possible reconstruction would be this: Judas hanged himself on a tree on the edge of a precipice that overlooked the valley of Hinnom. After he hung there for some time, the limb of the tree snapped or the rope gave way and he fell down the ledge, his body being mangled in the process.

The fall could have come before or after death as either would fit this explanation. This possibility is entirely natural when the terrain of the valley of Hinnom is examined. From the bottom of the valley, the rocky terraces are 25 to 40 feet in height and the cliffs below them are almost perpendicular.

There are still trees that grow around the ledges and a rocky surface at the bottom. Therefore it is easy to conclude that Judas struck one of the jagged rocks on his way down, tearing his body open. Matthew and Peter provide different perspectives of Judas's death but they are not contradictory.

Passage:

This fulfilled the prophecy of Jeremiah that says: "They took the thirty pieces of silver—the price at which he was valued by the people of Israel, and purchased the potter's field, as the Lord directed" (Matthew 27:9-10).

Difficulty: Why does Matthew quote from the prophecy of Zechariah 11:12-13, yet say it is the prophecy of Jeremiah?

Explanation: Matthew is speaking of the incident of the priests purchasing the potter's field after Judas threw the 30 pieces of silver on the floor in the Temple. This field was made into a cemetery for foreigners (see Matthew 27:6-7). Matthew goes on to quote from the prophet Zechariah but says it is the prophecy of Jeremiah. Did Matthew get the names of the prophets mixed up?

One possible answer is that Matthew was following a Jewish custom of citing books by referring to the first book in a particular scroll. The first book in the scroll containing Zechariah happened to be Jeremiah. Therefore he referenced Jeremiah when quoting from that scroll.

Another possible answer is that Matthew is combining two prophecies, one from Jeremiah and one from Zechariah, with a mention of only one author in the composite reference, namely Jeremiah, the major prophet.

Zechariah says nothing concerning the buying of a field, but Jeremiah states that God led him to buy a field as a solemn guarantee by God that fields and vineyards would be bought and sold in the future (see Jeremiah 32:6-8,15,43).

One of the fields God had in mind was the potter's field. Zechariah adds the details of the 30 pieces of silver and the money thrown down on the floor of the Temple. Matthew takes the detail from both prophets, but stresses the major prophet Jeremiah as the one who predicted the purchase of the potter's field.

Passage:

At about three o'clock, Jesus called out with a loud voice, [on the cross] "*Eli, Eli, lema sabachthani?*" which means "My God, my God, why have you abandoned me?" (Matthew 27:46).

Difficulty: Why would Jesus, God's Son, feel as though his Father God had abandoned him?

Explanation: Some scholars say that because "God made him [Jesus] who had no sin to be sin for us" (2 Corinthians 5:21 NIV), God turned away from Jesus on the cross. In other words because God's "eyes are too pure to look on evil" (Habakkuk 1:13 NIV) and at that moment in time Jesus became sin for all of us, God had to momentarily abandon his only Son.

Other scholars believe Jesus' humanity was simply being expressed. At one point Jesus said, "The one who sent me is with me—he has not deserted me. For I always do what pleases him" (John 8:29). Here Jesus is confident in his unity with his Father. And then as Jesus gets close to the crucifixion he prays to his Father, "'Abba, Father,' he cried out, 'everything is possible for you. Please take this cup of suffering away from me. Yet I want your will to be done, not mine'" (Mark 14:36).

It is evident that in his humanity Jesus didn't want to go through the torturous and brutal death of crucifixion. And if there had been another way to solve the human problem of sin and death without his dying for all humanity, it seems Jesus might have been open to it. He prayed, "Everything is possible for you." And it is natural to wonder in human terms why God couldn't have devised another way of dealing with the sin in the world. Why did the innocent Son of God, who had done no wrong, have to suffer such an excruciating death? Jesus' question, "Why have you abandoned me?" is pertinent, especially at any moment of severe suffering

Over 500 years before Jesus struggled on the cross, Habakkuk, the prophet of Judah, had a similar question about suffering. He lived at a time when the innocent were suffering. And he asked God, "How long, O LORD, must I call for help? But you do not listen! 'Violence is everywhere!' I cry, but you do not come to save" (Habakkuk 1:1-2). To Habakkuk it appeared God was ignoring the problem of pain and suffering.

King David had his questions for God too. He was misunderstood, mistreated, and betrayed; he suffered at the hands of his enemies. He cried out, "O LORD, how long will you forget me? Forever? How long will you look the other way? How long must I struggle with anguish in my soul, with sorrow in my heart every day?...Turn and answer me, O LORD my God!" (Psalm 13:1-3).

What was God's answer to David? What was God's answer to Jesus as he hung on the cross, dying a hideous death? When Jesus uttered: "My God, my God, why have you abandoned me?" (Matthew 27:46) he was actually quoting Psalm 22:1, where David asked that question. David followed up that question with "Why are you so far away when I groan for help? Every day I call to you, my God, but you do not answer. Every night you hear my voice, but I find no relief" (Psalm 22:1-2).

It is as if Jesus spoke on behalf of the entire human race with this question: "Why, God, have you abandoned us?" It was as if his cry was amplified to echo back to the expulsion of the first couple from the Garden of Eden and forward to the end of time, asking, *"Why don't you do something about the terrible sin and suffering in the world now?"*

We don't know if or how God answered his Son on the cross. The questions of Habakkuk and David were left unexplained. Search all of Scripture and you will find very few answers to why God seems to allow such suffering in the world. But Scripture doesn't leave us without direction on how to respond to God's apparent lack of response.

All throughout the Bible God calls on us to trust in him personally even if we don't understand his plan. King David understood this message. Right after he asked God, "Why have you abandoned me?" he declared, "Yet you are holy, enthroned on the praises of Israel. Our ancestors trusted in you, and you rescued them...They trusted in you and were never disgraced" (Psalm 22:3-5).

Psalm 22 was Jesus' faith passage of the moment. He realized the prophetic nature of what King David wrote:

> My enemies surround me like a pack of dogs; an evil gang closes in on me. They have pierced my hands and feet. I count all my bones. My enemies stare at me and gloat. They divide my garments among themselves and throw dice for my clothing. O Lord, do not stay far away! You are my strength; come quickly to my aid! (Psalm 22:16-19).

While Jesus as God knew that his suffering on the cross was the only solution for sin, pain, and death, he modeled in the human what we must do—wait for God, place our faith in him, and trust in him, who does all things right in his right timing. Peter said,

> God called you to do good, even if it means suffering, just as Christ suffered for you. He is your example, and you must follow in his steps. He never sinned, nor even deceived anyone. He did not retaliate when he was insulted, nor threaten revenge when he suffered. He left his case in the hands of God [he kept entrusting himself to God], who always judges fairly (1 Peter 2:21-23).

In Jesus' humanity he may have felt alone and forgotten for a moment. It is natural to wonder why there is suffering and where God is in the midst of it all. But in the end "Jesus shouted, 'Father, I entrust my spirit into your hands!' And with those words he breathed his last" (Luke 23:46). In his humanity Jesus too lived by faith and believed in the end his Father knew what he was doing. And Jesus knew the conclusion of Psalm 22:

> Royal power belongs to the LORD. He rules all the nations... Our children will also serve him. Future generations will hear about the wonders of the LORD. His righteous acts will be told to those not yet born. They will hear about everything he has done (Psalm 22:28-31).

Perhaps this Matthew 27:46 passage is to teach us to leave all our unanswered questions in "the hand of God who always judges fairly" (1 Peter 2:23). In the end he will rule the nations and make all things right, including abolishing all sin, pain, and suffering. But until that time comes we are to "live by faith." Yet we are not left alone or abandoned. After his resurrection Jesus made his disciples and all of us a solemn promise. He said, "Be sure of this: I am with you always, even to the end of the age" (Matthew 28:20).

Passage:

Suddenly there was a great earthquake! For an angel of the Lord came down from heaven, rolled aside the stone, and sat on it (Matthew 28:2).

Difficulty: Doesn't Matthew's report that there was an angel at Jesus' tomb contradict the report in Luke 24:4 that two angels were there?

Explanation: Luke does report that there were two angels at the tomb. But it is important to note that Matthew doesn't say there was *only* one angel. He simply identifies one, perhaps the one who spoke.

This is no more a contradiction than if you say that you went to the bank yesterday and then it is later reported that your best friend went with you to the bank. Your first statement may leave some people with the impression you went to the bank alone, while the other report explains someone was with you. But these are not contradictions. And neither are Luke's and Matthew's reports about one and two angels contradictory.

Passage:

A meeting with the elders was called, and they decided to give the soldiers [who were guarding Jesus' tomb] a large bribe. They told the soldiers, "You must say, 'Jesus' disciples came during the night while we were sleeping, and they stole his body'"...So the guards accepted the bribe and said what they were told to say. Their story spread widely among the Jews, and they still tell it today (Matthew 28:12-13,15).

Difficulty: How plausible is it that the disciples could have actually stolen the body of Jesus?

Explanation: To dispute Christ's resurrection, the Jewish leaders at the time claimed the disciples stole Jesus' body. That theory was held by many of the skeptics then and is still held by some today. But how plausible is the stolen-body theory?

This theory actually creates more problems than it solves. For example:

- It was the Roman guards who were bribed into accusing the disciples of stealing Jesus' body. If the guards had been sleeping, how could they have known whether the disciples—or anyone—stole the body? Sleeping sentinels can't reliably report what happened while they sleep.
- Roman soldiers were executed for sleeping on guard duty. This explains Matthew's report of the religious leaders

promising to protect the guards, saying, "If the governor hears about it, we'll stand up for you so you won't get in trouble" (Matthew 28:14). So how plausible is it that all the guards at the tomb would have decided to take a nap, knowing it would probably cost them their lives?

- Even if the Roman guards had slept, consider what it would have taken for thieves to remove the body from the tomb. The circular stone used to seal the tomb would have weighed between one and two tons! Thieves would have had to sneak past the guards, roll the large stone up a grooved incline, enter the dark tomb, and exit with the body...all without waking a single member of the Roman detachment!

The notion that the disciples stole the body while the Roman guards slept more than strains the bounds of believability. But the detachment of Roman soldiers is not the only problem with this theory. It's also difficult to imagine the followers of Jesus as being capable of pulling off such a feat. Consider this:

- It would have taken considerable daring—even outright foolhardiness—to go up against a detachment of Roman soldiers whether they were asleep or awake. Yet the historical record shows that in the days following the death of Jesus the disciples were a cowed and discouraged group. They ran away at the first sign of trouble, denied any association with Jesus, and cowered behind locked doors—hardly the picture of a group that would risk arrest to steal their dead teacher's body (see Mark 14:50; Luke 22:54-62; John 20:19).
- One of the first witnesses on the scene of the empty tomb reported that the linen wrappings from Jesus' body were still present, and that the grave cloth that had covered his head was neatly folded and arranged on the burial slab (see John 20:5-8). Can you imagine grave robbers taking the time to meticulously unwrap the body and neatly arrange

the cloth on the stone slab? On the contrary, if the body had been stolen, the burial wrappings would certainly have been removed along with the body.

- According to the historical accounts, the disciples were skeptical when they heard the news of the empty tomb. From all indications, they were not expecting an empty tomb, much less plotting to steal Jesus away.
- Why would a group of men who had run and hidden when Jesus was alive suddenly and courageously decide to steal his body and begin propagating a story that would certainly bring on them the very treatment (arrest, beatings, even death) they had fled just three days earlier?

Yet spreading the story of Jesus' resurrection is exactly what these disciples did. The historical record says that mere weeks after the death of Jesus, his followers were publicly preaching the news of his resurrection. During the week of Pentecost, in fact, thousands were "baptized and added to the church" as a result of this preaching (Acts 2:41).

Such preaching must have driven the Jewish leaders to the point of utter consternation. The fact they could do nothing to disprove the resurrection further attests to its truth. You can be sure that if Jesus' body hadn't been resurrected, the religious and political leaders of the day could have quickly and effectively quashed the rising sect of Christianity by locating Christ's corpse and wheeling it through the streets of Jerusalem. This would have been undeniable evidence that the resurrection was a hoax. It would have destroyed Christianity practically before it started. But that never happened, which further bolsters the case for Jesus' resurrection.

The enemies of Jesus had every reason to produce his body. On the other hand it is implausible to believe that the followers of Jesus could or would have stolen his body. It seems clear that subscribing to the stolen-body theory means climbing a mountain of implausibilities. (For a more comprehensive examination of the evidence of Christ's resurrection see *Evidence for the Resurrection* by Josh and Sean McDowell.)

Passage and Difficulty: Matthew 28:19—Is this the only passage that establishes the doctrine of the Trinity?

Explanation: See 1 John 5:7.

Difficult Verses *from* *the* Book *of* Mark

Passage:

Have you never read what David did when he and his companions were hungry and in need? In the days of Abiathar the high priest, he entered the house of God and ate the consecrated bread, which is lawful only for priests to eat (Mark 2:25-26 NIV).

Difficulty: Is Jesus incorrect here when he refers to the high priest as Abiathar, when it was actually Ahimelech who was high priest at the time?

Explanation: Jesus was referencing the incident in 1 Samuel 21:1-6. And it is true that Ahimelech was the high priest when David ate the sacred bread that was restricted to the priests. Immediately after that Saul had Ahimelech and the other priests killed for being allied with David. Abiathar, a son of Ahimelech, was the only survivor. And he went to David to tell him of Saul's killings. David protected Abiathar, who then became high priest.

With that as a background, Jesus was not inaccurate in saying "In the days of Abiathar the high priest" (verse 26). The incident did happen during the time of Abiathar—he just wasn't high priest when it happened. Also the Greek idiom used here can also mean "in the passage about Abiathar." And in that case Jesus would have simply been referring to the passage in the Hebrew Scriptures that recorded the story of David eating the sacred bread. In either case Jesus was neither misquoting the story nor inaccurate about who was high priest.

Passage and Difficulty: Mark 14:30—Doesn't this account in Mark contradict the Matthew 26 assertion about how many times the rooster crows during Peter's denial of Jesus?

Explanation: See Matthew 26:33-34.

> **Passage:**
>
> It was the third hour when they crucified Him [Jesus] (Mark 15:25 NASB).
>
> **Difficulty:** Isn't it contradictory for Mark to record the crucifixion of Jesus at the third hour, while John 19:14 puts the time when Pilate turned Jesus over to be crucified at "about the sixth hour" (NASB)?

Explanation: During the first century there were two different means of reckoning time. Some scholars believe Mark was following the Jewish reckoning of time while John was following the Roman reckoning. Mark has Jesus being crucified at the third hour, or nine o'clock in the morning, according to Jewish reckoning, while John places Jesus before Pontius Pilate at about the sixth hour, or about noon, according to Roman time.

John's use of time began at midnight. So if we calculate both John and Mark based on Jewish time, that puts Jesus before Pilate *at around* 6 a.m. or somewhere between 6 and 7 a.m. and being crucified by 9 a.m. This means that two to three hours would have elapsed between the time Pilate turned Jesus over to the Roman garrison and the time he was nailed to the cross. This is not an unreasonable time line at all.

Mark 15 references a beating of Jesus. This is possibly a second and more severe beating after his verdict of crucifixion. It was customary to give a severe beating to criminals once they had been condemned to the slow death of crucifixion. Then there was the long journey of carrying the cross out of town up to Golgotha. Jesus obviously struggled to carry the cross, and this slowed down the process. Eventually the Roman soldiers forced Simon from Cyrene to carry Jesus' cross (see Mark 15:21).

So it is not unrealistic for it to take two to three hours to beat Jesus a second time perhaps, move three crucifixion victims through the streets of Jerusalem with Jesus barely able to walk, get a substitute to carry his cross, and finally get to the out-of-town site for the actual crucifixion. So with harmonizing the Roman and Jewish reckoning of time and accounting for the time from Jesus' being released from Pilate and actually being crucified, Mark and John's time lines coincide.

Passage:

They briefly reported all this to Peter and his companions... And the disciples went everywhere and preached, and the Lord worked through them, confirming what they said by many miraculous signs (Mark 16:8-20).

Difficulty: Why are these verses omitted from some Bibles?

Explanation: Some Bibles end at the first sentence of verse 8, others add 2 more sentences to verse 8, and others add 12 more verses. Why?

Nearly all biblical scholars agree that Mark did not write either the shorter ending (the two last sentences of verse 8) or the longer ending (the last part of verse 8 through verse 20). There is a clear difference in style and vocabulary. And the oldest and most reliable Greek manuscripts, most notably the Codex Sinaiticus and Codex Vaticanus, do not have these endings.

However, most scholars doubt that Mark would have ended his Gospel with the one sentence of Mark 16:8. His narrative of Jesus' resurrection would then have ended with the women fleeing the tomb after the angel says Jesus is risen "and they said nothing to anyone because they were too frightened" (Mark 16:8). All the other three Gospels relate that Jesus was seen by many people after his resurrection.

Many scholars believe that Mark's original ending was torn out accidentally or lost. Others think Mark simply didn't get it finished. Whatever the case, the other Gospels fill in the ending and nothing in this added ending contradicts the other narratives.

Difficult Verses *from* *the* Book *of* Luke

Passage and Difficulty: Luke 3:23-38—Why does Luke's detailed family line from Jesus to Adam so radically differ from Matthew 1?

Explanation: See Matthew 1:1-17.

Passage:

Looking at his disciples, [Jesus] said: "Blessed are you who are poor, for yours is the kingdom of God" (Luke 6:20 NIV).

Difficulty: Why is Luke's account of Jesus' sermon (Luke 6:20-23) different from Matthew's account (Matthew 5:3-12)?

Explanation: These two authors seem to be seeing and hearing things differently. Luke seems to be saying Jesus is talking about the poor being blessed in a financial sense, while Matthew records it as poverty in a spiritual sense: "Blessed are the poor in spirit" (Matthew 5:3). Luke sees Jesus speaking to just the disciples, and Matthew sees Jesus speaking to the big crowd and the disciples. Luke's account of Jesus' sermon is rather brief and Matthew's is more extensive. If these two were inspired by God, why didn't they record Jesus' sermon in the exact same way?

When God inspired the writers to record his Word he didn't treat them as mindless dictation machines. God selected specific human authors, each with various backgrounds, different talents, certain educational training, and varied life experiences, for a very good reason. God being infinite wanted his Word to communicate clearly to finite humans. So he transmitted his thoughts and words through different humans with different personalities, styles, and voices.

Matthew, the recognized author of the Gospel according to Matthew, was a tax collector. Luke, the recognized author of the Gospel according to Luke, was a physician (Colossians 4:14). Matthew was a disciple of Jesus and saw and heard firsthand what went on. Luke most likely came to faith through the apostle Paul and wasn't present during Jesus' earthly ministry. Rather, he drew on eyewitness accounts and on written and oral testimony of what Jesus did and said. Matthew was Jewish; Luke was a Gentile. Matthew was a teacher and an accomplished writer, Luke was a historian with outstanding literary skills—considered one of the greatest writers of his time. Matthew emphasized Jesus' sermons, while Luke emphasized Jesus' parables.

The point is that God spoke through different men with their varied talents, knowledge, and experiences to give us a fuller and more comprehensive understanding of his truth. The different perspectives of Luke and Matthew do not contradict God's truth; they were simply delivering it to us through their unique human experience to convey a tapestry of meaning we could better understand.

God used 40-some authors to deliver us his Word. And as we stated in "How to Use This Handbook," it was as if God was composing a musical masterpiece using a 40-piece orchestra. Think of a master composer. He directs different instruments for different purposes: the various drums set the beat, the trumpets call us to action, the violins and cellos soothe us, the flutes lift our spirits, and so on. In the hands of the master the different and varied instruments produce a symphony of sounds that move the mind, heart, and emotions of the hearer with the message of the music. In a similar way, God used the different authors to be sure to impart his message clearly to us no matter who we are or what our human experience might be.

Passage:

Dear friends, don't be afraid of those who want to kill your body; they cannot do any more to you after that. But I'll tell you whom to fear. Fear God, who has the power to kill you and then throw you into hell. Yes, he's the one to fear (Luke 12:4-5).

Difficulty: If Jesus, as the Son of God, is so loving, why does he throw people into hell?

Explanation: Groups like the Jehovah's Witnesses claim it is against the loving nature of God to condemn people to hell. Other critics contend that the punishment of hell shows that God is an intolerant bully. Yet Jesus clearly confirms that there is a hell.

But is hell a place of eternal punishment as some people say? Is hell a "fire and brimstone" torture chamber where people suffer forever?

To understand what hell is we must first clarify how the words Jesus used were meant—literally or figuratively. Jesus referred to hell as a place where there is fire—which normally produces light (Matthew 5:22)—while at the same time calling it a place of "outer darkness" (Matthew 22:13). Obviously these words are figurative. If a literal meaning were attached to it, darkness and flames of light would cancel each other out. Jesus often used metaphors in his teachings and here he was probably talking about the indescribable nature of hell.

Hell is better understood by what is *not* there. Paul describes it as a place "away from the presence of the Lord and from the glory of His power" (2 Thessalonians 1:9 NASB). Try to imagine a place away from the God of relationships. A place without him is a place without relationships, without love, without joy, peace, beauty, satisfaction, contentment, acceptance, affection, fulfillment, laughter, and everything else that is called good. That would be hell—literally. A place void of all that God is would be a place of eternal aloneness—a place called hell. We believe that the "outer darkness" Jesus referred to describes this complete absence of relationship. And this eternal aloneness would be the source of indescribable anguish.

Likewise, we believe that the metaphor of eternal fire suggests the decomposition of the soul. It describes a never-ending disintegration of all that is good in a person. Truth is, we are living souls that are becoming something. We are either becoming a person who is unselfishly loving God and others, which is real life, or we are selfishly loving ourselves, which is real death. Pastor, apologist, and author Tim Keller provides insight into this concept:

> Even in this life we can see the kind of soul disintegration

> that self-centeredness creates. We know how selfishness and self-absorption leads to perceiving bitterness, nauseating envy, paralyzing anxiety, paranoid thoughts, and the mental denials and distortions that accompany them. Now ask the question: "What if when we die we don't end, but spiritually our life extends on into eternity?" Hell, then, is the trajectory of a soul, living a self-absorbed, self-centered life, going on and on forever.[1]

In sum, we believe hell is a place absent of relationship, which is absolute aloneness. Hell is a place of perpetual disintegration of the soul into greater and greater self-centeredness. It is hard to imagine the anguish of such a place—the absolute aloneness of the living dead. Yet is a loving God sending people to that place?

Scripture makes it clear that God "does not want anyone to be destroyed, but wants everyone to repent" (2 Peter 3:9). He loves the whole world and died that we might experience his presence and all the joy and goodness that brings. But he will not force us to love him and enjoy a relationship with him. So actually, God doesn't send people to hell; they make a free choice to reject him. He forces no one into a relationship with him. And his giving humans free choice has opened up consequences that can be extremely negative. And when people choose to serve themselves instead of serving God, they ultimately choose a place void of relationship and full of self—a place called hell.

C.S. Lewis said, "All that are in hell choose it...The door to hell is locked on the inside."[2] People make the choice to serve themselves because it is uncomfortable for them to serve God and others. Heaven—where God resides—is a place of perpetual worship and service to him (see Revelation 4). A person who has chosen a self-centered life would not tolerate heaven.

Hell is not where God wants anyone to end up. He won't force them to choose him in order to have an eternity of joy with him. He simply offers himself as their salvation from an eternity without him. (For a more comprehensive biblical view of hell see chapter 12, "Is Hell a Divine Torture Chamber?" in the book *Is God Just a Human Invention?* by Sean McDowell and Jonathan Morrow, described in the back pages of this book.)

Passage:

The Festival of Unleavened Bread arrived, when the Passover lamb is sacrificed. Jesus sent Peter and John ahead and said, "Go and prepare the Passover meal, so we can eat it together" (Luke 22:7-8).

Difficulty: Since Jesus celebrated the Jewish Passover meal, shouldn't Christians today participate in some form of Passover celebration?

Explanation: God commanded the children of Israel to celebrate the Festival of Unleavened Bread for a reason. "It will remind you that I brought your forces out of the land of Egypt on this very day. This festival will be a permanent law for you; celebrate this day from generation to generation" (Exodus 12:17). But this was a Jewish celebration. How does it relate to Christians today, if at all?

Most Christians do not celebrate the Passover described in Exodus 12 because it was directed to the children of Israel as part of the Levitical law. But it is important to understand the significance of the Jewish Passover to Christians, because the Passover wasn't simply a Jewish celebration of political freedom from the Egyptians. It was freedom from death, and that has significance to all humanity. And as Christians we do in fact celebrate a form of the Jewish Passover.

For hundreds of years Jewish families have celebrated the Passover Feast (*Pesach*). During the Passover meal a father with the assistance of his children retells the story of God redeeming Israel from Egyptian bondage. He explains how the death angel came over the land to kill the firstborn male of each family. But God had told his people they would be spared if they observed the Passover as he instructed. Each Israelite family was to choose a lamb or a young goat, kill it, and smear its blood on the top and sides of the door frame of their houses. In the evening they were to eat roast lamb with bitter herbs and bread made without yeast. That night at midnight God's death angel killed all the firstborn sons within Egypt. But those with the sacrificial blood placed on their houses were passed over (see Exodus 12).

The true significance of that Passover would not be fully revealed until some 1400 years later, when Jesus met with his disciples as recorded in Luke 22. "He took some bread and gave thanks to God for it. Then he broke it in pieces and gave it to the disciples" (Luke 22:19). That of course was not unusual. Jesus was doing what had been done for hundreds of years at the Passover meal. But what he said as he was observing this Passover was most strange.

"This is my body," he said, "which is given [or broken] for you. Do this to remember me" (Luke 22:19). Then he took the cup of wine, passed it around in customary Passover fashion, but again said the strangest thing. "This cup is the new covenant between God and his people—an agreement confirmed with my blood, which is poured out as a sacrifice for you" (Luke 22:20).

At that moment Jesus completely re-interpreted the entire Passover celebration. He was claiming metaphorically to *be* the bread and that the wine was *his* blood. This must have baffled those in attendance.

Previously Jesus had told his followers before that he was "the bread of life" (John 6:35). This was the same man about whom the prophet John the Baptist made a bold declaration when he saw him coming toward him. "Look!" John said. "The Lamb of God who takes away the sin of the world!" (John 1:29). Within hours of this momentous Passover celebration, the man called Jesus would be led away, brutally beaten, and cruelly nailed to a cross to bleed and die. Just over 1400 years after the very first redemption celebration by God's people, this Jesus of Nazareth, God's preeminent Son, celebrated himself being the Passover Lamb to be offered as redemption on behalf of a human race in bondage to sin. What a feast for Christians to celebrate!

The Passover is no longer just a Jewish celebration. It is a celebration for all those who have been redeemed by the atoning sacrifice of Jesus Christ. "God paid a ransom to save you from the empty life you inherited from your ancestors. And the ransom he paid was not mere gold or silver. It was the precious blood of Christ, the sinless, spotless Lamb of God" (1 Peter 1:18-19). And so lambs and bulls and goats no longer need to be sacrificed because "now, once for all time, he [Jesus] has appeared at the end of the age to remove sin by his own death as a sacrifice" (Hebrews 9:26). In effect the Passover is a celebration that we as Christians can celebrate when we observe Good Friday and

Resurrection Day (Easter) each spring. We also celebrate Jesus' atoning sacrifice for us when we participate in a communion service.

Some Christians are beginning to even follow many of the mealtime traditions of the Jewish Passover meal because it is so rich with symbolisms between Israel being freed from the slavery of Egypt and God's purpose to free the human race from the bondage of sin through Jesus' sacrificial death and resurrection.

Passage:

> He took some bread and gave thanks to God for it. Then he broke it in pieces and gave it to the disciples saying, "This is my body, which is given [broken] for you. Do this to remember me" (Luke 22:19).

Difficulty: Does bread eaten at communion actually become part of Christ's body for our forgiveness?

Explanation: Some people do believe that when the communion bread is consecrated it becomes the actual body of Christ. This is referred to as the doctrine of transubstantiation. But did Jesus literally mean that bread he was giving his disciples was actually his body?

How we interpret words of the Bible is important. Some we take literally, others we take figuratively. And this is where understanding the use of metaphors, grammar, and historical context comes into play.

Before this setting of the Passover meal when Jesus said the bread "is my body" he said, "I am the bread of life" (John 6:35). So what did he mean? How do we interpret his statement?

Part of interpretation is applying common sense, rather than taking words literally. We can understand passages better if we allow language to speak in ordinary ways, instead of imposing some kind of special, artificial standard for language usage in the Bible. The Bible is literature and the same linguistic principles apply to it as to other writings. This means we cannot take every word of the Bible as literal. While we are correct to believe the Bible is true, we must allow metaphors, similes, and analogies to be what they are, and not force them to be literal. (See "How to Use This Handbook" on page 9.)

So when Jesus says, "I am the bread of life," does he mean that he becomes a loaf of ground grain that has been baked? If not, then what does he mean? We can assume then that he is saying metaphorically that he provides sustenance for our spiritual life, just as a loaf of bread provides sustenance for our physical life.

Now let's put Jesus' statement within its cultural context. The historical setting was the first century during the Roman occupation of Israel. At that time bread was the main food source. It was not a supplement to the main meal as it is today—something to eat along with your steak, soup, or salad. Bread was the main meal. So Jesus' use of bread as the metaphor stresses his vital importance to the spiritual life of his hearers. Just as without bread they would die physically, without Jesus they would die spiritually.

With this as a background, how are we to take Jesus' statement that the bread was his body that was sacrificially broken for us? It becomes clear that Jesus was using a metaphor and wanted us to remember that he died that we might live. "Every time you eat this bread and drink this cup" the apostle Paul said, "you are announcing the Lord's death until he comes again" (1 Corinthians 11:26).

Passage:

Now I will send the Holy Spirit, just as my Father promised. But stay here in the city until the Holy Spirit comes and fills you with power from heaven (Luke 24:49).

Difficulty: What was so important about Jesus' followers staying in the city to receive the Holy Spirit?

Explanation: Prior to Jesus' death his devoted followers thought he was the Messiah who was going to overthrow the Romans and establish his earthly kingdom. Of course Jesus was taken from them and crucified. Their hopes and dreams were dashed. But then Jesus rose from the dead!

Their Messiah was back so they asked, "Lord, has the time come for you to free Israel and restore our kingdom?" (Acts 1:6). It was only ten days before the festival of *Shavuot* (*Pentecost* in the Greek), and what a perfect time for the Son of God to reveal himself as the powerful God of the heavenly kingdom! Pentecost celebrated the first fruits of the harvest and God's revelation at Sinai—why not the Son of God's revelation at Jerusalem and the first fruits of his kingdom?

But to the disciples' amazement, Jesus leaves them and ascends to heaven. Yet just before that, he told them to go back to the city and wait for the promise of the Father as described in Luke 24:49. The disciples were no doubt confused and maybe even frustrated by the fact Jesus left them before establishing his earthly kingdom. They would have no doubt disbanded and scattered to who knows where if Jesus hadn't told them to go back to the city and wait for God's promise of the Holy Spirit. Because without the Holy Spirit—the revealer of truth—they would not have realized the amazing and important truth about God's redemptive plan through Jesus.

So what did the disciples do? They went back to do what they would normally do—celebrate *Shavuot*/Pentecost. And in a real sense this is what Jesus wanted them to do—celebrate *Shavuot* or Pentecost. Typically it would be with readings and prayers and thanking God for his powerful revelation at Mount Sinai. Yet on this particular Pentecost something extraordinary took place.

As the disciples were gathered, the Holy Spirit was revealed like the roaring of a mighty windstorm and "what looked like flames or tongues of fire appeared and settled on each of them" (Acts 2:3). This festival changed from a celebration of God revealing himself through his Holy Word to God also revealing himself through his Holy Spirit. And instead of offering up their first harvest, the disciples *were* the first harvest—the beginning of the church, which would establish the kingdom of God in people's hearts.

The noise of the Holy Spirit's coming attracted a large crowd of those who had come to the city to celebrate Pentecost. And this band of Holy Spirit–filled followers of Jesus began speaking to them in their native languages. They asked how this could be and what it meant. Peter gave the answer:

> What you see was predicted long ago by the prophet Joel: "'In the last days,' God says, 'I will pour out my Spirit upon all people. Your sons and daughters will prophesy. Your young men will see visions, and your old men will dream dreams'" (Acts 2:16-17).

On the Festival of Pentecost (*Shavuot*) God fulfilled his promise made to Israel first through Isaiah the prophet in about 720 BC in Isaiah 32:15, then by the prophet Jeremiah quoted in Jeremiah 31:33, also by Ezekiel in Ezekiel 36:26-27, and finally by Joel the prophet in Joel 2:28-32. The coming of the Holy Spirit on the day of Pentecost ten days after Christ's ascension into heaven was no coincidence. Pentecost or *Shavuot* had been a required festival of all of the children of Israel from the time of their exodus out of Egypt (see Exodus 23:10-19). And this was the exact appointed time God sent his Holy Spirit to be the empowering source for his new church to take the gospel (the good news) to all the world.

Difficult Verses *from* *the* Book *of* John

Passage:

In the beginning the Word already existed. The Word was with God, and the Word was God (John 1:1).

Difficulty: Does this verse prove that Jesus isn't God as the Jehovah's Witnesses claim?

Explanation: In the Greek language the definite article "the" accompanies the word *God* the first time it is used in verse 1, but not the second time. Therefore shouldn't this verse read "and the Word was a god" as the Jehovah's Witnesses claim?

Jehovah's Witnesses assert that a noun with a definite article points to an identity or personality and when the definite article is not used (an *anarthrous* construction) it refers to the quality of someone. The correct translation, they say, is "the Word (Jesus) was a god." Therefore the scripture is telling us Jesus was with God but he does not share the substance and essence of being God.

The problem with the Jehovah's Witnesses' rendering of "a god" is that the usage of articles with nouns is being misapplied. When a definite article in the Greek language is used it often indicates the individual or personality, as they state. And when it is not presented it at times refers to the quality or nature of the person. So that would not render the latter part of the verse "the Word was a god," but "the Word was of the nature as God." That rendering of course reinforces the view that Jesus was of the same nature as God. But that would contradict their bias that Jesus was not part of the Godhead.

One need not look further than the first 18 verses of John to see that the word *God* appears six times without the definite article. Note verse 6: "There was a man sent from God [*Theos* (God) without a definite article]" (John 1:6 NIV). Yet even the Jehovah's Witnesses' own *New World Translation* renders this correctly as "God" not "a god." Neither is the definite article "the" used with *God* in verses 12, 13, and twice in

18. But in each case the Jehovah's Witnesses' translation renders it correctly "God" not "a god."

So why are the Jehovah's Witnesses inconsistent in their interpretation of the Greek grammatical usage? It's apparent that to render verse 1 as "the Word was God" would be to acknowledge Jesus was God and that would be contrary to their doctrinal position. And yet to consistently translate *Theos* without a definite article as "a god" in verses 6, 12, 13 and twice in 18 would be to say that Jehovah is "a god." And that would be contrary to their doctrine as well. This leaves the Jehovah's Witnesses with the choice of incorrectly translating verse 1 as "a god" because of their doctrinal bias. When the definite article is not used, one must translate the noun within context. Therefore when the word *god* is referring to the Lord God or the Son of God it is correct to translate *god* as *God.*

But for argument's sake, does the Bible ever refer to Jesus as "the God," using the definite article? Yes. In Hebrews God the Father is quoted as saying, "To the Son he says, 'Your throne, O God [*Theos* with definite article], endures forever and ever'" (Hebrews 1:8). Jesus was and always will be God.

When we are interpreting Scripture it is important to allow the context of a passage of the Bible to form our doctrinal positions rather than misinterpreting Scripture to fit our own biases. This of course invites error and, in some cases, results in heresy.

Passage:

When the master of ceremonies tasted the water that was now wine [miraculously done by Jesus]...he called the bridegroom over. "A host always serves the best wine first," he said. "Then, when everyone has had a lot to drink, he brings out the less expensive wine. But you have kept the best until now!" (John 2:9-10).

Difficulty: Did Jesus turn water into wine with alcoholic content?

Explanation: Jesus had six water jars filled with water. Each of them held 20 to 30 gallons. Then he miraculously transformed over 150 gallons of water into wine. But was this an alcoholic beverage?

In the cultural setting of the first century the phrase "best wine" was a reference to aged wine. In that day it would have alcoholic content. The "less expensive" wine would have been newer wine with a less developed taste and less alcoholic content. Typically a wedding host would serve the good wine at the beginning of the wedding feast. The good wine would numb the senses a bit so that the less expensive wine served later would tend to go unnoticed.

What Jesus produced was good, expensive wine that impressed the master of ceremonies at this wedding. It was undoubtedly an aged wine that did have alcoholic content.

Some would say that Jesus would not have created an alcoholic beverage because the Bible is against drinking alcohol in any manner. However, what the Bible speaks against is drunkenness (see Proverbs 20:1; 23:29-35). In the New Testament the apostle Paul warns, "Don't be drunk with wine, because that will ruin your life" (Ephesians 5:18). While wine was a part of society in biblical times and was drunk at practically every meal, the overuse of it to the point of drunkenness is what the Bible speaks against.

In North America the abuse of alcohol is widespread, especially among young people. Some Christians believe that condoning the use of alcoholic beverages in any way opens the door for people to abuse it, specifically young people. And with the addictive effect drinking has on people, many Christians simply abstain from consuming any alcoholic drink in an effort to discourage anyone from even starting to drink. They believe this policy is perhaps the best way to reduce the abuse of alcoholic drink. For more on the biblical position on alcoholic drink see *Explanation* of Proverbs 31:6-7.

Passage:

It was time for the Jewish Festival of Shelters, and Jesus' brothers said to him, "Leave here and go to Judea, where your followers can see your miracles!"...Jesus replied... "You go on. I'm not going to this festival, because my time has not yet come"...But after his brothers left for the festival, Jesus also went, though secretly, staying out of public view (John 7:2-3,6,8,10).

Difficulty: Was Jesus less than honest by telling his brothers he wasn't going to the festival, when in fact he intended to go all along?

Explanation: Jesus' brothers wanted him to go to the festival with fanfare, working miracles. They said, "You can't become famous if you hide this" (John 7:4). When Jesus told them he wasn't going he said, "Now is not the right time for me to go, but you can go anytime...my time has not yet come" (John 7:6,8).

It appears Jesus was making it clear he wasn't going to the festival to demonstrate he was the miracle-working Messiah—his time had not yet come. So he didn't go to the festival openly—he went secretly. Jesus may have left his brothers in the dark on whether he would show up at the festival at all, but he was not dishonest with them. He showed up "midway through the festival" (John 7:14) and didn't do any miracles as his brothers had suggested.

Passage:

Let any one of you who is without sin be the first to throw a stone at her...Then neither do I condemn you," Jesus declared. "Go now and leave your life of sin" (John 8:11 NIV).

Difficulty: Why do some people question whether the story of Jesus and the woman caught in adultery ever took place?

Explanation: The story of Jesus' encounter with the adulterous woman found in John 8:11 is reflective of Jesus' mercy and compassion. The problem is that the passage does not appear in the earliest and more reliable Greek manuscripts. And neither was the story included in the earlier translations like the Coptic, Gothic, or Old Latin ones. When the passage did surface in later manuscripts it was found after John 21:24 and after Luke 21:38, as well as after John 7:52.

For the above reasons some scholars believe the story to be questionable. Others acknowledge it was a late addition yet believe it is an authentic story about Jesus. Many translations today highlight the fact that most of the ancient manuscripts do not include the passage. Yet they include it because 1) it does not contain any doctrinal errors; and 2) it is consistent with the merciful and forgiving heart of Jesus.

Passage:

Don't let your hearts be troubled. Trust in God, and trust also in me. There is more than enough room in my Father's home. If this were not so, would I have told you that I am going to prepare a place for you? When everything is ready, I will come and get you, so that you will always be with me where I am (John 14:1-3).

Difficulty: Is the celestial home of God (heaven) where Christians will spend eternity?

Explanation: Many people think their eternal home in heaven is a city with streets of gold and gates of pearl. This is actually a reference to the holy city John saw in his vision coming down from God (see Revelation 21). But most scholars believe this is, so to speak, the capital city of a new heaven and a new earth.

The psalmist David declares, "The earth is the LORD's, and everything in it, the world, and all who live in it" (Psalm 24:1 NIV). God made the heavens and the earth and called them "very good," and he hasn't surrendered his title and right to them. They may be in ruins now, but Scripture states that he has definite plans to restore them back to a perfect world for us to live in.

Peter wrote, "In keeping with his promise we are looking forward to a new heaven and a new earth, where righteousness dwells" (2 Peter

3:13 NIV). Jesus also told us that "when the Son of Man comes in his glory," he "will say to those on his right, 'Come, you who are blessed by my Father; take your inheritance, the kingdom prepared for you since the creation of the world'" (Matthew 25:31,34 NIV).

God has not given up on his original plan. He has neither abandoned the idea of a perfect earth, nor has he laid aside his plan for his children to live in a perfect place forever. It is a questionable idea that he is taking us away to some distant heaven and then destroying this earth he designed to be our home. After his resurrection, Jesus ascended into heaven with a promise to return. He will return and restore this earth to his original design. God's perfect plan is "to bring unity to all things in heaven and on earth under Christ" (Ephesians 1:10 NIV).

Notice that in the verse above Paul tells us that the earth, as well as heaven, will be under Christ. If we who now live on the earth were to be taken into heaven, who would be left on the earth to be brought together under Christ? Scripture points out that heaven (the holy city) is God's home. The earth is our home, not only now, but forever, just as God originally intended. And it is Jesus who will eternally bring us together with God and connect his home with ours. In his revelation John saw the holy city, the New Jerusalem, coming down from God out of heaven and he heard a voice saying, "Look, the home of God is now among his people! He will live with them, and they will be his people. God himself will be with them" (Revelation 21:3).

Theologian Randy Alcorn in his book *Heaven* puts it this way:

> There will be one cosmos, one universe united under one Lord—forever. This is the unstoppable plan of God. This is where history is headed. When God walked with Adam and Eve in the Garden, Earth was Heaven's backyard. The New Earth will even be more than that—it will be Heaven itself. And those who know Jesus will have the privilege of living there.[3]

Scripture tells us that when God's restoration project is complete we will experience a renewed earth in the perfection of the Garden of Eden. "No longer will there be a curse on anything" (Revelation 22:3). No more thorns or thistles to prick our bodies. No more difficulty in getting things to grow. No more "survival of the fittest" among the animals. For they will all be at peace with one another. In fact, there will be no discord or fighting or evil anywhere, because "nothing evil will be allowed to enter, nor anyone who practices shameful idolatry and dishonesty—but only those whose names are written in the Lamb's Book of Life" (Revelation 21:27).

Passage and Difficulty: John 19:14—Why do John and Mark record different times in regard to Jesus' trial and crucifixion?

Explanation: See Mark 15:25.

Difficult Verses *from* *the* Book *of* Acts

Passage and Difficulty: Acts 1:18—Doesn't this account of Judas's death contradict the account found in Matthew 27:5?

Explanation: See Matthew 27:5.

Passage:

All the believers met together in one place and shared everything they had. They sold their property and possessions and shared the money with those in need (Acts 2:44-45).

Difficulty: Since first-century Christians seemed to practice a form of communism, are Christians today obligated to practice it?

Explanation: One of the characteristics of the church is that it is a family. "You are citizens along with all of God's holy people," Paul said. "You are members of God's family" (Ephesians 2:19). The church is also Christ's body "and since we are all one body in Christ, we belong to each other, and each of us needs all the others" (Romans 12:5 NLT). So "if one part suffers, all the parts suffer with it, and if one part is honored, all the parts are glad" (1 Corinthians 12:26).

When the first-century church was birthed with the outpouring of the Holy Spirit on the day of Pentecost, it reflected itself as one big family and a body that felt the needs of other members of the body. The truth of the church's family closeness and the members' needing one another was played out in Acts 2. And that truth is applicable today as taught in Ephesians, Romans, and 1 Corinthians. But does this mean the church today is to exactly replicate what the church did in the first century?

Acts 2 is describing what the newly birthed church did. It is a descriptive account, not necessarily a biblical directive for us to follow. We see they were united and unselfish, caring for the needs of others, and sacrificed to see that needs were met. This should be reflected in the church today. Yet this doesn't mean all new followers of Christ that become part of the body of Christ are to sell all their possessions and allow the church to distribute the proceeds as needed.

There is no indication that those in the early church were *required* to sell their property; it was all voluntary. This approach is clearly different from communism. Some have suggested that this mutual ownership could be called "commonism" but definitely not communism. In "commonism" one would voluntarily say, "What's mine is yours." But in communism the state says, "What's yours is mine."

This socialistic approach within the early church did seem to have its problems. The task of equitably distributing the money and food to those in need became an issue. "The Greek-speaking believers complained about the Hebrew-speaking believers, saying that their widows were being discriminated against in the daily distribution of food" (Acts 6:1). So a distribution committee was formed to address this problem.

We don't know how long the early church continued this practice, but the problem of meeting people's material needs without them earning it posed an increasing problem. In Paul's first letter to the church in Thessalonica he warned of people getting lazy (1 Thessalonians 5:14). Then in his second letter to the Thessalonians he told the church to "stay away from all believers who live idle lives and don't follow the tradition they received from us" (2 Thessalonians 3:6). Paul then goes on to say he had never accepted food from anyone without paying for it and said, "While we were with you we gave you this command: 'Those unwilling to work will not get to eat'" (2 Thessalonians 3:10).

As a family and body the church is certainly called upon to minister to the needs of others. Helping to provide for those who can't provide for themselves meets a special need in people's lives. But assisting those who are able-bodied and can earn their way may in fact prompt laziness. And Paul seemed to be addressing this issue.

Private ownership of property is implied in the Ten Commandments. We are told not to "steal" or even "covet" what rightly belongs to another (see Deuteronomy 5:19,21). And while all our possessions belong to God, he does call upon us to be wise stewards of what he grants each of us. (For more on giving out of what God grants us, see *Explanation* of Malachi 3:8.)

Passage:

Jesus is the one referred to in the Scriptures, where it says, "The stone that you builders rejected has now become the cornerstone." There is salvation in no one else! God has given no other name under heaven by which we must be saved (Acts 4:11-12).

Difficulty: Isn't this passage teaching a rather narrow-minded view—that Jesus is the only way to God?

Explanation: A major criticism leveled at Christians is that they are arrogant to say, like Luke in Acts 4, that Jesus is the only true religion and the only way to obtain eternal life. That view seems annoyingly exclusive and intolerant to many people. Consequently, most professed Christians in America no longer claim that Christianity is exclusive.

So is it narrow-minded for a Christian today to claim that Jesus is the only way to God? It would come across rather narrow-minded and arrogant of anyone to make that exclusive claim unless he or she was God. But the fact of the matter is, Jesus, as the Son of God, did make the claim of being the only way to obtain eternal life.

Most of the religious leaders of Jesus' time also thought he came across as narrow-minded and arrogant for saying what he said about himself. He claimed to be the Son of God who had existed eternally, who could forgive sin and give eternal life. And Jesus would have been not just narrow-minded but a deceiver for making such an outlandish claim of exclusivity if he wasn't God—but he was. And he gave extensive evidence to substantiate his claim.

Jesus fulfilled prophecies about God's Chosen One (the Messiah), being born of a virgin and performing many miracles before he actually said, "I am the resurrection and the life. Anyone who believes in me will live, even after dying. Everyone who lives in me and believes in me will never ever die" (John 11:25-26). He could make this seemingly arrogant declaration because he was the one and only Son of God, who could back it up. Read these words of his: "Unless you believe that I AM who I claim to be, you will die in your sins" (John 8:24). "I am the way, the truth, and the life. No one can come to the Father except through me" (John 14:6).

It was Jesus who made the exclusive claim to be the only way to God—and for good reason. No one else had the qualifications that a holy and just God would accept in redeeming a lost and sinful human race. However, Christ-followers need to be careful not to assert that *they* have a corner on truth or are the ones who have the only true religion. Rather, it is *Jesus* who is the way, the truth, and the life—his followers are simply sharing *his* message. So as Christians we can point back to him in the matter of obtaining eternal life. Our task is to spread the good news about him. And we are wise to share that news enthusiastically yet humbly.

Passage:

You must abstain from eating food offered to idols, from consuming blood or the meat of strangled animals, and from sexual immorality. If you do this, you will do well (Acts 15:29).

Difficulty: Does this passage forbid blood transfusions, as the Jehovah's Witnesses claim?

Explanation: God was very specific with the children of Israel when it came to how to sacrifice animals as an atonement for sin, a mandate that was eventually fulfilled in Christ's atoning death on the cross. There were laws regarding what to eat, what not to eat, what was clean and unclean. It was important that Israel follow these ceremonial laws, which represented how a holy God made it possible for his people to be transformed from death to life in relationship with him.

Blood was the symbol of life given by God. In the Old Testament, the blood of the animal sacrifice represented the life of the sinner coming before God. And when the priest sprinkled the blood of the animal sacrifice on the altar before God, it was considered an atonement—an exchange of a life for a life. "I have given you the blood on the altar to purify you," he said to Israel, "making you right with the Lord. It is the blood, given in exchange for a life, that makes purification possible... That is why I have said to the people of Israel, 'You must never eat or drink blood, for the life of any creature is in its blood.' So whoever consumes blood will be cut off from the community" (Leviticus 17:11,14).

This law of Moses regarding the eating of blood, along with many other Levitical laws, was being debated within the early church. As nonobserving Gentiles were coming into the church, certain Jewish followers of Christ were arguing for compliance with their traditions. They "insisted, 'The Gentile converts must be circumcised and required to follow the law of Moses'" (Acts 15:5). So Paul and Barnabas went to Jerusalem to meet with the whole church including the apostles and the elders to deal with the matter.

After long discussion the elders came to a compromise. James stood up in the meeting and said,

> My judgment is that we should not make it difficult for the Gentiles who are turning to God. Instead, we should write and tell them to abstain from eating food offered to idols, from sexual immorality, from eating the meat of strangled animals, and from consuming blood. For these laws of Moses have been preached in Jewish synagogues in every city on every Sabbath for many generations (Acts 15:19-21).

So the apostles and elders wrote the letter to confirm their position in an attempt to "lay no greater burden on you than these few requirements" (Acts 15:28). Then the requirements were laid out in verse 29. So are these requirements within the context in which they were given applicable today?

Certainly the requirement to abstain from sexual immorality is valid today because it is repeated throughout the Old Testament's moral law and in the New Testament. Yet the eating requirements the elders were prescribing were clearly from the Levitical laws or laws of Moses for the purpose of keeping unity among the Jewish and new Gentile followers of Jesus. Later the epistles of Paul and the writer of Hebrews made it clear that the blood sacrificial system of Moses was fulfilled in Christ's death and resurrection and such laws were no longer binding. Paul told the church at Colosse, "Don't let anyone condemn you for what you eat or drink...for those rules are only shadows of the reality yet to come. And Christ himself is that reality" (Colossians 2:16-17). (For further clarification on what laws of Moses are binding on us today see *Explanation* of Leviticus 11:46-47.)

The Old Testament regulation to not eat or drink the blood of animals was made for a reason, because "the life of any creature is in its blood" (Leviticus 17:14). And since the blood was the symbol of a sacred sacrifice for sin—a life for a life exchange, to ingest it was not allowing it to be offered to God as a substitute for a person's sin. But of course that perfect sacrificial substitute for our sins has been made once and for all. "Christ has now become the High Priest over all the good things that have come...With his own blood—not the blood of goats and calves—he entered the Most Holy Place once for all time and secured our redemption forever" (Hebrews 9:11-12). So it would seem that the prohibition against the eating of blood is not binding today. And that would of course mean there would be no scriptural regulation against a blood transfusion.

With that said, is having a blood transfusion even equivalent to "consuming blood"? Some scholars point out that even if eating or drinking the blood of animals was considered morally wrong from Scripture, a blood transfusion cannot be considered eating blood. Blood given by transfusion, as we know, is not absorbed through the digestive system. Transfusions are injected directly into the bloodstream, therefore bypassing the digestive system. And of course transfusions do not involve the blood of mere animals but of other human beings. So receiving a blood transfusion medically would appear to be acceptable even if eating or drinking blood were scripturally prohibited.

Paul's Letters

Romans–Philemon

Passage:

Moses writes that the law's way of making a person right with God requires obedience to all of its commands (Romans 10:5).

Difficulty: Can following the laws of God make a person right with God?

Explanation: Some have suggested that in the Old Testament time people were made right with God by obeying the law—meaning a person can become righteous by following God's commands. But the point Paul is making in Romans 10 is that the only way the law can make a person right with God is if they have never broken the law. In other words if you never sinned and you followed all the laws and obeyed God perfectly, you wouldn't need a Savior. But since Paul knew that was impossible he went on to say that his "message is the very message about faith that we preach: If you confess with your mouth that Jesus is Lord and believe in your heart that God raised him from the dead, you will be saved" (Romans 10:8-9).

A few chapters before chapter 10 Paul explained,

> No one can ever be made right with God by doing what the law commands. The law simply shows us how sinful we are [because we were all born sinners]. But now God has shown us a way to be made right with him without keeping the requirements of the law, as was promised in the writings of Moses and the prophets long ago. We are made right with God by placing our faith in Jesus Christ (Romans 3:20-22).

It might appear on the surface that Paul just contradicted himself. He says the law can't save us, yet he seems to imply that Moses and the prophets did promise that before Christ people were made right with God by obedience to the law. What Paul is saying is that in Moses' time the way of being made right with God *was* in obeying the instructions God gave including the sacrifices of animals. And by a sacrificial death of an animal the people were *provisionally* made right with God. This provisional status was based on the future death of Christ as the perfect sacrifice for all sin.

People of times past were not freed of their sins and made right with God because an animal was sacrificed—it was because of what Christ would accomplish in the future. The power of his death and resurrection not only reaches forward in time to free us from sin in the twenty-first century, it also reaches back in time to cover all those born prior to Jesus' sacrificial death. So God "did not punish those who sinned in times past, for he was looking ahead and including them in what he would do in this present time" (Romans 3:25-26). It is trust in God's perfect sacrifice (Jesus) that addresses the human dilemma of sin past, present, and future.

So is there nothing we can say to God or do for him that would merit our redemption? Is there nothing we can do to earn our justification? Paul asked and answered those questions when he wrote,

> Can we boast, then, that we have done anything to be accepted by God? No, because our acquittal is not based on our obeying the law. It is based on faith [in Jesus]. So we are made right with God through faith and not by obeying the law (Romans 3:27-28).

Performance-focused people who tend to earn what they get may find salvation by grace through faith hard to grasp, or at least hard to accept. But there is no human requirement to obtain God's offer of a relationship except to freely accept it. It is a gift based upon the requirements fulfilled by Jesus. That is why when speaking of salvation Paul said, "It does not depend on the man who wills or the man who runs, but on God who has mercy" (Romans 9:16 NASB).

Passage:

Just as our bodies have many parts and each part has a special function, so it is with Christ's body...In his grace, God has given us different gifts for doing certain things well (Romans 12:4-6).

Difficulty: Does this mean every Christian has at least one spiritual gift he or she should exhibit?

Explanation: Scripture is quite clear that God has given a spiritual gift to each of his children. "A spiritual gift is given to each of us so we can help each other" (1 Corinthians 12:7). "God has given each of you a gift from his great variety of spiritual gifts. Use them well to serve one another" (1 Peter 4:10).

The gifts God grants his followers are identified in Romans 12:3-13, 1 Corinthians 12:1-33 and 14:1-30, and Ephesians 4:11-13. Some Christians are confused about what these gifts are, which gifts they have, and how they are to exercise them. Various Christian groups take different positions on who receives what gifts, and when and whether some are to be used today. Also some make a distinction between a spiritual gift and a position or office in the church. But in general terms the gifts referenced in Scripture can be categorized as follows:

- administration (1 Corinthians 12:28)
- apostleship (Ephesians 4:7,11)
- discernment (1 Corinthians 12:7,10)
- encouragement/counseling (Romans 12:6,8)
- faith (1 Corinthians 12:7,9)
- giving (Romans 12:6,8)
- healing (1 Corinthians 12:7,9)
- helps (1 Corinthians 12:28)
- hospitality (1 Peter 4:9-10)
- interpretation of tongues (1 Corinthians 12:7,10)
- knowledge (1 Corinthians 12:7-8)
- leadership (Romans 12:6,8)

- mercy (Romans 12:6,8)
- miracles (1 Corinthians 12:7-8,10)
- pastor/shepherd (Ephesians 4:7,11)
- prophecy (Ephesians 4:7,11)
- teaching (Romans 12:6-7)
- tongues (1 Corinthians 12:7,10)
- wisdom (1 Corinthians 12:7-8)

(An excellent resource to help you discover your gifts is the book *LifeKeys—Discovering Who You Are, Why You're Here, What You Do Best* by Jane A.G. Kise, David Stark, and Sandra Krebs Hirsh. Check out this and other helpful resources at www.LifeKeys.com.)

Passage:

Fire will reveal what kind of work each builder has done. The fire will show if a person's work has any value. If the work survives, that builder will receive a reward. But if the work is burned up, the builder will suffer great loss. The builder will be saved, but like someone barely escaping through a wall of flames (1 Corinthians 3:13-15).

Difficulty: Does this passage teach the idea of purgatory?

Explanation: Some believe this passage is referring to a temporary place a person goes to after death to be purged for past acts of sin—purgatory. Roman Catholic Pope Gregory I taught that baptism takes care of original sin but we must remit payment for sins committed. And if there isn't enough payment made in life then further payment is to be made in purgatory. Once sufficient suffering has been paid the person moves on to heaven.

Those who hold to this doctrine cite a passage from 2 Maccabees 12, which is a book in the Apocrypha, not accepted as inspired Scripture by Protestants.

Romans 3 teaches that Christ's death on the cross atoned for all our sin committed, not just original sin. The apostle Paul said that God "declares that we are righteous. He did this through Christ Jesus when he freed us from the penalty of our sins" (Romans 3:24).

Nowhere in Scripture does it mention a place where we work out a payment plan for our sins. It does say we must give an account before God for our actions (see 2 Corinthians 5:10 and Romans 14:10-12) and that Jesus is our "single sacrifice for sins, good for all time" (Hebrews 10:12). For more on the idea of purgatory see *Explanation* of 1 Peter 4:6.

This 1 Corinthians 3 passage is thought to be referring to the rewards people will receive based on their accurate teachings and faithful works. James points out that "we who teach will be judged more strictly" (James 3:1). Therefore most scholars interpret this passage to mean that those whose teachings and works are in error will suffer a loss of reward but not a loss of their eternal salvation.

Passage and Difficulty: 1 Corinthians 6:18—Why is the Bible so negatively against sex?

Explanation: See 1 Thessalonians 4:3.

Passage and Difficulty: 1 Corinthians 7:12-13—Why did Paul say a married couple should not divorce an unbelieving spouse while in Ezra God required Jewish men to divorce their unbelieving wives?

Explanation: See Ezra 10:3.

Passage:

The head of every man is Christ, the head of woman is man, and the head of Christ is God (1 Corinthians 11:3).

Difficulty: Does this mean that women are inferior to men because men are their head or authority?

Explanation: Women are no more inferior to men than Christ is to God. Christ considered God his Father—that is, his head or authority—but this did not make Christ any less God. Christ shares the substance and essence of being God. In the same way a woman may consider her husband her head but this does not mean she is inferior, because all women share the same substance and essence of being a human of great worth and dignity.

Some have suggested that the curse upon Eve, "you will desire to control your husband, but he will rule over you" (Genesis 3:16), is somehow a permanent curse God put on all women and therefore they were destined to be inferior. This is a distorted interpretation of this verse (see *Explanation* of Genesis 3:16). The man, the woman, and the earth were all cursed as a result of sin. Yet God never intended for these curses to become a permanent part of our lives. In part he has been at work from the beginning to restore everything back to his original design. And he certainly doesn't will that a husband and wife engage in a battle for control one over the other.

There are those who contend on a practical level a wife must recognize that the husband makes the final decision in the home, otherwise there will be chaos. They will often quote 1 Corinthians 11:3. The point they make is that there is a chain of command that must be honored. Yet what is missed here is how the relationship between Christ and God isn't about authority, control, and who has the last say. It is about unity and oneness by serving one another.

The perfect oneness of God, his Son, and the Holy Spirit acts as a model of oneness for marriages and the church (see *Explanation* of Ephesians 5:21-23). Jesus prayed that "'they [Jesus' followers] will be one, just as you and I are one—as you are in me, Father, and I am in you'" (John 17:21). That oneness didn't come about by the Father barking out orders and claiming that the "buck stops here." Never once do we see the Father calling for his Son to recognize his "duty" to submit to the Father's authority and headship. The intimate oneness of the Father and the Son is a result of each loving and serving the other. This is a unique relationship. Jesus says, "The Son can do nothing by himself. He does only what he sees the Father doing" (John 5:19). This would first seem like the Son is submitting to the authority of the Father as a wife should submit to the authority of the husband. But read on!

"For just as the Father gives life to those he raises from the dead, so the Son gives life to anyone he wants" (John 5:21). Now it appears that the Father has authority to raise people from the dead independent of the Son and the Son can equally give life to anyone he wants. Then Jesus says, "The Father judges no one. Instead he has given the Son absolute authority to judge, so that everyone will honor the Son, just as they honor the Father" (John 5:22-23). So which is it? Does the Father have the authority or does the Son? Does the Father have the power to raise people from the dead or the Son? The chain of command and the hierarchical system seem to be blurred. And so they should, because a love relationship isn't about who is in charge or who gets the last say—it's about pleasing the other.

This headship or leadership concept continues to get even more confusing when we try to place it within the chain-of-command idea. Who was calling the shots on Jesus going to the cross? It's clear that "God loved the world so much that he gave his one and only Son" (John 3:16). The Father was in authority there, right? That seems correct because in his humanity, Jesus didn't really want to suffer on the cross but said to his Father, "I want your will to be done, not mine" (Matthew 26:39). Yet Jesus claimed that "no one can take my life from me. I sacrifice it voluntarily. For I have the authority to lay it down when I want to and also take it up again" (John 10:18). Jesus clearly seemed in charge. If he wasn't willing to go to the cross he could have called over 70,000 angels to rescue him (see Matthew 26:53).

As we study the relationship between the Father and the Son we see that the Father is pleased to give everything to the Son because he loves his Son. The Son is pleased to give everything to the Father because he loves his Father. This is clearly not a relationship in which power and authority are leveraged by one over the other. It is not some hierarchical chain of command. It is a circle of relationship that looks out for the best in each other because of a deep abiding love for one another. This is the relational picture God wants marriage to reflect. As Christ is to God so should the husband be to the wife. Each serving the other with Christ as the head of their marriage, resulting in an intimate oneness.

Passage:

A man dishonors his head if he covers his head while praying or prophesying. But a woman dishonors her head if she prays or prophesies without a covering on her head, for this is the same as shaving her head. Yes, if she refuses to wear a head covering, she should cut off her hair! But since it is shameful for a woman to have her hair cut or her head shaved, she should wear a covering (1 Corinthians 11:4-6).

Difficulty: Should Christian women today wear a head covering while praying or while worshipping in a church service?

Explanation: There have been differing views and interpretations of this passage by many scholars over the years. Some believe that Paul was mandating a material covering for a woman's head. Numerous churches today follow this interpretation, with women wearing a "prayer cap" at all times in public. Others hold the position that Paul was concerned about hairstyles. Specifically, they say he objected to women wearing their hair loose and flowing down their backs. Instead he wanted women to follow the usual custom of pinning their hair up on their heads. This interpretation, to some, means a woman's covering is her long hair fixed neatly on her head.

Most scholars today see this passage as a cultural injunction rather than a universal command. They see it as an issue in the first century on how Paul dealt with matters of authority. And he saw a woman's head covering as a symbol of respecting authority. Paul states his reason in verses 10 and 12. "A woman should wear a covering on her head to show she is under authority. But among the Lord's people, women are not independent of men and men are not independent of women. For although the first woman came from man, every other man was born from a woman, and everything comes from God" (1 Corinthians 11:10-12).

So to many the issue for us today isn't a covering for a woman's head, but an attitude of the heart—one of humility, submission, and service to one another. Some would contend that a head covering for a woman is a necessary symbol to reflect that servant heart, others would say the covering is symbolic, while still others say the heart attitude is all that is necessary. It would seem the primary focus of Paul's message was that when men and women are praying, teaching, or worshipping together they need to be mindful that we all are to humbly serve God and one another.

Passage:

Does not the very nature of things teach you that if a man has long hair, it is a disgrace to him, but if a woman has long hair, it is her glory? For long hair is given to her as a covering (1 Corinthians 11:14-15 NIV).

Difficulty: Is Scripture dictating the length of our hair?

Explanation: This passage follows Paul's discourse on women covering their heads while praying or prophesying. And he is stating that the long hair of a woman is her covering (see *Explanation* of 1 Corinthians 11:4-6).

In the book of Romans Paul talked about us knowing "by nature" certain things that are right or wrong (see Romans 2:12-15). God does make certain things known to us instinctively. Paul appears to be saying here that shorter hair for men and longer hair for women is somehow taught instinctively or by the nature of things.

In the Levitical laws to Israel it says "a woman must not put on man's clothing, and a man must not wear women's clothing. Anyone who does this is detestable in the sight of the LORD your God" (Deuteronomy 22:5). This restriction for Israel, perhaps like Paul with the different length of hair for men and women, is God's way of telling us that he wants a distinction to be kept between the sexes. In other words a man should look manly and a woman should look feminine. How this plays out culturally would of course be different, but distinguishing between the sexes seems to be the point here.

Passage and Difficulty: 1 Corinthians 12:7—Does this mean every Christian has at least one spiritual gift that he or she should exhibit?

Explanation: See Romans 12:4-6.

Passage:

I wish you could all speak in tongues, but even more I wish you could all prophesy (1 Corinthians 14:5).

Difficulty: Are all Christians supposed to speak in tongues (unknown languages)?

Explanation: There is not a consensus among evangelicals on Christians' speaking in tongues.

The book of Acts reports that when the Holy Spirit came upon Christ-followers on the day of Pentecost they "began speaking in other languages, as the Holy Spirit gave them this ability." The onlookers reacted. "'How can this be?' they exclaimed. 'These people are all from Galilee, and yet we hear them speaking in our own native languages!'" (Acts 2:4,7).

Pentecost was a festival that drew Jews from every nation. Obviously they spoke languages other than Greek or Aramaic. The Holy Spirit enabled these Galilean Christians to speak languages that were otherwise foreign to them. Many Christians today believe that speaking in tongues (an unknown language to the person speaking) is evidence of receiving the Holy Spirit. Some quote Jesus' directive as further support of this view: "Go into all the world and preach the Good News to everyone...These miraculous signs will accompany those who believe: They will cast out demons in my name, and they will speak in new languages" (Mark 16:15,17).

Others say that being gifted by the Holy Spirit to speak in a language that is not naturally familiar to the person was necessary for the first-century church to evangelize. But they would contend that this period or dispensation of miraculous giftedness of speaking in an unknown language (tongues) is over.

In 1 Corinthians 14 Paul is making the point that when someone speaks in tongues in a meeting someone should be there to interpret (verse 13). He points out that it is important that God's message or truth be understood by all. "In a church meeting I would rather speak five understandable words to help others than ten thousand words in an unknown language" (1 Corinthians 14:19).

Paul's major focus of 1 Corinthians 14 is that in public worship "one will sing, another will teach, another will tell some special revelation God has given, one will speak in tongues, and another will interpret what is said. But everything that is done must strengthen all of you" (1 Corinthians 14:26). Most Christians can agree on the point that a public worship service in the twenty-first century should also focus on everyone present being ministered to.

However, there is still disagreement on the idea of the gift of tongues. There are many who would interpret Paul's admonition in 1 Corinthians 14 about tongues as referring to someone speaking in a language unknown to anyone except God. And that he supernaturally gives another the gift to interpret the meaning of the unknown language. And so Paul is emphasizing that an interpreter be present to "strengthen all of you." Numerous Christian groups teach that the gift of tongues is a special "heavenly language" that only God understands and that this is what Paul meant when he said, "If I pray in tongues, my spirit is praying, but I don't understand what I am saying" (1 Corinthians 14:14) and "if no one is present who can interpret, they must be silent in your church meeting and speak in tongues to God privately" (1 Corinthians 14:28).

There has been much written on the "speaking in tongues" issue over the last few decades and it is clear there is no consensus. It would be wise for Christians to read up on the issue and study the Scripture with a sound interpretive process. (See "How to Use This Handbook" on how to effectively interpret Scripture.)

Passage:

Women should be silent during the church meetings. It is not proper for them to speak. They should be submissive, just as the law says. If they have any questions, they should ask their husbands at home, for it is improper for women to speak in church meetings (1 Corinthians 14:34-35).

Difficulty: Are women today not to verbally raise questions and get answers from church meetings?

Explanation: There are those who contend that Paul's prohibition of women speaking in church is universal and applies today. Their point is that women need to respect the authority of men as God's spokesmen of truth and should remain silent at church.

However, it seems that Paul was addressing a specific problem in the church of Corinth unique to them, with application for all of us. This would then be interpreting the passage in light of its cultural context (see "How to Use This Handbook" regarding scriptural interpretation).

Some recount historically how new women converts in the early church were hungry to know more about their faith and were asking questions in the formal meetings. Others say it was perhaps uneducated women raising irrelevant questions. Regardless of what was causing these women in Corinth to be speaking out it was resulting in disruption and chaos. In response Paul admonished them to keep quiet and ask their questions of their husbands at home. Paul precedes his admonition with this: "God is not a God of disorder but of peace, as in all the meetings of God's holy people" (1 Corinthians 14:33).

A prohibition for women to keep quiet in church then is not for all women in every age in every church. But rather this was a particular problem in the Corinthian church in the first century that needed to be addressed.

So what is the universal truth of this passage that is relevant to us today? God wants his message of truth to be heard and understood during the assembly of believers. Paul summarizes this universal truth in the closing verse of chapter 14.

> My dear brothers and sisters, be eager to prophesy, and don't forbid speaking in tongues. But be sure that everything is done properly and in order (1 Corinthians 14:39).

Passage:

If Christ has not been raised, then your faith is useless and you are still guilty of sins. In that case, all who have died believing in Christ are lost! (1 Corinthians 15:17-18).

Difficulty: Why does this Corinthian passage indicate that our faith is useless without the added element of Christ's resurrection?

Explanation: Some people would say that Jesus' death provides salvation for each of us who believe in him. And so his death is central to the Christian faith. But Scripture teaches that his resurrection is equally central to Christianity.

The resurrection of Jesus Christ and Christianity stand or fall together. One cannot be true without the other. Belief in the truth of Christianity is not merely faith in faith—ours or someone else's—but rather faith in the risen Christ of history. Without the historical resurrection of Jesus, the Christian faith is a mere placebo. That is why the apostle Paul said, "If Christ has not been raised, then your faith is useless" (1 Corinthians 15:17). Worship, fellowship, Bible study, the Christian life, and the church itself are worthless exercises in futility if Jesus has not been literally and physically raised from the dead. Without the resurrection, we might as well forget God, church, and following moral rules and "feast and drink, for tomorrow we die!" (1 Corinthians 15:32).

On the other hand, if Christ has been raised from the dead, then he is alive at this very moment, and we can know him personally. The whole of 1 Corinthians 15:1-58 gives us assurance that our sins are forgiven (see verse 3) and that Christ has broken the power of death (see verse 54). Furthermore, he promises that we too will be resurrected someday (see verse 22). We can trust him because he is sovereign over the world (see verse 27). And he will give us ultimate victory (see verse 57), as well as a plan for our lives (see verse 58).

Christ's resurrection is therefore central to Christianity. Contemporary theologian J.I. Packer puts it this way:

> The Easter event...demonstrated Jesus' deity; validated his teaching; attested the completion of his work of atonement for sin; confirms his present cosmic dominion and his coming reappearance as Judge; assures us that his personal pardon, presence, and power in people's lives today is fact; and guarantees each believer's own re-embodiment by Resurrection in the world to come.[1]

God is able to raise us to life in him because of the resurrected Jesus. The power of his resurrection not only overcame his own death, but it will one day defeat Satan and his hold of death on all of us.

> Christ must reign until he humbles all his enemies beneath his feet. And the last enemy to be destroyed is death... Then when he has conquered all things, the Son will present himself to God, so that God, who gave his Son authority over all things, will be utterly supreme over everything everywhere (1 Corinthians 15:25-26,28).

Passage:

> If the dead will not be raised, what point is there in people being baptized for those who are dead? Why do it unless the dead will someday rise again? (1 Corinthians 15:29).

Difficulty: Does this passage teach, like the Latter-day Saints (Mormons) claim, that baptism is necessary for salvation and if someone dies before being baptized a relative can be baptized by proxy for them?

Explanation: Apparently some first-century Christians were getting baptized either for believers who had died before they were baptized or for dead unbelievers they wanted to be saved. The idea was that a living believer could be baptized in place of someone else who had died—as a substitute.

This is the only place in Scripture that refers to this apparent practice. And Paul is neither condoning it or condemning it. He is, however, using it to make a point: Unless Christ has been raised, none of us will be raised to life eternal!

It is unwise to base a doctrinal position on an obscure and isolated passage of Scripture. Without other passages to clarify this one it is risky to interpret this to mean that a person can be baptized for another person. In fact, other passages make it clear we are saved by grace through faith in Christ (see Romans 4:4-5; Ephesians 2:8-9; Titus 3:4-7). To interpret 1 Corinthians 15:29 as a way for someone to do a work (be baptized) for a deceased person would contradict how Scripture teaches us we are made right before God.

Passage:

God made him who had no sin to be sin for us, so that in him we might become the righteousness of God (2 Corinthians 5:21).

Difficulty: How could Jesus be sin when he is said to be sinless?

Explanation: It is true that the Scripture states that Jesus "faced all the same testings we do, yet he did not sin" (Hebrews 4:15). So how is it that God made Jesus sin?

Jesus was *actually* sinless yet God made him sin for us *judicially* or *substitutionally*. In other words Jesus' death substituted for our death. Scripture says even though the "wages of sin is death" (Romans 6:23), "God paid a ransom [your wages]...And the ransom he paid was not mere gold or silver. It was the precious blood of Christ, the sinless, spotless Lamb of God" (1 Peter 1:18-29). It is Jesus' death on the cross that atoned for our sins. He became our sacrifice for sin. A clearer translation of 2 Corinthians 5:21 is "God made Christ, who never sinned, to be the offering for our sin, so that we could be made right with God through Christ" (2 Corinthians 5:21).

Some scholars say that Jesus' death as the "spotless Lamb of God" satisfies the demands of both God's holiness and his justice. His holiness is satisfied because Jesus was sinless—a perfect sacrifice without sin. His justice is satisfied in that Christ's death paid our "wages of sin," which is death. There are various views on the doctrine of atonement, with substitutionary atonement the most widely accepted by Protestant and evangelical churches. That is, God's perfect justice demanded that the penalty for sin be paid, and Christ stepped in and paid it. Others see his sacrifice more as a ransom. That is, when we sin we become enslaved to Satan. Christ ransoms us by saying, in effect, "Take me instead." And Satan jumped at the offer. Biblically speaking, both views are true.

While there is some disagreement over the distinction as to whether Christ "suffered for us" or whether he was "punished instead of us," there is common agreement that through Jesus' death we are redeemed—forgiven of our sin, raised to new life, and reconciled to God.

Passage and Difficulty: 2 Corinthians 11:2—If it is wrong to get jealous, why is Paul jealous?

Explanation: See Exodus 34:14.

Difficult Verses *from* *the* Book *of* Galatians

Passage and Difficulty: Galatians 1:15-16—Is this teaching the idea of reincarnation?

Explanation: See Jeremiah 1:5.

Passage:

Bear one another's burdens, and thereby fulfill the law of Christ (Galatians 6:2 NASB).

Difficulty: To what extent are Christians to take on the burdens and problems of others?

Explanation: A Christian friend comes to you and explains that he has maxed out his five credit cards. He says he has overspent for a big vacation and Christmas gifts for his family. He wants to know if you could help bear his financial burden. He says that $300 a month for a year would really help. According to Galatians 6:2 aren't you supposed to help? It's true it is his financial responsibility, but doesn't the "law of Christ" make your friend's financial responsibility yours too?

Scripture doesn't teach that bearing another person's burden means taking responsibility for that person's problem or hurt. Rather, it means coming alongside and gently helping a person lift the weight. Bearing the burdens of others doesn't mean taking responsibility *for* their problem; it means being responsible *to* them—to comfort, encourage, and support them in their pain or difficulties.

Galatians 6:2 does tell us that we are to "bear one another's burdens." But the context of the entire passage gives us insight into the proper interpretation of verse 2. Because just three verses down the page declares, "Each one will bear his own load" (Galatians 2:5 NASB).

The meaning of these verses comes together when we consider that there is an important difference between a "burden" and a "load." The

Greek word for *burden* is *baros,* which denotes a heavy weight. Jesus used this word when describing the workers toiling in the vineyard who have "borne the burden [*baros*] and the scorching heat of the day" (Matthew 20:12 NASB). This was a heavy burden to bear.

We all face situations that bear down heavily on us, and God is pleased that others experience Galatians 6:2 with us by coming alongside to support us in our difficulty. Consider the image of a man carrying a heavy beam across his shoulders. Now watch as two friends come alongside him. They put their shoulders on either side of the beam and help lift his load. That is the picture here. When we are burdened down with an injury, an illness, the loss of a job, or loss of a loved one, we need comfort and support; we need others to help us lift our heavy load.

In verse 5 Paul uses a different word for *burden* or *weight.* He says, "Each one shall bear his own load" (Galatians 6:5 NASB). This is the Greek word *phortion,* which refers to something with little weight that is carried, like the supply pack a first-century soldier would carry into the field. A more idiomatic translation is given in the New Living Translation: "We are each responsible for our own conduct" (Galatians 6:5). In other words, this load is your assignment and bearing it is your responsibility alone. It's the idea Paul was conveying when he said, "Each of us will give a personal account to God" (Romans 14:12).

We all have personal responsibilities, and when we fail in our responsibilities—by using poor judgment or making wrong choices or harboring bad attitudes—we must face up to the consequences. To step in and remove the natural and corrective consequences of people's irresponsible behavior may rob them of valuable lessons—lessons which may be critical for their continued growth and maturity.

Experiencing Galatians 6:2 with others doesn't mean being responsible *for* other people—like for the bills they pile up irresponsibly. It means being responsible *to* others—to be there for them to encourage and support them. That may involve financial support, but whatever load-lifting we do it shouldn't interfere with a person's facing his or her own responsibilities.

Difficult Verses *from* *the* Book *of* Ephesians

Passage:

This is God's plan. Both Gentiles and Jews who believe in the Good News share equally in the riches inherited by God's children. Both are part of the same body, and both enjoy the promise of blessings because they belong to Christ (Ephesians 3:6).

Difficulty: Since Gentiles receive God's inheritance, does this mean Christians can claim all the promises made to the children of Israel?

Explanation: The "riches inherited by God's children" includes a resurrected new body that will live forever, a recreated heaven and earth, a place of eternal peace where there is no more sin, pain, or suffering, a home where God dwells, and so on (see Matthew 25:31-34; Romans 8; 1 Corinthians 15; Revelation 21). All those who have been redeemed by God and transformed into a relationship with him share in this rich inheritance. However, there are promises given to the children of Israel that are specific to that family.

God made a promise—a covenant—with Abraham that includes God raising up a nation. Through Abraham's descendants he would send a Savior, the Redeemer of the world. The Old Testament is the story of God's faithful and loving relationship with his people, the children of Israel. And so it is understandable that certain promises, conditions, and instructions to Israel would not apply to everyone. God made an "everlasting covenant" with Abraham and promised him and his descendants a land (see Genesis 17:2-8); he promised they would conquer their enemies and through his family "all the nations of the earth will be blessed" (see Genesis 22:16-18); and he foretold they would be scattered but would return to their land (see Ezekiel 47:13-23; Hosea 14:4-7; Amos 8:11-15; Obadiah 19-21; and Zephaniah 3:18-20). So these tangible promises seem to belong specifically to Israel and can of course be considered an inheritance.

However, some believe once Jesus fulfilled the promise of the Messiah, that his body—the church—equally inherited the promises made to Israel. In other words all Christians can now spiritually claim the promises made to Abraham. While there are differences of opinion as to what degree Christians can claim those promises, Scripture does make it clear that every child of God is spiritually born into his family and can claim the inheritance of eternal life in a new heaven and a new earth.

Passage and Difficulty: Ephesians 5:3—Why is the Bible so negatively against sex?

Explanation: See 1 Thessalonians 4:3.

Passage:

Submit to one another out of reverence for Christ. For wives, this means submit to your husbands as to the Lord. For a husband is the head of his wife as Christ is the head of the church (Ephesians 5:21-23).

Difficulty: What does it mean that the husband is the head or the authority of his wife?

Explanation: Some people have used this verse to say the Bible teaches that husbands are to be the "CEO of their home," "the ruler of their house," and "the king of their castle." They imply then that the man is the leader and the woman is the follower—the husband is the boss and the wife is the employee or maybe the executive secretary.

A misunderstanding of the biblical idea of "head" or "authority" has created a distorted concept for many men as to how they are to relate to their wives. Has God established that a husband is to teach, direct, and guide his wife? How much of a say does the wife have in how their home operates? What should the hierarchical structure of a marriage look like according to Ephesians 5?

The mistake many people make in interpreting Ephesians 5 or any passage is taking verses out of context. The context of this passage is Paul explaining how God's people are to praise their Lord for his amazing grace (Ephesians 2:8-9), how he has brought us together as one in his body—the church (Ephesians 2 and 3), how we are to put on a "new nature, created to be like God—truly righteous and holy" (Ephesians 4:24), and how we are to "imitate God, therefore, in everything [we] do" (Ephesians 5:1) by living in the power of his Spirit (Ephesians 5:15-20). Paul is not attempting to give us insights on an authoritative hierarchical structure, but rather on our relationships with each other. He is saying we are now to start acting Godlike, be one in our relationship, and imitate God in all our actions. Then he says, "Submit to one another out of reverence for Christ" (Ephesians 5:21). This admonition is for all of us to submit to one another, not just a certain group of people to submit to those in authority. And Paul is in fact implying that submitting is somehow key to developing a healthy relationship.

Paul then says that wives are to submit to their husbands, "for a husband is the head [authority] of his wife as Christ is the head of the church" (Ephesians 5:23). At first this may not seem very relational. This passage appears to be saying that wives are to submit to the authority figure of their husband, and that doesn't project a picture of a warm and intimate love relationship between husband and wife. For most of us submission isn't viewed as one of our "love languages." And husbands setting themselves up as the one in authority probably isn't attractive to their wives. So how is this passage to be interpreted in light of relational oneness and imitating God?

We get an insight into the relational dimension of authority by looking at how Christ is head of the church. But Jesus' idea of being in authority and how to use the position of leadership is very much different than most commonly thought and taught. Read Jesus' summary of true leadership. He said,

> In this world the kings and great men lord it over their people, yet they are called "friends of the people." But among you it will be different. Those who are the greatest among you should take the lowest rank, and the leader should be like a servant. Who is more important, the one who sits at the table or the one who serves? The one who

> sits at the table, of course. But not here! For I am among you as one who serves (Luke 22:24-27).

Jesus was espousing a whole new concept of authority and leadership. The common worldview was that people are subservient to leaders and those in authority. But Jesus' worldview was that leaders are to serve. Jesus shared this revolutionary concept of how to lead during the Passover meal just before he gave his life for the church. John records him getting up from the meal and starting to wash the disciples' feet just as a servant would do. When he finished he said, "Do you understand what I was doing? You call me 'Teacher' and 'Lord,' and you are right, because that is what I am. And since I, your Lord and Teacher, have washed your feet, you ought to wash each other's feet. I have given you an example to follow. Do as I have done to you" (John 13:12-15).

Then how does a husband exercise his authority or headship? By living out Jesus' worldview on leadership—serving the needs of the wife. This concept of headship as described by Jesus is perhaps difficult for many husbands to grasp. It turns the idea of leading on its head, so to speak. How *do you* effectively lead by serving? How *do you* "call the shots" by taking on the "lowest rank"? This approach is confusing if you try to implement it as a hierarchical structure for marriage. But it really makes sense when you see this in light of developing an intimate relationship with your spouse.

Paul goes on and states in Ephesians 5, "As the Scripture says, 'A man leaves his father and mother and is joined to his wife, and the two are united as one'" (Ephesians 5:31). Paul was quoting Genesis 2:24 which defines one of the primary purposes of marriage—a unity or intimacy factor. Paul concludes by saying, "This is a great mystery, but it is an illustration of the way Christ and the church are one. So again I say, each man must love his wife as he loves himself, and the wife must respect her husband" (Ephesians 5:32-33).

Jesus wants the husband and wife to experience oneness and intimacy in the way that Christ and his people (the church) experience intimacy. Jesus accomplished that by serving the needs of his church. A husband can accomplish that by being a servant leader and meeting the needs of his wife.

When couples truly understand how Jesus exercised his servant leadership for the purpose of expressing his love and experiencing oneness, they are more apt to experience the oneness God intended in marriage. This then "is an illustration of the way Christ and the church are one" (Ephesians 5:32).

Passage:

In the same way, husbands ought to love their wives as they love their own bodies. For a man who loves his wife actually shows love for himself (Ephesians 5:28).

Difficulty: How is this kind of love not a self-serving or selfish love?

Explanation: Paul is admonishing husbands to "love your wives, just as Christ loved the church. He gave up his life for her" (Ephesians 5:25). That is why verse 28 starts out with "In the same way, husbands ought to love their wives." Husbands ought to replicate a sacrificial love, not a selfish one.

But at first blush it does seem odd to say when you love like Christ it is actually like loving yourself. Jesus advocated this kind of love when he said, "Love your neighbor as yourself" (Matthew 27:39) (see full *Explanation* of Matthew 27:37-39).

But this is far from a selfish love. It is a love that looks out for the interest of the other, just like a person looks out for the interests of their own bodies. Paul said, "No one hates his own body but feeds and cares for it" (Ephesians 5:29). In other words, this kind of *love makes the security, happiness, and welfare of another person as important as your own.*

Feed and *care for* are key terms in understanding how a husband is to make the security, happiness, and welfare of his wife as important to him as his own. Just as all of us are concerned and active to make sure our physical, emotional, and spiritual needs are met, so we are to be concerned and active to meet the needs of others, not just our spouses as Paul instructs, but everyone, as Jesus commands elsewhere (see Matthew 27:37-39).

The King James Version uses two beautifully descriptive words in this verse: *nourish* and *cherish*. Just as we are careful to nourish and cherish our own bodies, we are to nourish and cherish others in love.

To *nourish* means to bring to maturity. It pictures the growth of young Jesus in Nazareth as described in Luke: "Jesus grew in wisdom and stature and in favor with God and all the people" (Luke 2:52). To nourish means to care for and contribute to the whole person: relationally, physically, spiritually, and socially. Love is a provider. It requires that we provide for the security, happiness, and welfare of others in order to bring them to maturity, just as we provide for our own security, happiness, and welfare.

To *cherish* means to protect from the elements. Imagine a nest of newborn eaglets high on a mountain crag, exposed to the sky. An angry thunderstorm is rolling in. The mother eagle swoops down to the nest and spreads her wings over the eaglets to protect them from the pounding rain and swirling wind. That's a picture of what it means to cherish.

Ephesians 5:29 tells us that it is natural for us to cherish ourselves, that is, to protect ourselves from anything that may endanger our mental, physical, spiritual, and social well-being. We buckle up and drive safely to prevent physical injury or death on the highway. We monitor our fat and calorie intake to keep our bodies healthy. We learn to turn away when tempted to compromise our obedience to Christ. We stay away from people who are a bad influence on our beliefs or behavior. In short, we generally guard ourselves against anything that negatively affects our lives. Love is a protector as well as a provider.

So for a husband to love his wife like he loves himself means he does whatever he can to *provide for* (nourish) the security, happiness, and welfare of his wife relationally, physically, spiritually, and socially, just as he would provide for himself. And he is to *protect* (cherish) his wife from anything that might detour her from or hinder her maturity, just as he would protect himself.

As we stated earlier, this is the same kind of love Jesus describes in the Great Commandment of Matthew 27. Everyone is to love their neighbor as themselves. So interestingly enough a wife should be loving her closest neighbor—her husband—with a providing and protecting love as well. When two committed married people love each other this way, it creates an intimate bonding and oneness that God designed. Jesus said, "'This explains why a man leaves his father and mother and is joined to his wife, and the two are united into one.' Since they are no longer two but one, let no one split apart what God has joined together" (Matthew 19:5-6).

Passage and Difficulty: Ephesians 6:5—Does the Bible condone or at least allow for the owning of slaves?

Explanation: See Leviticus 25:44-45 and Philemon 15-16.

Difficult Verses *from* *the* Book *of* Philippians

Passage:

Let us therefore, as many as be perfect, be thus minded: and if in anything ye be otherwise minded, God shall reveal even this unto you (Philippians 3:15 KJV).

Difficulty: Are Christians supposed to be perfect?

Explanation: Some Christians tend to be performance-oriented and are perfectionistic in their efforts to please God. So they may be tempted to interpret Philippians 3:15 with perfection as the standard, but that only deepens their frustration, because no one can live perfectly.

Reading verse 15 within context clears up the notion that any of us can reach perfection in this life. Earlier in the chapter Paul says, "I want to know Christ and experience the mighty power that raised him from the dead" (Philippians 3:10). Then he goes on to say, "I don't mean to say that I have already achieved these things or have already reached perfection" (Philippians 3:12). So Paul is admitting he hasn't reached perfection in the Christian life.

With that as a context let's read verse 15 from a different translation that more clearly renders the verse. "Let all who are spiritually mature agree on these things. If you disagree on some points, I believe God will make it plain to you. But we must hold on to the progress we have already made" (Philippians 3:15).

When we trust Christ as our Savior we are transformed from death to life and become a child of God (Romans 8:15-17). Paul talked about being built up so "we will be mature in the Lord, measuring up to the full and complete standard of Christ...growing in every way more and more like Christ" (Ephesians 4:13,15). There is an instant in time when a person is "born" into the family of God and transformed into his child. But that transformation continues in a process of spiritual growth.

Paul wrote in the letter to the Philippians, "I am certain that God, who began the good work within you, will continue his work until it is finally finished on the day when Jesus Christ returns" (Philippians 1:6).

The work has begun in us, but it must be continued day in and day out as God's nature is unleashed through our attitudes and actions. Peter said, "May God give you more and more grace and peace as you grow in your knowledge of God and Jesus our Lord. By his divine power, God has given us everything we need for living a godly life" (2 Peter 1:3).

There is a very important principle here about the transformation process of becoming more and more like Christ. As new followers of Christ we *do* live differently from our old lives. But the doing isn't what continually transforms us. It is living in relationship with Christ and his nature, which is being imparted by and empowered by the Holy Spirit, that continually transforms us. So the process isn't so much in learning to do all the right things perfectly as it is learning who Christ is and acting according to our new nature.

Difficult Verses *from* *the* Book *of* Colossians

Passage:

He [Jesus] is the image of the invisible God, the firstborn of all creation (Colossians 1:15 NASB).

Difficulty: If Jesus was a created being, how could he be the eternal Son of God?

Explanation: Some people, namely the Jehovah's Witnesses, use this verse to teach that Jesus was the first being that God created and therefore could not be the eternal God. They also use Proverbs 8:22-23 to say that Jesus was created (see *Explanation* of Proverbs 8:22-23). That is why they teach that only God, not Jesus, should be worshipped. For additional proof that Jesus is not God they point out that Jesus referred to himself as the Son of Man, not the Son of God (see *Explanation* of Matthew 20:28).

Those that claim Jesus was a created being using Colossians 1:15 grossly misinterpret the passage. Their interpretation that Jesus was a created being is based on the word *firstborn*. They assume the word means "first in order." In other words, Jesus was the first thing God created. But the Greek word used here does not carry such a narrow meaning.

The word *firstborn* in the Greek is *prototokos* and can mean 1) first in order or 2) first in priority; superiority of position. The apostle Paul was not implying that Jesus was the first to be created, but rather that he was the highest priority or supreme over all creation.

Notice in verse 18 Paul uses the same word to say Jesus was "the firstborn from the dead" (Colossians 1:18 NASB). Was Jesus the first to ever be raised from the dead? Of course not. Jesus himself raised Lazarus from the dead (see John 11). The proper interpretation within context again is that Jesus was the supreme one or the most important one to rise from the dead. A more idiomatic and clearer translation of both these verses is made in the New Living Translation: "He [Jesus] existed before anything was created and is supreme over all creation...

He is the beginning, supreme over all who rise from the dead" (Colossians 1:15,18).

Further, when you read verse 15 within context it is clear Jesus couldn't be a created being. Because verse 17 says, "He [Jesus] existed before anything else, and he holds all creation together" (Colossians 1:17). Jesus couldn't have been a created thing as the Jehovah's Witnesses claim if, as this verse states, he existed before anything else, including himself. Other verses that support the correct interpretation of the word *firstborn* are found in Romans 8:29 and Revelation 1:5. (For more on a passage Jehovah's Witnesses use to claim that Jesus was created see *Explanation* of Proverbs 8:22.)

Passage:

Don't let anyone capture you with empty philosophies and high-sounding nonsense that come from human thinking and from spiritual powers of this world, rather than from Christ (Colossians 2:8).

Difficulty: Does this mean it is wrong to study and engage in philosophy?

Explanation: The apostle Paul wrote this letter to the Colossian church primarily because of the false teachings that were circulating there. Colosse was a key commercial center within the region. So the Christians within the Colossian church were no doubt exposed to many philosophies of the day.

Gnosticism was a particular philosophy and teaching that was beginning to develop at the time of Paul's writing. And it was influencing the church. Gnostics espoused dualism: The spiritual was good, while all matter was evil. Salvation for a Gnostic came through a series of spiritual intermediaries that could only be accessed by those with "revealed knowledge." It was this philosophy that Paul was probably referring to, not the study of philosophy in general.

Paul himself was well versed in the philosophies of his day. "He went to the synagogue to reason with the Jews and the God-fearing Gentiles, and he spoke daily in the public square...He also had a debate with some of the Epicurean and Stoic philosophers" (Acts 17:17-18). It was Paul's study and understanding of the philosophies and religions of his day that enabled him to explain why and how the various teachings were false. And today it would be wise for Christians to also study the philosophies and other religions of our time so we will "always be prepared to give an answer to everyone who asks you to give the reason for the hope that you have" (1 Peter 3:15 NIV).

Passage:

> Don't let anyone condemn you for what you eat or drink, or for not celebrating certain holy days or new moon ceremonies or Sabbaths (Colossians 2:16).

Difficulty: Is worshipping together with Christians each week optional?

Explanation: The apostle Paul was addressing Christians, especially Jewish followers of Christ, who were feeling the pressure to continue to observe all the Jewish customs and traditions of Moses. Some Jewish Christians were conducting worship services on the Sabbath. Others were meeting on the first day of the week (the Lord's Day) primarily because that was the day Jesus rose from the grave (see Matthew 28:1). Many were observing both days plus other Jewish festivals and traditions. And Paul was releasing them from those regulations. "These rules," he said, "are only shadows of the reality yet to come. And Christ himself is that reality" (Colossians 2:17). (For more on worshipping on Saturday rather than on Sunday see *Explanation* of Exodus 20:11.)

But Paul by no means was suggesting that believers not meet together as the body of Christ—the church. Paul and the other apostles and traveling teachers were consistently meeting with believers at their gatherings. It was at these church meetings that people were being taught; it was where they prayed for one another, sang together, worshipped together, encouraged one another, understood each other's needs, and so on. Not being a part of these meetings largely meant a person couldn't receive the spiritual and relational support to grow and mature in Christ. That's why the writer of Hebrews said, "Let us not neglect our meeting together, as some people do, but encourage one another, especially now that the day of his return is drawing near" (Hebrews 10:25).

Today's Christians also need the support, encouragement, and teaching of God's Word that comes with attending a church gathering. We certainly have access to more tools than the early church had. There are so many books, so much Christian radio and TV, so many online studies and resources today that can help a person grow spiritually. But none of those tools take the place of personal and relational interaction. That is why Paul said, "Since we are all one body in Christ, we belong to each other, and each of us needs all the others" (Romans 12:5 NLT). Not being connected to other believers is not really an option because we all need one another to grow in our spiritual life.

Passage and Difficulty: Colossians 3:21—How does a father not aggravate his child?

Explanation: See Proverbs 22:6.

Passage:

After you have read this letter, pass it on to the church at Laodicea so they can read it, too. And you should read the letter I wrote to them (Colossians 4:16).

Difficulty: Is there another letter from the apostle Paul that didn't make it into the New Testament?

Explanation: Laodicea was a very important city in the Lycus River valley, which was part of Asia Minor. It was not far from Ephesus and

Colosse. Laodicea had many believers living there. And some scholars believe Paul wrote to these believers as he says in verse 16, but the letter somehow got lost over time. Not being preserved, it would have never come up for consideration as part of the canon of the New Testament.

But the letter Paul is referring to is most likely what we know as Ephesians. Today most translations render Ephesians 1:1 as "I am writing to God's holy people in Ephesus..." But the most ancient manuscripts do not include the words "in Ephesus." Therefore, many scholars believe that the letter originally was meant for a number of the churches in Asia Minor, including Laodicea. And that is the letter Paul was referring to—the one we now know as Ephesians.

It is possible that Paul or other of the apostles did write some letters that were lost. But if you believe that God inspired men to write all that he intended for us to have, then you believe we do in fact have all of God's Word in 66 books of the Bible. For more on what was included and left out of the Bible and why, see *Explanation* of Jude 14.

Difficult Verses *from* *the* Books *of* 1 & 2 Thessalonians

Passage:
God's will is for you to be holy, so stay away from all sexual sin (1 Thessalonians 4:3).

Difficulty: Why is the Bible so negative about sex?

Explanation: Some people view the negative commands of the Bible, especially those related to sexual relationships, as taking all the fun out of life. Actually the reason God says no—"don't do this" or "don't do that"—is for our good. The reason he gives negative commands is to establish boundaries and to provide for us and protect us. Consider Psalm 145. It describes God as a gracious provider and protector. And when it comes to the matter of sex, God also wants to be our Provider and Protector. But to enjoy his provision and protection we must honor the boundaries and prohibitions for sexual behavior. In other words, we must avoid sexual immorality.

In biblical terms, sexual immorality is all sex that occurs outside of a marriage between one man and one woman (extramarital and premarital sex).

Respecting the boundaries of sexual morality does bring protection and provision. Here are just a few.

Protects from

- guilt
- unplanned pregnancy
- sexually transmitted diseases
- sexual insecurity
- emotional distress

Provides for

- spiritual rewards
- optimum atmosphere for child-raising

- peace of mind
- trust
- true intimacy

Sex as God designed it was meant to be lived within the context of healthy boundaries—prohibitions before marriage and fidelity after marriage. Following God's design then allows a couple to experience the beauty of sex as it was meant to be experienced. And it is these boundaries and limits that make the "negatives" such a positive answer.

Passage:

The Lord himself will come down from heaven with a commanding shout...First, the Christians who have died will raise from their graves. Then, together with them, we who are still alive and remain on earth will be caught up in the clouds to meet the Lord in the air. Then we will be with the Lord forever (1 Thessalonians 4:16-17).

Difficulty: If the Christians who have died won't get resurrected bodies until Christ returns, are they existing somewhere consciously without bodies?

Explanation: Some say that Christians who have died are simply "asleep" and will remain in an unconscious state until the return of Christ. Since Paul makes reference to those "who have fallen asleep in him" (1 Thessalonians 4:14 NIV), and other such passages use similar language (see Matthew 9:24; John 11:11; 1 Thessalonians 5:10), some believe we go into what they call a "soul sleep." They say that those in Christ who are "sleeping" will be awakened at the resurrection and receive new bodies.

However, most evangelicals consider the "fallen asleep" phrases in Scripture as euphemisms for death that describe the body's outward appearance. The physical body is "sleeping" until the resurrection, while our nonphysical souls enjoy a conscious existence with the

Lord. The Old Testament declares, "You were made from dust, and to dust you will return" (Genesis 3:19) and "The dust will return to the earth, and the spirit will return to God who gave it" (Ecclesiastes 12:7).

But is this actually a conscious spirit existence with God even before we are bodily resurrected? It would appear so. Jesus told the dying thief on the cross, "I assure you, today you will be with me in paradise" (Luke 23:43). Obviously, the thief wouldn't be getting his spiritual body until Christ returned, yet Jesus said that the man would be with him. Paul said he preferred "to be absent from the body and to be at home with the Lord" (2 Corinthians 5:8 NASB). All the references in Revelation to humans prior to the resurrection of the dead depict them as conscious souls.

As these passages indicate, when Christians die they enter into what theologians refer to as an "intermediate state." This is considered a transitional existence spanning the period between a believer's death and Christ's return, when all who are dead will be bodily resurrected. This moment of resurrection when the spirit is reunited with a transformed body is sometimes referred to as "going to heaven." But there is a difference between an intermediate heaven and the eternal heaven (see *Explanation* of John 14:1-3).

If our souls are with the Lord in an intermediate heaven prior to the resurrection of the dead, do we function as physical human beings during that time? These are issues that Scripture simply doesn't address. Yet theologians such as Randy Alcorn have ventured to say,

> Given the consistent physical description of the intermediate Heaven and those who dwell there, it seems possible—though this is certainly debatable—that between our earthly life and our bodily resurrection, God may grant us some physical form that will allow us to function as human beings while in that unnatural state "between bodies," awaiting our resurrection.[2]

Passage:

Women should learn quietly and submissively. I do not let women teach men or have authority over them. Let them listen quietly (1 Timothy 2:11-12).

Difficulty: Does this passage mean women today are not to hold teaching or ministry positions in the church that teach men?

Explanation: Some today consider the above verses to restrict women from teaching men the truths of Scripture in a church setting. This would mean women would be prohibited from becoming elders or pastors to a congregation in general. Many of those who hold this view would say, however, that women could minister to children and other women. They simply couldn't teach men and overall should not speak in the public service (see *Explanation* of 1 Corinthians 14:34-35).

To properly interpret this passage, as well as any other passage of Scripture, one must understand it within the cultural context of that day. (See "How to Use This Handbook" on page 9.) So before we apply God's truth for the role of women in the church today, it is wise to understand the truth Paul was getting at for his original readers.

Paul had been to Ephesus a number of times to speak and teach at the church there. Timothy had accompanied Paul for much of his ministry in Ephesus. Timothy was tasked with dealing with new and troubling developments there within the church. False teachings were cropping up and Paul was instructing Timothy in his letters on how to deal with it.

Ephesus had the largest temple in Asia Minor that was dedicated to Artemis, the goddess of fertility. Women served as "sacred" priestesses and reportedly fulfilled the role of "sacred" prostitutes.

Alvera Mickelsen, a respected author on women's role in the ancient church, also points out in addition to the influence of the Artemis temple in Ephesus that

> there were also hundreds of *hetaerae*, the most educated of Greek women who were the regular companions and often the extramarital sexual partners of upper-class Greek men. Possibly some of these women had been converted and were wearing their suggestive and expensive clothing to church. Since *hetaerae* were often respected teachers of men in Greece (many are named in Greek literature), they would be more likely to become teachers after they became part of the church.[3]

The false teaching that was prevalent in Ephesus, propagated perhaps by some women, was apparently successful at influencing other women. Paul warned Timothy about these false teachers and said, "They are the kind who work their way into people's homes and win the confidence of vulnerable women" (2 Timothy 3:6). Paul spoke of younger widows with sexual problems (1 Timothy 5:6,11-16), women of weak faith (2 Timothy 3:7), and those with modesty issues (1 Timothy 2:9-10). These women were learning from false teachers and Paul was instructing Timothy to correct it.

With that as a context, it was necessary that "women should learn quietly and submissively" from the orthodox teaching of the men in the church. Women had been "learning in submission" to false teaching, now Paul was instructing that they "learn submissively" to correct teaching. This was Paul's solution to the false teachings and errant living that was becoming prevalent.

Based on the above interpretation, this would not appear to be a timeless prohibition for all women in all churches in every age. Rather it was a directive applicable to the church of Ephesus at the time. The universal truth applicable to us today is that if a person is to teach others they must know what they are talking about. This is the context of Paul's entire letter to Timothy. Notice how Paul sets up his instructions by saying,

> The purpose of my instruction is that all believers would be filled with love that comes from a pure heart, a clear conscience, and genuine faith. But some people have missed the whole point...They want to be known as teachers of the law of Moses, but they don't know what they are talking

about, even though they speak so confidently (1 Timothy 1:5-7).

Additionally, Paul's involvement with women as co-workers in the gospel would have precluded him forbidding *all* women to speak or officially serve in the church. In the church at Philippi, Paul cites two women, Euodia and Syntyche, as his co-workers. He explained that "they worked with me in telling others the Good News. They worked along with Clement and the rest of my co-workers, whose names are written in the Book of Life" (Philippians 4:3).

Paul specifically identifies another woman co-worker in his letter to the believers in Rome. In this case Paul refers to her as a deacon of a specific church. "I commend to you our sister Phoebe, who is a deacon in the church in Cenchrea" (Romans 16:1).

The word translated *deacon* from the Greek is *diakonos,* which in a general sense means "to minister or serve." But it is used here, as it is in 1 Timothy 3:8-13, to refer to those serving in a leadership role or office of the church. Specifically, Phoebe is identified as serving in some important official capacity in the church at Cenchrea. If Paul was against women speaking, teaching, and serving in leadership roles he certainly wouldn't be commending Phoebe to the believers in Rome as a deacon.

Paul also says to "greet Andronicus and Junia, my fellow Jews, who were in prison with me. They are highly respected among the apostles and became followers of Christ before I did" (Romans 16:7). Junia, a woman, was either recognized by Paul as an apostle, an authoritative governor of the churches, or at least exercising certain authority within the church.

Additionally, throughout history God has elevated women to places of authority and godly leadership. So interpreting Paul's injunction to women as temporary would be consistent with the context of Scripture. For example, in the Old Testament women were to be present at the reading of Scripture (Deuteronomy 31:9-13), which was highly honored. Women served at the entrance of the Tabernacle (Exodus 38:8), which was an honorable duty, and they offered sacrifices (Leviticus 12:1-8), which demonstrated God's recognition of the worship rights of women. God appointed Miriam, Moses' sister, as a prophet

(Exodus 15:20-21). Deborah was both a prophet and a judge. She spoke and judged publically in the name of God (Judges 4:4-7). And Huldah equally was a prophet of God. She too spoke on behalf of God (2 Kings 22:14-20). It is clear God did not regard women as inferior and unable to lead and speak for him to both men and women.

Passage and Difficulty: 1 Timothy 5:23—Does the Bible condone alcoholic drinks?

Explanation: See Proverbs 31:6-7 and John 2:9-10.

Passage:

All Scripture is inspired by God and profitable for teaching, for reproof, for correction, for training in righteousness, so that the man of God may be adequate, equipped for every good work (2 Timothy 3:16-17 NASB).

Difficulty: What is the true purpose of Scripture?

Explanation: The English phrase "inspired by God" is translated from the Greek *theopneustos*, which means "God-breathed." God personally "breathed" out his words for a purpose, and this passage gives us three clear reasons he gave Scripture to us. Keep in mind that Paul was referring to the Old Testament in this passage, as the New Testament documents were not yet complete at the time 2 Timothy was written. Yet these truths still apply since Paul is making a general statement about the efficacy of *all* Scripture.

First, Scripture is given to "teach us." The word rendered *teaching* in this passage is the Greek word *didaskalia*, which means "doctrine," or "correct teaching." Paul is telling us that God gave us his Word so we can believe rightly. There is a *doctrinal purpose* for God's Word. His truths actually make up our theology.

Many people shy away from the idea of theology. Yet theology is actually the study of God. So in a sense, we are all "theologians." We all have ideas about who God is and what he is like, though we rarely think of that as knowing "theology." But one of the clear purposes of Scripture is unabashedly theological—to reveal God for who he is. He wants us to know what he is like, how his ways differ from ours, and how he sees life in contrast to how we see it.

Secondly, Paul says here that God gave us his Word "for reproof, for correction." So we can say that the Bible is his way of correcting us when we're wrong and restoring us to living rightly. The Bible is full of teachings in the form of laws, commands, and instructions for living. That is why we can say there is a *behavioral purpose* for God's Word. When the Bible says, "Follow this way," "Avoid those places," "Abstain from those actions," or "Embrace those thoughts," it is instruction in how to live rightly.

God's laws and instructions act as a boundary to tell us what is right and wrong and that living out God's ways is in our best interest. As Moses told the nation of Israel, "Obey the LORD's commands and laws that I am giving you today for your own good" (Deuteronomy 10:13). Obeying God's Word is always in our long-term best interest. It directs us down the correct path of living. King Solomon said that it is God who "guards the paths of the just and protects those who are faithful to him. Then you will understand what is right, just, and fair, and you will find the right way to go" (Proverbs 2:8-9). So the Bible shows us how we are to live.

But there is a third purpose for Scripture that many people miss. The religious leaders of Jesus' time missed it as well. The Pharisees and other religious leaders had seemingly grasped the doctrinal and behavioral purpose of Scripture. But what they failed to do is connect right beliefs and right behavior with right relationships.

The Hebrew Scripture is filled with the connection between truth and relationships. King David said in one of his psalms, "I am always aware of your unfailing love, and I have lived according to your truth" (Psalm 26:3). He prayed, "Teach me your ways, O LORD, that I may live according to your truth!" (Psalm 86:11). The Old Testament writers understood truth within the context of relationships. When Jesus quoted the greatest of commands to love God and others in Matthew

22 he was framing doctrinal beliefs and obedience within the context of relationship. He was proclaiming that there was a *relational purpose* for God's Word.

In 2 Timothy it says the third purpose of Scripture is "for training in righteousness" (2 Timothy 3:16). The word *training* is translated from the Greek word *paideia*—to "bring up," as in to "raise" or "parent" a child. This passage suggests that God's Word is designed to "parent" us.

But how? How can a set of words in a book "raise" us? Parenting is a person-to-person function. Jesus explains how the Word of God in fact does that. He said, "I will ask the Father, and he will give you another Advocate, who will never leave you. He is the Holy Spirit, who leads into all truth" (John 14:16-17). It is God the Father who has sent his Holy Spirit to "parent" us. The Holy Spirit comes to show us God himself and his truth in the words he has written. He helps us understand who God wants us to be and how he wants us to love and live.

Scripture was given to "parent" us by the Holy Spirit. But not by just directions, instructions, and "behavioral guidelines." These things don't raise us any more than they raise children. Parents—relational human beings—are the ones that raise children. That is the way God designed it. He wants kids to be brought up through loving relationship. Without relationship, all attempts to instill values, beliefs, and right behaviors will be ineffective because they are detached from the necessary elements of personal love and care. Truth without relationship leads to rejection, and discipline or correction without relationship leads to anger and resentment. But when you place truth within the context of a loving relationship, you almost always get a positive response.

The Holy Spirit administers Scripture to us like a loving parent in order to provide us with wisdom through its lessons (Proverbs 3:5), security through its boundaries (Exodus 20), caution through its warnings (Ephesians 4:17-22), and reproof through its discipline (Philippians 2:3-4). We may study God's Word for correct beliefs. We may even obey it for right behavior. But we must not forget why. The relational God of the Bible wants us to relationally experience his love and the love of those around us. We can then say that *God gave us the Bible so we can relationally love him, know his ways, be like him, live and love like him, and enjoy all the benefits that relationship offers.* (For more information on how to experience and study your Bible check out *Experience Your Bible* by Josh McDowell and Sean McDowell, described in the back pages of this book.)

Difficult Verses *from* the Book *of* Titus

Passage:

Appoint elders in every city as I directed you, namely, if any man is above reproach, the husband of one wife, having children who believe, not accused of dissipation or rebellion (Titus 1:5-6 NASB).

Difficulty: Are people who are divorced today unable to become leaders in the church?

Explanation: In Paul's first missionary journey he visited the island of Crete. He planted a church there but did not appoint leaders. It was clear that the community of believers was being negatively influenced by false teachings. So Paul sent Titus to establish decisive and mature leadership within the infant church in Crete. This letter was to Titus.

Within that context Paul wanted to be sure the most mature and capable teachers of the true faith were leading the churches there. That is why he set a very high standard for those church leaders—he wanted to counter those coming into the church that had been predisposed to false teachings. The list of elder qualifications was stringent: a blameless life, faithful to his wife (literally, the husband of one wife), children that were not rebellious, not arrogant or quick-tempered, nor a heavy drinker, not violent or dishonest with money, hospitable; he must live wisely and justly, be devout and disciplined, have strong beliefs in the true faith that he was taught, and have the ability to communicate the message with confidence and not be intimidated by those who oppose him.

This is still wise counsel today for someone who is going to lead an unestablished church where the people who are attending have been influenced by false doctrine. It makes sense that in those kinds of situations a leader needs to live up to a higher standard than some others. But does every leader in the church need to be held to this high standard today? There are levels of leadership that no doubt require different levels of qualification. A person leading a choir or musical group in church would naturally require a different level of maturity and leadership than one conducting a couple's class on marriage, a doctrinal class on the atonement, or a discipleship class on how to study and interpret Scripture. It would be wise to choose leaders that match the maturity and spiritual understanding of the task required.

Difficult Verses *from* *the* Book *of* Philemon

Passage:

It seems Onesimus ran away for a little while so that you could have him back forever. He is no longer like a slave to you. He is more than a slave, for he is a beloved brother, especially to me (Philemon 15-16).

Difficulty: Does the Bible condone or at least allow for the owning of a slave?

Explanation: This entire letter from Paul to Philemon centers on Onesimus, who was no doubt Philemon's runaway slave. Onesimus had come in contact with Paul and became a believer.

Paul wrote this letter from prison and had Onesimus deliver it to Philemon. This was much like a recommendation of Onesimus to Philemon along with instructions on how each of us are to forgive, accept, and treat one another, regardless of economic, ethnic, gender, or social standing.

So Paul knew Onesimus was a slave, yet he didn't explicitly call for his freedom. Does this mean Paul and the whole of the Bible condoned slavery?

Slavery during the first century was widespread. The Roman world was almost entirely dependent on slave labor. It appears that Paul, along with most early Christians, accepted the traditional structure of their society. What was radically different about Christianity and these followers of Christ was their worldview.

Paul and the other apostles reflected a view of life propagated by Jesus, which was equally a part of the Old Testament worldview. That view of the world—a biblical worldview—included that humans were created in God's image and as such each individual was a person of dignity, value, and worth.

Jesus said, "Do to others whatever you would like them to do to you. This is the essence of all that is taught in the law and the prophets" (Matthew 7:12). This treatment of others based upon how we want to be treated was the essence of all the law of the Old Testament. The word *law* that Jesus used was the Greek word *nomos*, which is a noun meaning a governing principle or set of rules that creates a system or way of dealing with life. Jesus was saying his entire worldview and that of all of Scripture focused on loving God and loving others as yourself. He repeated this worldview later by saying specifically to 1) love God with your everything, and 2) love your neighbor as yourself. Again he said, "The entire law and all the demands of the prophets are based on these two commands" (Matthew 22:40).

So while slavery was an accepted norm in the culture of the Old Testament and during the first century, the law of love addressed how to treat others. In the Old Testament God's command to the children of Israel was specific: "Do not take advantage of foreigners [slaves] who live among you in your land. Treat them like native-born Israelites, and love them as you love yourself" (Leviticus 19:33-34). These slaves were to be considered more as employees by Israel rather than as property to be mistreated. "You must not mistreat or oppress foreigners in any way," the Scripture told Israel, "Remember, you yourselves were once foreigners [slaves] in the land of Egypt" (Exodus 22:21). (For more on the Old Testament view of slavery see the *Explanation* of Leviticus 25:44-45.)

As a Jew, Paul was well versed in the law. And when he became a transformed Christ-follower he emphasized over and over again how we are to treat one another as people of dignity, value, and worth. He wrote, "Are you a slave? Don't let that worry you—but if you get a chance to be free, take it. And remember, if you were a slave when the Lord called you, you are now free in the Lord" (1 Corinthians 7:21-22). Paul then emphasized what the new Christians, slave or free, were to do with that freedom:

> You have been called to live in freedom, my brothers and sisters. But don't use your freedom to satisfy your sinful nature. Instead, use your freedom to serve one another in love. For the whole law can be summed up in this one command: "Love your neighbor as yourself" (Galatians 5:13-14).

As far as Paul's worldview was concerned there was "no longer Jew or Gentile, slave or free, male and female. For you are all one in Christ" (Galatians 3:28). In other words with a biblical worldview there was to be no discrimination regarding gender, economic or social standing, free or slave—everyone was to be treated as they wanted to be treated.

While Paul didn't explicitly call for Philemon to liberate Onesimus, he did hint at it. "So if you consider me your partner," he wrote Philemon, "welcome him as you would welcome me. If he has wronged you in any way or owes you anything, charge it to me" (Philemon 17-18).

No one knows exactly what happened to Onesimus the slave. The name Onesimus did show up in a letter by Ignatius, a Christian martyr some 50 or 60 years later. He was referred to as a well-respected bishop of the entire province of Asia. This may have been the same person. If it was it reinforces the point that God is a champion of social justice. (For more on the biblical view of social justice see *Explanation* of Amos 2:6-7.)

We do know when it came to the cruel practice of human trafficking, Paul was outspoken. When forming a list of vile evildoers he identifies "people who are sexually immoral, or who practice homosexuality, or are slave traders, liars, promise breakers..." (1 Timothy 1:10). So from a biblical worldview perspective the mistreatment of others is wrong on every level, including enslaving others and denigrating their value, dignity, and worth as individuals created in the image of God.

(For more on the issue of slavery in the Bible see chapter 11 of *Is God Just a Human Invention?* by Sean McDowell and Jonathan Morrow, described in the back pages of this book.)

General Letters

Hebrews–Revelation

Passage:

Because God's children are human beings—made of flesh and blood—the Son also became flesh and blood. For only as a human being could he die, and only by dying could he break the power of the devil, who had the power of death. Only in this way could he set free all who have lived their lives as slaves to the fear of dying (Hebrews 2:14-15).

Difficulty: Is there any scientific proof that there is life after death?

Explanation: This passage explains that as humans we are slaves to death and we all will die. But Jesus took on human form to break the power of death so we could have eternal life after death. As Christians we accept the biblical testimony for life after death. And yet it is interesting that every culture from the very dawning of civilization has believed in a life beyond the grave, a life in which some type of soul survives the death of the body. Why is it that a belief in the afterlife has been affirmed almost universally among every culture in history?

It seems clear that we humans instinctively sense that there is a life after death because it has been implanted deeply within our hearts. Wise King Solomon said that God "has planted eternity in the human heart, but even so, people cannot see the whole scope of God's work from beginning to end" (Ecclesiastes 3:11). Though humans cannot see into the next life, the vast majority believe it's there, and they have believed that since the dawn of time.

Additionally there are stories of people who have seemed to peer into the next life and come back to tell of it. These stories are referred to people having "near-death experiences."

Pam Reynolds had little option left. She had an aneurysm on her brain stem that could not be removed through conventional medical procedures. So she chose an experimental procedure called "cardiac standstill." Surgeons put her under general anesthesia to get her brain into a nonresponsive state. Then they lowered her body temperature to 60 degrees, stopped her heart to prevent blood flow to her brain, and put her into a "clinically dead" state.

With blood drained from Pam's brain, surgeons quickly removed the aneurysm and brought her back from the brink of death. *USA Today* featured the story in a June 22, 2009, article titled "The God Choice."[1] The article quoted Pam as saying she consciously left her body and witnessed the entire operation from above the surgeons. She was able to describe intimate details of the operating room procedure, including how many surgeons and attendants were involved. She described the Midas Rex bone saw used to cut open her skull, the drill bits, blade containers, and so on. She was also able to relay specific details of conversation between the surgeons she overheard. All the details were confirmed from the official hospital records. The doctors had no scientific explanation for Pam's "out of body" experience.

In his book *Life After Death: The Evidence,* Dinesh D'Souza references thousands of documented near-death experiences that reach as far back as the writings of Plato, 300 years before Christ. In recent times, the International Association for Near Death Studies was founded to study the phenomenon and has gathered a wide body of data from around the world. "Near death research," D'Souza points out, "now involves separate tracks of inquiry into the various categories of the near death experience—the out of body phenomenon, the tunnel of darkness, the bright light, the sensation of love and warmth, the life review, and the subsequent life transformation. What emerges from this work is how vivid and real these experiences are to the people who have them."[2]

Yet we agree that while near-death experiences may refute the position held by some who say, "Nothing exists after death," they still do not provide empirical evidence that the soul is immortal or indicate what the afterlife is really like. Some would contend, like the apostle Thomas after the resurrection, that they will not believe until they see better proof. And of course Jesus provided such proof.

The apostle Paul talked about the fact that as Christians we are pitted against "evil rulers and authorities of the unseen world" (Ephesians 6:12). He is speaking here of a world on a dimension that is real yet invisible to us humans. And after Jesus died and rose from the grave, he demonstrated his ability to pass from the "seen world" into this "unseen world" at will (see Luke 24:13-16).

Jesus had a real body that could move from the physical dimension in which we exist into an unseen physical dimension—the "unseen world" that Ephesians 6 refers to. Scripture reliably documents what the disciples saw and what Jesus did and said after he rose from the dead. That alone enables us to believe with confidence there is life after death as Jesus promised.

Passage:

With his own blood—not the blood of goats and calves—he entered the Most Holy Place once for all time and secured our redemption forever (Hebrews 9:12).

Difficulty: Did Jesus actually offer himself in heaven as a sacrifice for our sins?

Explanation: God gave Moses very specific instructions on building the Tabernacle along with the ark of the covenant, the altar of burnt offering, the Most Holy Place where God would reside, and so on (see Exodus chapters 25–30). The high priest would go into the Most Holy Place once a year and offer the blood of an animal. This was on the Day of Atonement. But what the Jewish high priest did was simply an illustration of what one day would happen literally.

The earthly priests and the earthly Tabernacle were to "serve in a system of worship that is only a copy, a shadow of the real one in heaven. For when Moses was getting ready to build the Tabernacle, God gave him this warning: 'Be sure that you make everything according to the pattern I have shown you here on the mountain'" (Hebrews 8:5).

What Moses built was a replica of what exists in the dwelling place of God. Hebrews is telling us there is a literal Tabernacle, with a literal altar that houses the real ark of the csovenant with "the cherubim of divine glory, whose wings stretched out over the ark's cover, the place of atonement" (Hebrews 9:5).

Just as the priests of old took the sin offering into the holy Tabernacle and made a sacrifice to God to redeem the people,

> so Christ has now become the High Priest over all good things that have come. He has entered that greater, more perfect Tabernacle in heaven, which was not made by human hands and is not part of this created world. With his own blood—not the blood of goats and calves—he entered the Most Holy Place once for all time and secured our redemption forever (Hebrews 9:11-12).

The book of Hebrews gives us this picture of Jesus, our great High Priest, entering the Temple before his Father God to "once for all time… remove sin forever by his death as a sacrifice" (Hebrews 9:26). What the priests of the Old Testament did as they sacrificed animals year after year in order to atone for sin was a continuing, ritualistic picture foreshadowing the real sacrifice to come. The true sacrifice was completed in Jesus' final act as High Priest when he "offered himself to God as a single sacrifice for sins, good for all time. Then he sat down in the place of honor at God's right hand" (Hebrews 10:12).

This underscores the absolute necessity of Jesus' bodily resurrection, because there was the need of a holy and blameless High Priest to offer the Holy Lamb on the altar before God. For if Jesus did not break the power of death over his own body by rising to life, he could not enter the Most Holy Place, offer himself on our behalf, and cancel our death sentence. Jesus' bodily resurrection was a historical and literal necessity.

"Because God's children are human beings—made of flesh and blood—the Son also became flesh and blood. For only as a human being could he die, and only by dying could he break the power of the devil, who had the power of death" (Hebrews 2:14). Jesus had to rise physically, bodily, from the dead "so that he could be our merciful and faithful High Priest before God. He then could offer a sacrifice that would take away the sins of the people" (Hebrews 2:17).

That is one of the reasons why Paul the apostle was so emphatic about the bodily resurrection of Jesus being the foundation of our faith. He said, "If Christ has not been raised, then all our preaching is useless, and your faith is useless" (1 Corinthians 15:14). Jesus' promise to forgive us of our sins and be the atoning sacrifice that would allow us to have a relationship with God was based, not only upon his death, but also upon his resurrection. Because as a risen High Priest, "with his own blood...he entered the Most Holy Place [in heaven] once for all time and secured our redemption forever" (Hebrews 9:12).

Passage:

Marriage should be honored by all, and the marriage bed kept pure (Hebrews 13:4 NIV).

Difficulty: What does it mean for a husband and wife to keep their marriage bed pure?

Explanation: Keeping the marriage bed pure has nothing to do with sanitary procedures or abiding by certain limits and guidelines on sexual intercourse techniques. Hebrews 13:4 is referring to a sexual purity before and after marriage. But what does it really mean to be sexually pure?

Have you ever had a candy bar that identified itself on the wrapper as "pure milk chocolate"? What about a jar of honey? Some labels read, "Pure honey—no artificial sweeteners." Purity of a substance like chocolate or honey means there is no foreign substance to contaminate it or to keep it from being what authentic chocolate or pure honey is supposed to taste like.

To be pure sexually is to "live according to God's original design," without anything coming in to ruin his authentic, perfect plan for sex. Sex was designed to be expressed between a husband and a wife. To have more than one sexual partner—whether physically or through the use of pornography—is to bring a foreign substance into the relationship and make it cease to be pure. If you were to drop a dirty pebble into a glass of pure water, it would become adulterated—or impure. A glass of water without any impurities in it is an unadulterated glass of water. God wants our sex lives to be unadulterated.

God's design is that sex be experienced within an unbroken circle, a pure union between a man and a woman entering into an exclusive relationship. That pure union can be broken even *before* marriage if one or both of the partners has not kept the marriage bed pure by waiting to have sex until it can be done in the purity of the husband–wife relationship. When we remain sexually pure before marriage and after marriage, we can enjoy the protection and provision of sex and experience it as it was meant to be experienced. (For more on the biblical view of sex see *Explanation* of 1 Thessalonians 4:3.)

Difficult Verses *from* *the* Book *of* James

Passage:

Look here, you rich people: Weep and groan with anguish because of all the terrible troubles ahead of you (James 5:1).

Difficulty: Is it wrong to be rich?

Explanation: Jesus said, "I tell you the truth, it is very hard for a rich person to enter the Kingdom of Heaven" (Matthew 19:23). Why is that? It is hard for a rich person to enter the kingdom because riches tend to consume the heart of the rich. But it is not what we possess materially that is the problem; it is what possesses us. When possessions take hold of us and become our master, riches become a problem.

Jesus said, "Don't store up treasures here on earth...Store your treasures in heaven...No one can serve two masters. For you will hate one and love the other; you will be devoted to one and despise the other. You cannot serve both God and money" (Matthew 6:19-20,24). It is apparent then if a rich person didn't make riches his or her master, being rich materially wouldn't be wrong. Jesus said, "Use your worldly resources to benefit others and make friends. Then, when your earthly possessions are gone, they will welcome you to an eternal home" (Luke 16:9).

What James is condemning is the misuse of riches. "You have spent your years on earth in luxury, satisfying your every desire" (James 5:5), he writes. Jesus taught that it was in giving that we receive, and what we try to keep for ourselves we lose. "If you try to hang on to your life, you will lose it. But if you give up your life for my sake, you will save it. And what do you benefit if you gain the whole world but are yourself lost or destroyed?" (Luke 9:24-25).

So if one accumulates material wealth and recognizes that it belongs to God and uses it accordingly he or she is following Jesus' worldview to "seek the Kingdom of God above all else, and live righteously, and he will give you everything you need" (Matthew 6:33).

Passage:

Above all, my brothers, do not swear—not by heaven or by earth or by anything else. All you need to say is a simple "Yes" or "No." Otherwise you will be condemned (James 5:12 NIV).

Difficulty: Is it wrong to take an oath, as when we "swear to tell the truth" in court?

Explanation: James is essentially repeating what Jesus taught in Matthew 5:33-37, to not take an oath. This wasn't a prohibition of committing to tell the truth, rather an improper practice of swearing that something was true when in fact a person was using the oath to deceive another. People still do that today. When someone is confronted with a wrong a person might say, "I swear on my mother's grave I didn't do it." The person is often hoping the oath or swearing will convince you he or she is telling the truth, when in fact he or she is using it to try to deceive you.

What James and Jesus were saying was to merely be honest and let your "yes" be an honest yes or let your "no" be an honest no. Honest oath-taking was done in the Old Testament with God's blessing in Deuteronomy 6:13, with an angel in Revelation 10:6, and by God himself in Genesis 22:16-17. Paul swore a mild oath in his second letter to the Corinthian church when he said, "I call upon God as my witness that I am telling the truth" (2 Corinthians 1:23). This is what we, in essence, do when giving a promise in court to "tell the truth, the whole truth, and nothing but the truth, so help me God." We promise to be truthful and don't use the oath in an effort to be deceitful.

Difficult Verses *from the* Books *of* 1 & 2 Peter

Passage:

Christ...died for sins once for all, the just for the unjust, in order that He might bring us to God, having been put to death in the flesh, but made alive in the spirit (1 Peter 3:18 NASB).

Difficulty: Was Jesus simply made "alive in the spirit"—having a spiritual resurrection as the Jehovah's Witnesses contend instead of being bodily resurrected?

Explanation: There are those today who claim that Jesus' body decayed in the grave and his real resurrection was a spiritual one. Jehovah's Witnesses espouse a form of this theory. Rather than believing that Jesus' body decayed in the grave, however, they believe that God destroyed the body in the tomb and that Jesus rose in an immaterial body. Both of these "spiritual resurrection" theories have insurmountable problems.

Jesus himself defeated the spiritual-resurrection theory. When his startled disciples thought they were seeing a spirit, Jesus admonished them, "See My hands and My feet, that it is I Myself; touch Me and see, for a spirit does not have flesh and bones as you see that I have" (Luke 24:39 NASB). Later, Christ ate fish with his followers, further demonstrating his flesh-and-bone mode of existence. Matthew records that when the disciples met Jesus they took hold of his feet and worshipped him (see Matthew 28:9). You don't grab the legs of a spirit! Some have argued that Jesus temporarily manifested himself in a physical body so the disciples would recognize him. While this is a creative response, it is arbitrary—and what is worse, it would involve deception on Jesus' part, which is clearly inconsistent with his character and nature.

Paul also refuted the spiritual-resurrection theory in his discussion of the resurrection body in 1 Corinthians 15:29-58. As a former Pharisee, Paul firmly believed in a physical resurrection. Basing his theology on the resurrection of Christ, Paul argues that we too will be physically raised someday. While our resurrected bodies are physically different from our current bodies, the difference involves enhancement; they are still thoroughly physical.

Some have disagreed with this interpretation of this passage, basing their argument on Paul's claim in 1 Corinthians 15:44 that "it is sown a *natural* body, it is raised a *spiritual* body" (NIV). They claim that Paul believed in an immaterial resurrection. What this objection fails to consider is that the word *spiritual*, in this context, does not connote *immaterial*. We often refer to the Bible as a "spiritual" book, yet we clearly don't mean that it is immaterial!

Author and researcher Michael Licona did a quite exhaustive historical investigation of the Greek terms translated *natural* and *spiritual* in 1 Corinthians 15:44. After searching ancient texts from the eighth century BC through the third century AD he concluded, "Although I did not look at all of the 846 occurrences, I viewed most. I failed to find a single reference where *psuchikon* [the word translated *natural* in 15:44] possessed a meaning of 'physical' or 'material.'"[3] It is simply incorrect to assume that Paul was contrasting a physical body with a nonphysical body.

Others object to a physical resurrection because in 1 Corinthians 15:50 Paul says that "flesh and blood cannot inherit the kingdom of God." They believe that Jesus' body had to be immaterial so he could be in heaven. But the phrase, "flesh and blood," in this context is referring to *mortal* flesh and blood, or a mere human being. This interpretation is supported throughout Scripture. For example, in Matthew 16:17 Jesus says, "Blessed are you, Simon Barjona, because *flesh and blood* did not reveal this to you, but My Father who is in heaven" (NASB).

For Jesus' resurrection to be relevant to his promise that we will be resurrected, he had to have been bodily resurrected. Because when Christ returns he not only plans to resurrect us into real bodies; he will restore this material earth to his original design. For God plans "to bring to unity all things in heaven and on earth under Christ" (Ephesians 1:10 NIV). We will then reign with him, not spiritually, but literally (see *Explanation* of Revelation 21:5-7 of what Christians will eternally inherit from God).

Passage:

The gospel has for this purpose been preached even to those who are dead, that though they are judged in the flesh as men, they may live in the spirit according to the will of God (1 Peter 4:6 NASB).

Difficulty: Can non-Christians be saved after they die?

Explanation: Is this passage suggesting there is some type of purgatory? Does this mean that after a person dies he or she might still get another chance?

The writer of the book of Hebrews made it clear that "each person is destined to die once and after that comes judgment" (Hebrews 9:27). So it is unlikely Peter is explaining that the dead have a second chance of repentance. He is saying that the gospel "has been preached" (past tense) to those "who are dead" (present tense). A clearer translation reads, "That is why the Good News was preached to those who are now dead—so although they were destined to die like all people, they now live forever with God in the Spirit" (1 Peter 4:6). This then means people who have died had the gospel preached to them so they would be saved.

However, some scholars believe this passage might be referring to Christ offering salvation following his death to those who died accepting the blood sacrifices of the Old Testament. This interpretation sees Jesus preaching to those who had died observing the Levitical sacrificial system and explaining to them that such sacrifices were based upon him being the perfect Lamb of God. Others tie this passage to 1 Peter 3:19 that indicates Jesus "went and preached to the spirits in prison—those who disobeyed God long ago when God waited patiently while Noah was building his boat" (1 Peter 3:19-20). But scholars point out that these verses still do not claim that Jesus offered salvation or "evangelized" the unrepentant dead. Some contend that he preached or announced the victory of his resurrection but with no opportunity to repent.

Passage:

This letter is from Simon Peter, a slave and apostle of Jesus Christ (2 Peter 1:1).

Difficulty: Did Peter actually write 2 Peter?

Explanation: Because the letter of 2 Peter is different in style and tone from 1 Peter, some interpreters believe that Peter didn't write it at all. They assert that someone else probably wrote 2 Peter in his name.

First, Peter is dealing with a very different subject matter than in his first letter. That would account for a language shift. Also in his first letter he says, "I have written and sent this short letter to you with the help of Silas" (1 Peter 5:12). Silas apparently helped write the letter and so his writing style could account for the differences between 1 and 2 Peter. Either Peter wrote his second letter himself or used a different secretary. Whatever the case, the book of 2 Peter is ascribed to Peter and many scholars believe him to be the rightful author.

Passage:

God did not spare even the angels who sinned. He threw them into hell, in gloomy pits of darkness, where they are being held until the day of judgment (2 Peter 2:4).

Difficulty: If fallen angels (demons) are in hell, how can they tempt people today?

Explanation: Peter's reference to "the angels who sinned" might be referring to only a small group of angels. As early as AD 500 writers of ancient and Jewish literature held to the view that the "sons of God" described in Genesis 6:2-4 were actually fallen angels. These "sons of God" took wives from the daughters of man and produced the

Nephilites, who were giants. And some scholars believe that these "sons of God" are the "angels who sinned" that Peter is referring to.

Jude elaborates on this view when he writes, "I remind you of the angels who did not stay within the limits of authority God gave them but left the place where they belonged. God has kept them securely chained in prisons of darkness, waiting for the great day of judgment" (Jude 6). A detailed explanation of this view is found in 1 Enoch chapters 7–10. According to this writing there were 200 such angels that came to earth and had intercourse with the "daughters of men" (see 1 Enoch 7:1-7). (For more on the book of Enoch and other writings that are not part of the canon of Scripture see *Explanation* of Jude 14.)

Jude later does quote from Enoch. So it is probable that he and perhaps Peter were referring to these "sons of God" mentioned in Genesis 6 as the angels that God "chained in prisons of darkness." This view would leave many more fallen angels or demons who are not yet chained and are presently fighting against Christians. Paul states that we are not fighting against a human enemy "but against evil rulers and authorities of the unseen world, against mighty powers in this dark world, and against evil spirits in the heavenly places" (Ephesians 6:12).

Other scholars believe that Peter is possibly referring to the ultimate judgment of fallen angels, which hasn't yet been handed down. In other words, they can still operate together with Satan, who maintains power and control of this world (1 John 5:19), but are awaiting a final judgment in which the devil and his demons will be bound forever (Revelation 20:10).

Passage:

The Lord isn't really being slow about his promise [to return], as some people think. No, he is being patient for your sake. He does not want anyone to be destroyed, but wants everyone to repent...And remember, our Lord's patience gives people time to be saved (2 Peter 3:9,15).

Difficulty: Is Christ deliberately delaying his return so that more people will be saved?

Explanation: Jesus told his disciples that he was going to prepare a place for them and "when everything is ready, I will come and get you, so that you will always be with me where I am" (John 14:3). And then after Jesus was crucified and rose again, his disciples asked, "Lord, has the time come for you to free Israel and restore our kingdom?" (Acts 1:6).

The disciples of course were thinking of God's kingdom being established then, in the first century. But Jesus ascended into heaven, and angels told the disciples that "someday he will return from heaven in the same way you saw him go!" (Acts 1:11). And Jesus never did explain to them when he would return or what specific conditions had to be met before he would come back and set up his eternal kingdom.

Peter does, however, suggest a condition for Christ's return. He first introduced this condition when preaching right after Pentecost. He was urging people to repent and added, "Then times of refreshment will come from the presence of the Lord, and he will again send you Jesus, your appointed Messiah" (Acts 3:20). Here Peter seems to link Jesus' return with people repenting.

In 2 Peter a similar linkage is made between Christ's return and living godly. "Since everything around us is going to be destroyed like this, what holy and godly lives you should live, looking forward to the day of God and hurrying it along" (2 Peter 3:11-12). The writer seems to suggest we can hurry Christ's return by being living witnesses of holiness and godliness. And he further suggests that God is waiting to give "people time to be saved" (2 Peter 3:15).

Studies do confirm that the longer Christ waits to return, the more people are coming to him. Research by Operation World reported in the book *Perspectives* shows that by 1887, after 100 years of Christian missionary work around the world, there were 3 million Protestant converts out of a world population of a billion and a half. Today, over 100 years later, those numbers have dramatically changed.

Christianity may have declined as a proportion of the West's population, but this is not so in other major population areas of the world. For example, in 1900 there were 8 million Christians in Africa; by 2000 there were 351 million. Christianity has now become the major religion across sub-Saharan Africa. In 1900 there were 22 million Christians in Asia; by 2005 there were around 370 million. From 1900 to

2000, evangelicals in Latin America grew from about 700,000 to over 55 million. And more Muslims are turning to Christ in the Middle East than at any other time in history. The 2006 Operation World report summarized it thus:

> Evangelical Christianity is currently the fastest growing religious movement in the world today. Evangelical growth represents more than double the growth rate of the next closest religion (Islam) and more than triple the world's population growth rate.[4]

Does this mean that as long as the earth is being populated and people are coming to Christ, God will wait to bring an end to it all? We don't know. But God does, and it seems he has chosen not to fully explain when he is returning. Jesus said, "The Father alone has the authority to set those dates and times, and they are not for you to know" (Acts 1:7). But we do know we are to continue to be faithful and, as Jesus said, "Be my witnesses, telling people about me everywhere" (Acts 1:8).

Difficult Verses *from* *the* Books *of* 1, 2, & 3 John

Passage:

There are three who bear witness in heaven: the Father, the Word, and the Holy Spirit; and these three are one (1 John 5:7 NKJV).

Difficulty: Does the fact that this reference to the Trinity cannot be found in any of the early Greek manuscripts mean that the doctrine of the Trinity is not biblical?

Explanation: It is true that the early Greek manuscripts did not include this longer version of verse 7. The longer addition showed up in some Latin editions, including later copies of the Latin Vulgate. Eventually Erasmus incorporated it into the Greek Textus Receptus, which is why the King James and New King James translations include it.

So it is true that this longer version of the verse is not recognized by scholars as part of the authentic text. But this does not mean the Trinity is not taught elsewhere in the Scriptures. However, groups like the Jehovah's Witnesses, the United Church of God, and other organizations use this improper inclusion as evidence that the Trinity was an "add-on" doctrine, introduced by certain church leaders wanting to push their ideology of a Triune God.

Various groups today assert that the Scripture teaches that "the LORD our God, the LORD is one" (Deuteronomy 6:4 NIV) and not three persons existing as one being.

The Jehovah's Witnesses contend that God the Father is eternal but Jesus was the first in God's creation (see *Explanation* of Colossians 1:15). Others who equally don't believe in the Trinity, like the Apostolic Church, claim the Bible does not teach that the one God exists in three Persons. They contend there are three manifestations of only one God. In other words, the Father, Jesus the Son, and the Holy Spirit are all the same person, who simply manifests himself in different forms.

The doctrine of the Trinity is not an "add-on" idea. Christians have taught the doctrine that God is a triune Godhead—one God in three persons—from the first century on. Scripture teaches that God has always existed as three divine Persons.

Jesus is the divine Son of God. This does not mean that Jesus was created by God. In fact, Scripture tells us plainly that he has always co-existed with God (see John 1:1-3). Jesus himself declared he had eternally co-existed with his Father God. And on the basis of that declaration the Jewish leaders plotted to kill him. They said that "he called God his Father, thereby making himself equal with God" (John 5:18). Paul the apostle declared Jesus to be deity. "Christ himself was an Israelite as far as his human nature is concerned. And he is God, who rules over everything and is worthy of eternal praise!" (Romans 9:5). The writer of Hebrews says, "The Son radiates God's own glory and expresses the very character of God" (Hebrews 1:3).

Therefore, God the Father co-exists with God the Son and it was the Son who created everything.

> Christ is the visible image of the invisible God. He existed before God made anything at all and is supreme over all creation, for through him God created everything in the heavenly realms and on earth...He existed before everything else, and he holds all creation together (Colossians 1:15-17).

The apostle Paul refers to both the Father and Jesus as God. "It is by the command of God our Savior that I have been entrusted with this work for him...May God the Father and Christ Jesus our Savior give you grace and peace" (Titus 1:3-4). God the Father is deity. God the Son is deity.

God the Holy Spirit is also deity. The apostle Peter recognized this when he pointed out the wrongdoing of a man in the Jerusalem church. He said: "Ananias, why have you let Satan fill your heart? You lied to the Holy Spirit...You weren't lying to us but to God!" (Acts 5:3-4). The Spirit has eternally co-existed with the Father and the Son and was present at creation (see Genesis 1:2). Jesus said, "I will ask the Father, and he will give you another Advocate...He is the Holy Spirit, who leads into all truth...When the Father sends the Advocate as my representative—that is, the Holy Spirit—he will teach you everything" (John 14:16,17,26). Paul said, "When you believed in Christ, he identified you as his own by giving you the Holy Spirit, whom he promised long ago" (Ephesians 1:13). Jesus called his co-existing Spirit holy because he is the Spirit of the Holy God. The Holy Spirit is the third Person of the triune Godhead.

The Scriptures quoted above tell us clearly that God is not merely one God with three different roles or relationships. He is one God in three Persons interacting both with each other and with us. God the Father is a distinct Person. God the Son is a distinct Person. And God the Holy Spirit is a distinct Person.

We have clear evidence that Jesus, God's Son, is a distinct Person, because he took on a human form while God the Father did not. But Jesus referred many times to his Father God as a Person. He said he was with a Person—his Father—before he was born a man (John 8:38). He said this Person—his Father—sent him into the world (John 17:18). He said there were many rooms in his Father's house (John 14:2). He prayed to his Father (John 17:1).

Jesus also referred to the Holy Spirit as a Person many times. He used the pronoun "he" when referring to him. Jesus said,

> When the Spirit of truth comes, he will guide you into all truth. He will not speak on his own but will tell you what he has heard. He will tell you about the future. He will bring me glory by telling you whatever he receives from me. All that belongs to the Father is mine; this is why I said, "The Spirit will tell you whatever he receives from me" (John 16:13-15).

Jesus also referred to all three Persons of the Trinity when he told his followers to make disciples, "baptizing them in the name of the Father and the Son and the Holy Spirit" (Matthew 28:19).

Additionally when people claim the Holy Spirit is not a Person, but only an influence or power force, it flies in the face of Jesus referring to him as a Person. Other Scripture also refers to the Holy Spirit as a distinct Person. Paul the apostle attributes characteristics of a Person to him. He indicates the Holy Spirit has a mind, saying, "He who searches our hearts knows the mind of the Spirit" (Romans 8:27 NIV). Scripture also tells us he can feel. We are not to "bring sorrow to God's Holy Spirit by the way you live" (Ephesians 4:30). The Holy Spirit makes choices as to who will receive what spiritual gifts. "It is the one and only Holy Spirit who distributes these gifts" (1 Corinthians 12:11). As noted earlier, Peter told Ananias, "You lied to the Holy Spirit" (Acts 5:3). Ananias wasn't lying to an influence; he was lying to a Person. Peter said to him, "You weren't lying to us but to God" (Acts 5:4).

The Trinity is one God who eternally co-exists as three Persons. The Father, Son, and Holy Spirit as three distinct Persons share the one substance and essence of being God.

Passage:

> There is a sin that leads to death, and I am not saying you should pray for those who commit it. All wicked actions are sin, but not every sin leads to death (1 John 5:16-17).

Difficulty: What is "a sin that leads to death" or the unforgivable sin?

Explanation: Biblical scholars have different views as to what John is referring to as "a sin that leads to death." Some believe it is apostasy, which involves leaving the apostolic faith and becoming part of a heretical and anti-Christian group. Some say apostates are people who learn all about Christ and what he offers yet turn their back on it all and join a movement that is anti-Christ. This would be a sin that definitely leads to death. Others say an apostate could include people who once experienced a relationship with God but turned their back on Christ and the church. Yet others say it could be people who were once Christians who turned away from Christ; their sin will lead to a premature death but their soul will be saved.

Jesus himself made reference to a sin that could not be forgiven. "Anyone who speaks against the Holy Spirit will never be forgiven, either in this life or in the world to come" (Matthew 12:32). Jesus said, "Every sin and blasphemy can be forgiven—except blasphemy against the Holy Spirit" (Matthew 12:31). Blaspheming is speaking contemptuously of or strongly in defiance against someone.

So why is blasphemy against the Holy Spirit unforgivable? Jesus said his Father will send the Holy Spirit to "convict the world of its sin, and of God's righteousness, and of the coming judgment" (John 16:8). And if someone resists the Holy Spirit's conviction of sin and refuses to accept Jesus' sacrifice as God's righteousness, how can he or she be forgiven? Without agreeing with the Holy Spirit regarding sin and Jesus' offering for sin, forgiveness can never be granted. Therefore it is the unforgivable sin.

The writer of Hebrews makes the same point: "If we deliberately continue sinning after we have received knowledge of the truth [by the Holy Spirit], there is no longer any sacrifice that will cover these sins" (Hebrews 10:26). If we reject the convicting agent of the Holy Spirit and keep on deliberately sinning we simply can't obtain forgiveness.

Passage:

I am writing to the chosen lady and to her children, whom I love in the truth—as does everyone else who knows the truth (2 John 1:1).

Difficulty: Who is the chosen lady to whom John is writing?

Explanation: A number of the apostles' letters were written to individuals. So is this letter written to a particular lady John knew?

The Greek word *lady* in verse 1 is *kuria* and can be a proper name. Some believe this letter could have been written to a particular woman named Kyria and her biological children. John does later offer "greetings from the children of your sister" (2 John 1:13).

However, others think John is referring to a particular local church as "the chosen lady." He says that everyone else who knows the truth loves her. That doesn't seem like he is referring to a person because it's doubtful everyone who knows the truth would love her—because not everyone would be acquainted with her as a person. But if John is referring to the body of Christ—his church—then all believers that love the truth would love Christ's body.

Bottom line, it is unclear who the "chosen lady" is that John was writing to—a particular person or the church at large.

Passage:

Dear friend, you are being faithful to God when you care for the traveling teachers who pass through...For they are traveling for the Lord, and they accept nothing from people who are not believers. So we ourselves should support them so that we can be their partners as they teach the truth (3 John 5,7-8).

Difficulty: Should traveling evangelists not accept donations from non-Christians?

Explanation: John was writing this letter to reinforce the true teachings of the gospel and the authority of the apostles. False teaching was prevalent within the early church. Diotrephes was a teacher who broke away from the fellowship of the apostles. He was rejecting the traveling teachers sent by the apostles and was telling others not to welcome them or support them in any way (see 3 John 1:9-10).

So John was countering that by writing to his friend Gaius, thanking him for welcoming the traveling teachers and encouraging his further support of them. John was merely reporting the fact that these traveling teachers were not accepting anything from nonbelievers. There is nothing in the text that indicates they did the right thing or that it would have been wrong if they did accept help from nonbelievers. It would appear that lodging or other material support would be welcome no matter who it came from as long as no strings were attached. If receiving support didn't influence the true message these teachers were declaring, it's doubtful the apostles would have objected.

Difficult Verses *from* *the* Book *of* Jude

Passage and Difficulty: Jude 6—If fallen angels (demons) are in hell how can they tempt people?

Explanation: See 2 Peter 2:4.

Passage:

Enoch, who lived in the seventh generation after Adam, prophesied about these people. He said, "Listen! The Lord is coming with countless thousands of his holy ones to execute judgment on the people of the world" (Jude 14-15).

Difficulty: Since Jude is quoting from the book of Enoch, why isn't that book considered part of Scripture? Are there other books left out of the "official" Bible?

Explanation: Jude quotes from 1 Enoch 1:9, which was part of Jewish literature at the time. No doubt most of the early church was familiar with the book of Enoch.

It was not uncommon for the apostles to quote from sources other than the Hebrew text, which was the accepted Scripture. Not everything in Enoch was accepted fully by Jewish scholars. But that doesn't mean that men like Jude couldn't quote from it. He obviously felt certain portions were valid. Even Paul quoted from secular poets in Acts 17:28 and 1 Corinthians 15:33 and a secular philosopher in Titus 1:12. So quoting from Jewish literature in no way diminishes or distorts the truth of Scripture. The larger question is, why isn't a book like Enoch accepted as Scripture? And are there other books that should have been considered part of the official Bible? And why isn't God still inspiring people to write his Word today?

There are many people throughout history who have written spiritually inspiring books and letters. But there is good reason they are not considered equal to Scripture. It is true that the Holy Spirit is alive today and does guide people to write inspiring literature. Yet Jewish and church leaders long ago concluded that the period of what is called God's special revelation and inspiration is past.

Over 100 years before Christ was born all 39 books of the Old Testament had been written, collected, and officially recognized (canonized) as God's inspired Scripture by the Jewish leaders. By the late 300s the 27 books of the New Testament had been recognized as God-inspired. The writer of the book of Hebrews said, "Long ago God spoke many times and in many ways to our ancestors through the prophets. And now in these final days, he has spoken to us through his Son" (Hebrews 1:1-2). And once God delivered his complete message through his prophets he "closed the book" on the Old Testament.

Jesus confirmed the completeness and authority of the entire Hebrew Scriptures (the 39 books of our current Old Testament) when he said that "everything written about me in the law of Moses, and the prophets and in the Psalms must be fulfilled" (Luke 24:44). Jesus was referring to the entire Hebrew Old Testament. Additionally, Jesus never cited any books other than the current 39 books of the Old Testament to indicate there was any other literature that was also God-inspired. And by using the phrase "all the Scriptures" (Luke 24:27) in regard to the Old Testament he showed that he accepted the same completed Jewish canon as did Judaism at that time.

The New Testament centers around the revelation of God through his Son, Jesus Christ, as written by his apostles. Obviously the best and most accurate writing about Jesus and all he revealed would be done by those who were in direct contact with him. Thus the men inspired by God to reveal the truth about his Son and his message would either be eyewitnesses or would know those who had personally heard the message of the gospel. By the end of the first century it became clear to the early church that God's special revelation and inspiration of Scripture was complete.

Yet early on there were some writings that emerged that some thought should be considered Scripture. After the Old Testament canon had been recognized by Jewish leaders and officially closed, certain literature of a spiritual nature remained or appeared. Today these writings are referred to as the *Apocrypha*, which means "that which is hidden."

There were 14 books that some people added to the 39 canonized books in the Greek Septuagint translation of the Old Testament. These 14 books—the Apocrypha—were not accepted by the early church, but they were eventually included in the Old Testament by the Roman Catholic Church in AD 1546.

These added books surfaced between about 200 BC and some time in the 100s AD. They are

- First Esdras
- Second Esdras
- Tobit
- Judith
- Additions to Esther
- The Wisdom of Solomon
- Ecclesiasticus
- Baruch
- Susanna
- Bel and the Dragon (additions to Daniel)
- The Song of the Three Hebrew Children (additions to Daniel)
- The Prayer of Manasseh
- First Maccabees
- Second Maccabees

The books of the Apocrypha are not part of the Protestant Bible today. The reason cited by Protestant scholars for rejecting these books are that none of the 14 books of the Old Testament Apocrypha claimed divine inspiration—in fact some actually disclaimed it. Also various credible historians, philosophers, and translators such as Josephus, Philo, and Jerome rejected them. And the early Church Fathers excluded these added books entirely.

There were also certain letters or books that some thought should have been included in the New Testament. By the end of the first century Paul's epistles and the four Gospels were widely accepted by the new Christian church as divinely inspired. Peter even wrote around AD 65 that all of Paul's known writings belonged in the category of Scripture (see 2 Peter 3:15-16). But by the middle of the second century there were a growing number of other writings that gained attention, and some wondered if they too were God-inspired. These became known as New Testament apocrypha and Gnostic writings (*Gnostic* meaning having to do with knowledge).

However, the Gnostic writings were rejected by the early church because they largely contradicted the Gospels and epistles of Paul. Some of these included *The Infancy Gospel of Thomas, The Gospel of Judas, The Gospel of Peter,* and *The Gospel of Thomas*. These writings taught that there were multiple creators; that ignorance was the ultimate problem—not sin; and that salvation was by "spiritual knowledge" for only a few. One Gnostic writing depicts a young Jesus striking other children down for bumping into him.

So by the late 300s, when the Church Fathers had established a clear means to recognize the authoritative Word of God, these works had been long rejected. In AD 367 Athanasius of Alexandria offered the first official list of the 27 books of the New Testament we have today. And by AD 397 the church councils of Hippo and Carthage accepted them as well.

Difficult Verses *from* *the* Book *of* Revelation

Passage:

This is a revelation from Jesus Christ, which God gave him to show his servants the events that must soon take place (Revelation 1:1).

Difficulty: Since there are a number of people who interpret the book of Revelation differently, what is the message of Revelation to Christians today?

Explanation: The book of Revelation is confusing to many Christians. It is written in an apocalyptic style that transports us to a spiritual realm of strange beasts, symbolic names and numbers, and cataclysmic events. It reveals a different vision of our present reality. And all this sets up questions as to how we should interpret its meaning.

Generally speaking scholars have aligned themselves in one of three perspectives regarding how a thousand-year period (the millennium) relates to the coming of Christ as described in Revelation 20. This is immediately following Christ's coming to earth in power with a heavenly army to defeat the beast and false prophet in the battle of Armageddon. Then an angel "seized the dragon—the old serpent, who is the devil, Satan—and bound him in chains for a thousand years" (Revelation 20:2). It is then that Christ is to rule the world for a millennium. The three perspectives people take on the millennial reign of Christ largely governs how they interpret the entire meaning of John's vision in Revelation.

Amillennialism. This view rejects the notion that Christ has a literal thousand-year physical reign on earth. Interpreting the thousand years in Revelation 20 as a symbolic or metaphoric number, amillennialists believe the spiritual millennium is the current age between Christ's first and second coming. Some even believe this period ended with the destruction of Jerusalem in AD 70.

The overall focus of this view is that Christ reigns spiritually with his people and at the end of this age he will return in final judgment to establish a perfect and sinless kingdom throughout eternity with "those whose names are written in the Lamb's Book of Life."

Premillennialism. This view perceives Christ rapturing his church from the earth, sending judgment upon those who remain for a period of three-and-a-half to seven years, and then returning to literally reign on earth for a thousand years. After that period a final judgment will come, after which Christ will establish his eternal kingdom with all those who have trusted in him.

The premillennialist view is generally incorporated in a system of theology known as dispensationalism. A common tenet of dispensationalism is that the nation of Israel will see a literal fulfillment of God's promise made to Abraham. In this view the church is distinct from Israel. And while the church plays an evangelistic role in the end time, this view sees God literally fulfilling the Old Testament promises made to Israel.

Postmillennialism. This view holds that the millennium is an era, not necessarily a literal thousand-year reign of Christ. Through a gradual increase of the gospel influence over the world, postmillennialists believe Christ will eventually return to judge the wicked and establish his kingdom forever. This view, similar to amillennialists, considers much of the vision of John as a metaphor for Christ's eventual triumph over Satan.

As indicated, there has been considerable debate over the way Christians should interpret the book of Revelation. In fact Christians have divided sharply over the issue. What the majority of Christians do agree on is the theme and basic message of the book.

The message of Revelation is that despite all the evil in the world and Satan's attack on God's people, ultimately Christ triumphs over sin and death. God through his Son restores his original plan of a perfect world, where he has an unobstructed relationship with his creation of humans and Planet Earth. Yes pain, sin, and suffering dominate a fallen world. But the great victory over evil has already been won through the death and resurrection of Christ. We therefore must be patient and live by faith in God who will reward those who are faithful.

The apostle Paul actually shared a parallel theme of Revelation when he wrote,

> Christ was raised as the first of the harvest; then all who belong to Christ will be raised when he comes back. After that the end will come, when he will turn the Kingdom over to God the Father, having destroyed every ruler and authority and power. For Christ must reign until he humbles all his enemies beneath his feet. And the last enemy to be destroyed is death...Then, when all things are under his authority, the Son will put himself under God's authority, so that God, who gave his Son authority over all things, will be utterly supreme over everything everywhere (1 Corinthians 15:23-26,28).

The message of Revelation should prompt us to respond like Solomon about the whole of life. "Here now is my final conclusion: Fear God and obey his commands, for this is everyone's duty. God will judge us for everything we do, including every secret thing, whether good or bad" (Ecclesiastes 12:13-14).

Passage and Difficulty: Revelation 21:1-2—Is the celestial home of God (heaven) where Christians will spend eternity?

Explanation: See John 14:1-3.

Passage:

I am the Alpha and Omega—the Beginning and the End. To all who are thirsty I will give freely from the springs of the water of life. All who are victorious will inherit all these blessings, and I will be their God, and they will be my children (Revelation 21:6-7).

Difficulty: What will Christians actually inherit from God for all eternity?

Explanation: "God will give us our full rights as his adopted children, including the new bodies he has promised us" (Romans 8:23). This means we inherit a body that will live forever. It also means we will enjoy a new heaven and a new earth (2 Peter 3:13) that will no longer be cursed. In fact there will no longer "be a curse upon anything" (Revelation 22:3). "Nothing evil will be allowed to enter" (Revelation 21:27) into this new world and "there will be no more death or sorrow or crying or pain. All these things are gone forever" (Revelation 21:4).

The inheritance God will grant his children for all eternity will be a pristine, glorious new home, yet it will retain the comfortable familiarity we love. God is not creating a strange place that will require us to completely readjust ourselves and change who we are. Rather, he is restoring the old—getting rid of the scars, damage, and malfunctions inflicted by the Fall. We will no doubt enjoy the restored beauty of the earth with its lush forests, majestic mountains, sparkling water, and an animal kingdom in which the multitude of species are no longer at odds with each other.

But more than that, our future home will be a place where we will be with our loved ones, a place where the word *family* takes on a whole new meaning. Our earthly families and friends can be great. But we can tire at times of being with family and friends. Yet in our new home these relational imperfections will be removed along with the imperfections of the environment. People will relate to each other exactly as they should have related all along. Indeed, there will be nothing but bliss in every aspect of our lives because we will be entering into the pure joy of God himself.

Jesus gave an illustration of what it will be like to inherit the kingdom of heaven. He said that the Master would pay us the greatest of compliments by saying, "Well done, my good and faithful servant." But there would be even more. He will go on to add, "You were faithful with a few things, I will put you in charge of many things; enter into the joy of your master" (Matthew 25:23 NASB). Our eternal inheritance is so much more than just a reward; it is our initiation into a whole new realm of meaning and significance for our lives.

One of the things our inheritance includes is something to be "in charge of." Some people think heaven is one long extended vacation. Obviously Matthew 25:23 suggests we are not merely spectators, but participants in our inheritance. There will be things to do, projects we will be "in charge of."

Randy Alcorn quotes theologian Dallas Willard, who comments on Matthew 25:23:

> A place in God's creation order has been reserved for each one of us from before the beginning of cosmic existence. His plan is for us to develop, as apprentices to Jesus, to the point where we can take our place in the ongoing creativity of the universe.

Alcorn then goes on to say:

> God is grooming us for leadership. He's watching to see how we demonstrate our faithfulness. He does that through his apprenticeship program, one that prepares us for Heaven. Christ is not simply preparing a place for us; he is preparing us for that place.[5]

After God created the original earth he told Adam and Eve, "Be fruitful and increase in number; fill the earth and subdue it. Rule over the fish of the sea and the birds in the sky and over every living creature that moves on the ground" (Genesis 1:28 NIV). God had a responsibility in mind for his original created family of humans, and he seems to have a responsibility in mind for his future redeemed children. In his vision John saw those who were washed in the blood of the Lamb given a place at "the throne of God," where they will "serve him day and night" (Revelation 7:15 NIV). So our present faithfulness to God is rewarded with future responsibilities in our new home. At first glance, this promise may not immediately appeal to some. You might think, *I'm stressed out with all the responsibilities piled on me here. I was hoping that heaven would free me from all that.*

Randy Alcorn answers this fear with an insightful perspective:

> Service is a reward, not a punishment. This idea is foreign to people who dislike their work and only put up with it until retirement. We think that faithful work should be rewarded by a vacation for the rest of our lives. But God offers us something very different: more work, more

> responsibilities, increased opportunities, along with greater abilities, resources, wisdom, and empowerment. We will have sharp minds, strong bodies, clear purpose, and unabated joy. The more we serve Christ now, the greater our capacity will be to serve him in Heaven.[6]

There are many things we may not know about our future inheritance. What exactly we can expect to be doing for all eternity is still veiled in mystery. It is a great secret yet to be revealed. But we do know this: Whatever task he has planned for you will fit you exactly. When you receive your assignment, you will suddenly understand just what your particular talents were meant to accomplish. It will be your dream job—the path to fulfillment of all your deepest ambitions. A perfect place, where you perfectly fit, for all eternity.

Notes

INTRODUCTION

1. Josh McDowell and Sean McDowell, *The Unshakable Truth* (Eugene, OR: Harvest House Publishers, 2010), 96.
2. Josh McDowell, *More Evidence That Demands a Verdict* (Nashville, TN: Thomas Nelson Publishers, 1999), 21-22.
3. McDowell, *More Evidence*, 26.
4. Josh McDowell, *The New Evidence that Demands a Verdict* (Nashville, TN: Thomas Nelson Publishers, 1999), 38-39.

THE PENTATEUCH (Genesis–Deuteronomy)

1. Simon Singh, *Big Bang: The Origin of the Universe* (New York: Harper-Collins, 2004), 144-61, 249-61.
2. P.C.W. Davies, "Spacetime Singularities in Cosmology," *Study of Time II*, ed. J. T. Fraser (Berlin: Springer Verlag, 1978), 78-79.
3. Richard N. Ostling, "The Search for the Historical Adam," *Christianity Today* magazine, June 11, 2011, 25.
4. Ann Gauger, "The Science of Adam and Eve," in Ann Gauger, Douglas Axe, and Casey Luskin, *Science and Human Origins* (Seattle, WA: Discovery Institute Press, 2012), 117.
5. Gauger, 115.
6. Ostling, 25.
7. Lee Irons and Meredith G. Kline, "The Framework View," *The Genesis Debate*, ed. David G. Hagopian (Mission Viejo, CA: Crux Press, 2001), 217-53.
8. As quoted in Ostling, 26.
9. As quoted in Ostling, 27.
10. As quoted in Ostling, 27.
11. As quoted in Ostling, 27.
12. Fazale R. Rana and Hugh Ross, "New Discoveries in Biochemistry of Aging Support the Biblical Record," 2001, accessed at www.godandscience.org/apologetics/longlife.html#senescence.
13. Rana and Ross.
14. As reported at www.thecomputerwizard.biz/lightning.htm.
15. Josh McDowell, *Answers to Tough Questions* (Wheaton, IL: Tyndale House Publishers, 1991), 211.
16. McDowell, *Answers*, 212.
17. McDowell, *Answers*, 212.
18. McDowell, *Answers*, 212.
19. McDowell, *Answers*, 213.

20. McDowell, *Answers*, 213.
21. McDowell, *Answers*, 213.
22. Paul Copan, *How Do You Know You're Not Wrong?* (Grand Rapids, MI: Baker Books, 2005), 126.
23. Henri Blocher, *In the Beginning: The Opening Chapters of Genesis* (Downers Grove, IL: InterVarsity, 1984), 209.
24. Josh McDowell, *The New Evidence that Demands a Verdict* (Nashville, TN: Thomas Nelson Publishers, 1999), 378.
25. Gerald F. Hawthorne, Ralph P. Martin, and Daniel G. Reid, *Dictionary of Paul and His Letters* (Downers Grove, IL: InterVarsity Press, 1993), 881.
26. Sean McDowell and Jonathan Morrow, *Is God Just a Human Invention?* (Grand Rapids, MI: Kregel Publications, 2010), 151-52.
27. Harold L. Willmington, *Willmington's Bible Handbook* (Wheaton, IL: Tyndale House Publishers, 1997), 889.
28. "Archaeology and Sources for Old Testament Background," *New Living Translation Study Bible* (Wheaton, IL: Tyndale House Publishers, 2008), 8.
29. McDowell, *New Evidence*, 476-477.

THE HISTORICAL BOOKS (Joshua–Esther)

1. Joel Kramer, "Bible Expedition: Jericho Unearthed" DVD, Exploration Films, Sourceflix, Inc.

POETRY AND WISDOM (Job–Song of Songs)

1. *Ryrie Study Bible*, Charles Caldwell Ryrie, ed. (Chicago: Moody Press, 1976), 25.

THE PROPHETS (Isaiah–Malachi)

1. Pergamon Museum, Berlin, accessed at http://en.wikipedia.org/wiki/file:Pergamon_Museum_Berlin_2007085.jpg.

THE GOSPELS/NARRATIVES (Matthew–Acts)

1. Timothy Keller, *The Reason for God: Belief in an Age of Skepticism* (New York: Dutton, 2008), 76-77.
2. C.S. Lewis, *The Abolition of Man* (New York: Macmillan, 1947), 69.
3. Randy Alcorn, *Heaven* (Wheaton, IL: Tyndale House Publishers, 2004), 101.

PAUL'S LETTERS (Romans–Philemon)

1. As quoted in Ravi Zacharias and Norman Geisler, *Who Made God?* (Grand Rapids, MI: Zondervan, 2003), 97.
2. Randy Alcorn, *Heaven* (Wheaton, IL: Tyndale House Publishers, 2004), 57.
3. As quoted by Stanley J. Grenz and Denise Muir Kjesbo, *Women in the Church* (Downers Grove, IL: InterVarsity Press, 1995), 126.

GENERAL LETTERS (Hebrews–Revelation)

1. Barbara Bradley Hagerty, "The God Choice," *USA Today*, June 22, 2009, 9a.
2. Dinesh D'Souza, *Life After Death: The Evidence* (Washington, DC: Regnery Publishing, 2009), 63.

3. Michael Licona, "Paul on the Nature of the Resurrection Body," in *Buried Hope or Risen Savior: The Search for the Jesus Tomb*, ed. Charles L. Quarles (Nashville, TN: B&H Academic, 2008), 177-98.
4. Institute of International Studies, *Perspectives on the World Christian Movement* (Pasadena, CA: William Carey Library, 2009), 362-64.
5. Randy Alcorn, *Heaven* (Wheaton, IL: Tyndale House Publishers, 2004), 215.
6. Alcorn, 226.

Index by Scripture Passage

The Pentateuch:

Genesis–Deuteronomy

The Historical Books:
Joshua–Esther

The Prophets:
Isaiah–Malachi

The Gospels/Narratives:
Matthew–Acts

Index by Topic

Apparent Contradictions

Christian Apologetics

Miscellaneous

Science and the Bible

Unorthodox Doctrines

About the Authors and the Josh McDowell Ministry

As a young man, **Josh McDowell** was a skeptic of Christianity. However, while at Kellogg College in Michigan, he was challenged by a group of Christian students to intellectually examine the claims of Jesus Christ. Josh accepted the challenge and came face-to-face with the reality that Jesus was in fact the Son of God, who loved him enough to die for him. Josh committed his life to Christ, and for 50 years he has shared with the world both his testimony and the evidence that God is real and relevant to our everyday lives.

Josh received a bachelor's degree from Wheaton College and a master's degree in theology from Talbot Theological Seminary in California. He has been on staff with Cru (formerly Campus Crusade for Christ) for almost 50 years. Josh and his wife, Dottie, have been married for more than 40 years and have four grown children and five grandchildren. They live in Southern California.

Sean McDowell is an educator, speaker, and author. He graduated summa cum laude from Talbot Theological Seminary with a double master's degree in philosophy and theology. He is the head of the Bible department at Capistrano Valley Christian School and is presently pursuing a PhD in apologetics and worldview studies at Southern Baptist Theological Seminary. You can read Sean's blog and contact him for speaking events at www.seanmcdowell.org.

Sean and his wife, Stephanie, have been married for more than ten years and have two children. They live in Southern California.

Other Resources from Josh and Sean McDowell

Go Beyond Mere Study...
Experience Your Bible

In *Experience Your Bible,* Josh and Sean McDowell delve into God's original design for the Scriptures—revealing himself to you so you can experience him and a deepened relationship with others.

With this in mind, Josh and Sean show you how the Bible can radically transform your life:

- The only hope of a life of joy is in a relational experience with God. The Bible is designed to guide you into that kind of relationship.
- God wants you to relationally experience things like acceptance, security, and comfort with him and others...not just mechanically obey commands.
- Your encounter with God's book can become a journey into what relationships with God and others were meant to be.

Is God Just a Human Invention?
And Seventeen Other Questions Raised by the New Atheists
Sean McDowell and Jonathan Morrow

Sean McDowell and Jonathan Morrow believe that the current religious landscape is both an opportunity and a challenge for people of faith. In an accessible yet rigorous look at the arguments of the New Atheists, such as Richard Dawkins and Christopher Hitchens, McDowell and Morrow honestly discuss both scientific (philosophical) and biblical (moral) questions, such as "Are Science and Christianity at Odds?"; "Is Hell a Divine Torture Chamber?"; and "Why Jesus Instead of the Flying Spaghetti Monster?" Find out what you need to know to engage your atheist peers. *From Kregel Publishing. Visit your local Christian bookstore or go to www.DidHumansInventGod.com.*

The Unshakable Truth®

How You Can Experience the 12 Essentials of a Relevant Faith

As a Christian, you may feel unsure about what you believe and why. Maybe you wonder if your faith is even meaningful and credible.

Unpacking 12 biblical truths that define the core of Christian belief and Christianity's reason for existence, this comprehensive yet easy-to-understand handbook helps you discover…

- the foundational truths about God, his Word, sin, Christ, the Trinity, the church, and six more that form the bedrock of Christian faith
- how you can live out these truths in relationship with God and others
- ways to pass each truth on to your family and the world around you

Biblically grounded, spiritually challenging, and full of practical examples and real-life stories, *The Unshakable Truth®* is a resource applicable to every aspect of everyday life.

The Unshakable Truth® Study Guide

This study guide offers you—or you and your group—a *relational experience* to discover…

- 12 foundational truths of Christianity—in sessions about God, his Word, the Trinity, Christ's atonement, his resurrection, his return, the church, and five more
- "Truth Encounter" exercises to actually help you live out these key truths
- "TruthTalk" assignments on ways to share the essentials of the faith with your family and others

Through twelve 15-minute Web-link videos, Josh and Sean McDowell draw on their own father-son legacy of faith to help you feel adequate to impart what you believe with confidence. *Includes instructions for group leaders.*

The Unshakable Truth™ DVD Experience

12 Powerful Sessions on the Essentials of a Relevant Faith

What do I believe, and why do I believe it? How is it relevant to my life? How do I live it out?

If you're asking yourself questions like these, you're not alone. In 12 quick, easy-to-grasp video sessions based on their book *The Unshakable Truth*, Josh and Sean McDowell give a solid introduction to the foundations of the faith.

Josh and Sean outline 12 key truths with clear explanations, compelling discussions, and provocative "on-the-street" interviews. And uniquely, they explain these truths *relationally*, showing you how living them out changes you and affects family and friends—everyone you encounter. *Helpful leader's directions included.*

Apologetics for a New Generation

A Biblical and Culturally Relevant Approach to Talking About God

Sean McDowell, general editor

This generation's faith is constantly under attack from the secular media, skeptical teachers, and unbelieving peers. You may wonder, *How can I help?*

Working with young adults every day, Sean McDowell understands their situation and shares your concern. His first-rate team of contributors shows how you can help members of the new generation plant their feet firmly on the truth. Find out how you can walk them through the process of...

- formulating a biblical worldview and applying scriptural principles to everyday issues
- articulating their questions and addressing their doubts in a safe environment
- becoming confident in their faith and effective in their witness

The truth never gets old, but people need to hear it in fresh, new ways. Find out how you can effectively share the answers to life's big questions with a new generation.

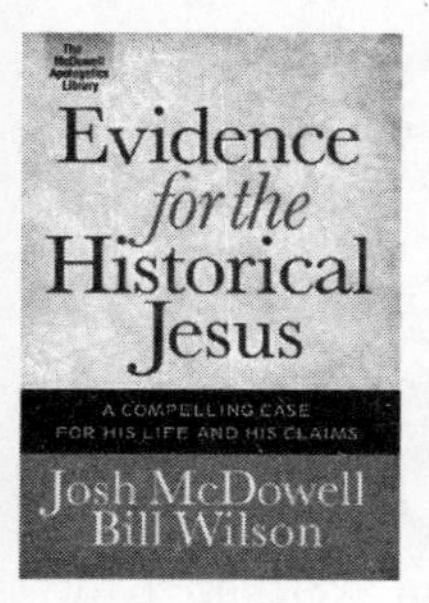

Evidence for the Historical Jesus
A Compelling Case for His Life and His Claims
Josh McDowell and Bill Wilson

After two years of intensive research, the agnostic Josh McDowell was convinced of the reliability of the historical evidence showing that Jesus of Nazareth existed and was precisely who he said he was—God in the flesh. Confronted by the living Lord, Josh accepted the offer of a relationship with him.

In *Evidence for the Historical Jesus,* Josh teams with writer-researcher Bill Wilson to provide you with a thorough analysis to document that Jesus Christ actually walked on this earth—and that the New Testament accounts are incredibly reliable in describing his life. The authors' broad-ranging investigation examines

- the writings of ancient rabbis, martyrs, and early church leaders
- the evidence of the New Testament text
- historical geography and archaeology

Detailed and incisive but accessible, this volume will help you relate to people who distort or discount Christianity and its Founder. And it will strengthen your confidence in Jesus Christ and in the Scriptures that document his words, his life, and his love.